Far Off in Sunlit Places

Stories of the Scots in
Australia and New Zealand

JIM HEWITSON

D0790112

CANONGATE

To the thousands of bairns who never saw their new homes

First published in Great Britain in 1998
by Canongate Books, 14 High Street,
Edinburgh EH1 1TE

British Library Cataloguing-in-Publication Data
A catalogue record for this book is available on request from the British Library

ISBN 1 86241 775 9

Typeset by Carnegie Publishing Ltd, Lancaster
Printed and bound by GraphyCems

Acknowledgements

Over the past three years I have had much assistance and goodwill from the people of Australia and New Zealand in compiling this book – from the mayors of the great cities to the residents of far-flung communities with proud Scottish connections, from libraries, museums, the media, churches, national parks, historical societies, and, of course, Scots-interest groups who have been happy to share their stories.

I am especially indebted to: The High Commissions of New Zealand and Australia, London; Orkney Library, Kirkwall; Clydebank Central Library; The Australian Tourist Commission; New Zealand Tourism; Westland National Park; Cliff Hanley/ Kerr Music Corporation Limited T/A James S. Kerr Music Publishers.

A. W. Cameron, Shirley Roberts, Netta Curnow, Ron Hewitson, Douglas Campbell, Kerr Johnston, Malcolm Prentis (NSW); Belle Avery, Ron Kirkwood, Jane Tuwhare, Paula Preston, Lyndsay Brock, Gordon Smart, Ron Boyd, John Murray, Noel Robinson (AD); Janet McKenzie, Joe Adams, Tom Brooking, Trevor Ross, Tania Connelly, Beryl Miller, Jim Johnstone, Nancy Whittlestone, Eleanor Leckie, Lyn Young, Alan and Joan Cooke, Elspeth Lumsden, Wally and Rosalie Fisher, Margot McLean, Pat Inder, Gordon Gray, Lester Flockton (OO); Cyril Hart, Bournemouth, Owen Henry, Anne Ralston, Dorothy Law, Janet Henderson, D. Robbins (TI); Vince Boyle, Frederick Miller, Alan and Heather Duthie, Patricia Williams, Westray Manson (SD); Gordon Seatter, Donald McFarlane (CY); Craig and Bill Traill, Leigh McKinnon, Stuart Wilson, Jeff Burgher, Dave Cowper, Stuart Bryan, Christine Laskowski, Owen McKenzie, Don Macreadie, Bette Bilton, Marj Smith, Joan Fraser, Margaret Burslem, Keith Murray, Margaret Thompson, John Davidson, Ian Hyndman, Barbara Yuill (VA); Joan Pearce,

Ruth Amos, Margaret Long, Jock Inglis, David Needham (TA); Paddy Clark (BoP); Bill Scott, Betty Markwell, Laura Scott, Dorothy Nealie, Sandy Pearson, Barbara Wolff, Ruth Inglis, John Mackenzie-Smith, Helen Taylor, Angela Collyer, Colin Campbell, Jill Freshwater (QD); Christina Powell, Heather Mathie, Marie Moncrieff, Wayne McKirdy, Doris Arrowsmith (WN); Eric Richards, Barbara Medhurst, Connie Fraser (SA); Bill Smith, Lily Baker, Heather Chalmers, Robin Barker, Heather Mitchell (HB); Helen Dyson, Allan Muntz, Paul Melody (MW); Allan Drummond, Bruce Farrell, Marion Stringer (NM); Dee Skewes, Ron Ross, Jenny Michel (NT); Marjory Harper, Aberdeen; Inverary Jail; Alistair Isdale, Kay Te Huia, Myfanwy Taylor (WO); Billy Tierney, Joy Dench, Dee Nairn, Bill Tannock, Chris Milroy, Bonnie Hicks, Phylis Kutzer, Jessie Duckworth, Don Ross, Edna Carruthers, Helen Muir-Richardson, Bill Bennie, Deanna Milburn, Margaret Kissane, Marjory Johnston, Alan Campbell, Steve Howell (WA). Jean Hansen (WC).

Mayors: Vicki Buck, Christchurch; Wynne Raymond, Timaru; Paul Rieger, Palmerston North; J. P. Wilson, Rangitikei; Paul Ruger, Tennant Creek (NT); John Miller, Barcaldine; Jim Sorley, Brisbane: Nita Cunning, Bundaberg; Tony Peck, Launceston; Sandra French, Burnie; Megan Weston, Bendigo; Gerry Smith, Geelong; Alisdair Thompson, Thames/Coromandel; Ken Thomas, Matamata Piako; John Terris, Lower Hutt; Mark Blumsky, Wellington; Del Mills, Shire President, Carnarvon.

Libraries/Museums: Corangamite (VA), Launceston (TA), Invercargill (SD), Mount Gambier (SA), Penola Community (SA), Whanganui Museum (MW), Rotorua (WO), National Library of Australia, La Trobe Library (VA), Mortlock Library (SA), Waipu Museum (ND), Otago Settlers Museum (OO), Glasgow Museums, Mary McKillop Place, Nelson Provincial Museum, Alexander Turnbull Library (WN), Northern Territory Library, John Oxley Library (QD), National Library of Scotland, University of St Andrews Library, Dundee City Library, Newcastle Region Public Library (NSW), Mackenzie Community Library (CY), Battye Library, Perth (WA), Mitchell Library, Sydney (NSW), Kapiti District Library (WN), Mount Barker Community Library (SA), Karratha Community Library (WA), Fremantle City Library (WA), Geraldton Library (WA).

Local Authorities/Historical Societies: Evandale HS, Rodney District Council, Glen Innes HS, Franklin DC, Inverell Shire Council, Shire of Flinders, Beaudesert HS, Gore DC, New Plymouth DC, South Taranaki DC, Central Highlands Council, Greater Shepparton City Council, City of Monash, Wyndham CC, South Waikato DC, Paeroa and District HS, Albany HS, Broome HS.

A Brief Chronology

1750 East Lothian's Alexander Dalrymple, hydrographer with the East India Company, was advocating and was prepared to lead extensive exploration in the Pacific. Cook eventually preferred by the Admiralty for the job because of his practical experience.

1766 John Callender publishes at Edinburgh his *Terra Australis Cognita* emphasising the value of the distant lands and Britain's role as natural leader of expansion in the region.

1769 Cook's first sighting of New Zealand; several Scots seamen and officers among crew of the *Endeavour*.

1788 Foundation Day in Australia as the First Fleet, the convoy of prison and supply ships, arrives.

1801 A small settlement is established at mouth of Hunter River for convicts undergoing secondary punishment; it grew into industrial centre of Newcastle (NSW).

1807 Lord Castlereagh first suggests free passage, land grants and convict labour for well-heeled and responsible immigrants to New South Wales.

1808 Macarthur and Johnston among Scots involved in deposing Governor Bligh, who stood accused of influencing judicial system and betraying the King's trust.

1809 Australian colony's sheep population is 25,888.

1810 Lachlan Macquarie from Mull takes up post as Governor of New South Wales; white population of mainland Australia put at 10,454 while 1,321 live in Van Diemen's Land.

1813 Expedition finds way through the Blue Mountains behind Sydney but importance of vast new lands does not seem to have been immediately realised.

1814 Captain Matthew Flinders, pioneer explorer of Australia, dies; Gospel is preached for first time in New Zealand by Rev. Samuel Marsden.

1817   Governor Macquarie recommends Australia be used as official name for the island continent, instead of New Holland; first bank opens its doors in Sydney.

1824   Foundation stone of the Scots kirk in Sydney is laid.

1826   Failed expedition to Hokianga in New Zealand's North Island leaves Leith.

1827   First Governor of Western Australia, Lanarkshire's Sir James Stirling, arrives off the Swan River where Perth now stands.

1828   Sturt and Hume name the River Darling on expedition into Australian interior; first census shows 36,598 white persons living in New South Wales (20,930 free and 15,668 convicts).

1829   New opportunities for settlers as Western Australia is opened up.

1831   John Dunmore Lang arrives in Australia with 140 immigrants, chiefly skilled Scots 'mechanics' and their families, to help build Lang's Australian College.

1834   Lord Melbourne takes office as Britain's Prime Minister; Glasgow's James Busby, resident administrator in New Zealand, survives attack on his home by Maori marauders.

1835   In the face of French interference Busby persuades thirty-five northern Maori chiefs to sign declaration of independence and adherence to British protection.

1836   Port of Adelaide founded by Colonel William Light; City of Melbourne founded to provide additional land for Tasmanian settlers.

1837   Third ship of season left Tobermory for Australia with 300 immigrants – a piper played during emotional scenes on the quayside.

1838   Formation of reconstituted New Zealand Company.

1839   First Caledonian Society in Australia organised in Sydney; among first actions is to switch St Andrews Day to June – for climatic reasons.

1840   First Governor of New Zealand landed, Treaty of Waitangi signed and New Zealand declared a British colony; *Bengal Merchant* arrives at Wellington with boatload of Scots pioneers.

1841   New Zealand declared independent of New South Wales administration; New Zealand Company's latest settlements at Nelson on South Island and at New Plymouth in Taranaki established; population of Auckland is 2,000, swollen the following year by several hundred Scots migrants; first Gaelic sermon in New Zealand preached by the Rev. John Macfarlane at Kaiwarra.

1842   George Rennie, Scots member of UK parliament, suggests a Scottish settlement sponsored by New Zealand Company; Jane Gifford and Duchess of Argyle arrive at Auckland with contingent of Scots settlers.

1843   Disruption in the Church of Scotland sees creation of the Free Kirk which soon shows interest in New Zealand settlement.

1846   Governor Grey of New Zealand receives word from London that a parliament to be called the House of Representatives is to be elected by colonies themselves; it was 1852, however, before this came to pass.

1848   First settlers for Free Church of Scotland settlement in Otago arrive.

1850   Canterbury colony founded.

1851   Gold discovered in New South Wales, the fever soon spreading to Victoria; Otago Settlers Association formed and quickly begins to agitate for self-government; *Margaret*, carrying first of the Waipu settlers, leaves Canada; Crown Lands Ordinance makes leaseholds in New Zealand with low rentals widely available, encouraging more Scots and Australian sheep farmers to New Zealand; a catastrophic bush fire sweeps across Victoria, remembered as Black Thursday.

1853   Land prices lowered throughout colonies to encourage development; province of Otago established with Captain William Cargill elected superintendent; taking office, Provincial Council did not have control of Crown lands for first three years; Murihiku Block (Southland) purchased from Maoris.

1854   After wandering the globe the Nova Scotian Highlanders finally land at Waipu; first colonial parliament of New Zealand meets in Auckland on Queen Victoria's birthday.

1855   Women's Christian Temperance Union formed in New Zealand; total of 60,000 sheep recorded in Otago but by beginning of next decade there were 700,000.

1856   Province of Auckland's decision to offer free land grants to intending settlers proves popular with Scots; first settlement of Mackenzie Country in New Zealand's South Island.

1857   Dunedin's population only 890 but within two years increased to over 2,000.

1858   Caledonian Society of Victoria formed; New Zealand's New Provinces Bill allows areas to become provinces if they submit a petition by 150 registered voters (Hawkes Bay and Marlborough created within months); Militia Act sees creation of many distinctively Scots volunteer units in New Zealand sporting Highland dress and pipe bands.

1859   Invercargill's population reaches almost 1,000, its prosperity tied very much to the sheep runs to the north; large runs in South Australia broken up for smaller farms.

1860   James Mackay, originally from Sutherland, purchases, on behalf of government, entire vast West Coast of New Zealand's South Island from Maoris.

1861   Census figures show one third of New Zealand's population to be of Scottish birth – some 30,000 people; conference to discuss unification of different Presbyterian churches in New Zealand; province of Southland – the Maori district of Murihiku – breaks away from Otago; South Island gold rush sees Otago's population double to 30,000 within few months; Robertson Land Act cuts up large runs in New South Wales.

1862   Otago Caledonian Society formed.

1863   Otago gold rush sees more than 35,000 rough and ready immigrants flood goldfields; disastrous winter in South Island sees many lives lost including recently arrived Otago miners; Canterbury completes first four miles of railway track in colony; outbreak of long-running Maori Wars.

1864   Thanks to gold rush, Dunedin could claim to be New Zealand's largest town with population of almost 16,000.

1865   Dunedin stages huge international fair highlighting Otago's prosperity.

1866   Death of Rev. Norman McLeod, charismatic leader of the Waipu colonists.

1867   Bluff to Invercargill rail line in Southland completed.

1868   Australia ceases to be convict settlement with end of transportation to Western Australia. Over 165,000 were transported over an eighty-year period.

1870   British military forces withdrawn from Australia; Otago's offer of reunion with Southland gratefully accepted by financially troubled southern province.

1871   Otago Girls' High School established; latest census indicates that 36,861 New Zealanders claim Scottish birth; red deer from Forfarshire released in Otago and within a few years populate a vast area.

1874   Westland, New Zealand, becomes province with James Alexander Bonar elected superintendent.

1875   Despite vocal opposition from Auckland and Otago, Abolition of the Provinces Bill becomes law.

1878   Serious flooding in Southern Otago when the Clutha (Clyde) bursts its banks.

1879   Soup kitchens set up in Christchurch as economic slump with falling wages and unemployment spreads.

1880   Ned Kelly and gang mopped up in shoot-out near Melbourne.

1881   Mail services from London to Brisbane are inaugurated by British Indian Steamship Company as the *Merkera* leaves Victoria Docks.

1882   The *Dunedin* carries first cargo of frozen meat from New Zealand to UK.

1883   Population of Queensland estimated to be less than 300,000.

1885   New South Wales contingent leaves for the Sudan – first time a British colony sent troops at own cost to aid mother country.

1888   Exodus of unemployed from New Zealand to Victoria and United States in full swing; talk of sweated labour in clothing industry, something immigrants thought they had left behind.

1889   Queensland dock strike against loading wool sheared by non-union labour is first major success for Australian trade unions.

1891   One-year expedition led by Scots descendant David Lindsay maps 80,000 square miles of central Australia; population of New Zealand reaches 668,000.

1893   Women in New Zealand win right to vote after lengthy campaign spearheaded by Scots-born Kate Sheppard.

1901   Proclamation of Commonwealth and first Australian Parliament.

1902   Australia introduces Immigration Restriction Act.

1907   Dominion Day for New Zealand.

1913   Foundation of Canberra where Federal Parliament meets for first time in new capital in 1927.

1915   Australian and New Zealand forces figured prominently in Gallipoli campaign during World War I.

1924   Major trade treaty signed between Australia and Canada.

1926   Self-governing dominion status granted to Australia and New Zealand, although changes in constitution require approval of British Parliament.

1931   First official air mail run from United Kingdom to Australia takes twenty days.

1932   Sydney Harbour Bridge completed; Australian Broadcasting Commission formed.

1935   First regular air service between London and Australia begins.

1941   War with Japan in aftermath of Pearl Harbor.

1954   Queen Elizabeth II tours the Antipodes, first such visit by a reigning British monarch.

1962   Australian Aboriginals are given right to vote.

Chapter One
Drawn by the Southern Cross

U NDER COVER of the night Otago's modern bravehearts crept stealthily
along Cumberland Street, Dunedin, replacement street signs tucked
under their arms. They were not about to let the 250th anniversary of the
defeat at faraway Drummossie Moor pass unmarked. After a session of skilful
balancing on shoulders, adjustment of kilts for modesty and the tuneful
twanging of elastic bands all twenty-eight signs had been replaced and the
thoroughfare which once reminded expatriate Scots of 'Butcher' Cumberland, government commander in 1746, had been magically transformed into
Culloden Road.

Traders complained about potential loss of business, the *Otago Daily
Times* had a lot of fun with the story and the council ordered the illegal
signs taken down, threatening a $1,000 fine for non-compliance. Having
bowed the knee a promise was made by the Scottish raiders that a more
orthodox approach would soon be made to the transport department in an
attempt to persuade them that the name change should be permanent – and
official.

Merely a prank, of course, but remember Dunedin is the Scots capital of
the southern hemisphere; therefore it's the sort of happening you might
expect thereabouts. However, I suspect that no other European immigrant
group in either Australia or New Zealand gets quite so stirred up about
perceived injustices connected with their heritage as do the Scots; on this
occasion it was a militant wee Jacobite cell calling themselves Clann Albain
or Children of Scotland.

Whether or not this WallacetheBruceism, as the playwright James Bridie
styled it, is the surface froth of something more fundamental and important
or a sad, pointless longing by 'professional' Scots descendants for a mythical

The Children of Scotland make their Culloden anniversary protest in Dunedin.
(*Otago Daily Times*)

land of haggis and heather, we may be in a better position to judge by the end of this book. The fact is that, apart from the Caledonians, this sort of civic protest nowadays is almost exclusively the domain of the Aborigines, the Maoris and their supporters.

One cynical speaker at a Burns Supper in the same South Island city recently spoke of this persistent, Janus-like quality of the legion of expatriates:

> The Scots have a deep, abiding love of their country. They sing about it, write poems about it, even greet over it after a few drams; they'll do everything but damned well stay in it.

Of course, in that thrawn Scottish way, the speaker was poking fun at himself as much as the assembled company. Mind you, if only it was that simple and straightforward. Often there was no choice for the folk who left Scotland behind. Certainly some climbed the gangplank filled with anticipation but others left choked with bitterness, refugees from, and victims of, a changing world. But the point is valid enough. How is it, as Kenneth McKellar asked on New Zealand TV recently, that the further Scots get from home the more Scottish they seem to become? Ah, yes, another great Scottish conundrum. Almost as puzzling as the age-old question – what exactly is a Scot?

But first things first. To start researching a book which looks at the Scots settlement of the great island nations at the bottom of the world, Australia and New Zealand, just when everything appeared to be splitting apart at the seams, may strike you as a bit perverse. We can blame the French, of course. There they were, in 1995, determined to unleash their nuclear muscle in the Muraroa Atoll tests. Britain's support or at least lack of official criticism of the French stance infuriated the peoples of the Pacific nations. There was talk of old relationships being strained to breaking point, of a common wealth no more. The ba' was almost on the slates.

Within a few weeks, however, the political crisis was over. The French managed to bodyswerve further criticism by limiting the number of tests and Australia and New Zealand emerged having shown a solidarity and strength of purpose which marked them out, on the threshold of the 21st century, as no far-flung soft touches. Normal service was resumed. The ba' was back in play. I would not, at least for the moment, be observing the Scots in New Zealand and Australia in the context of a final break up of the Commonwealth. The Queen was apologising to the Maoris for some shady colonial dealing in the 19th century, a Maori Scot was leading New Zealand's campaign for immigration control; in Australia the general election saw a step back – perhaps only temporarily – from republicanism; Australia resumed efforts to palm off her nuclear waste on Scotland and a group of impudent tykes suggested moving Governor Lachlan Macquarie's ancient family home on Mull to Sydney. Sadly, the best and most accurate indicator of normality was that the Scots rugby tourists were getting a gubbing from the All Blacks.

PALNACKIE NO MORE

As my inquiries began to bear fruit, and information began to bounce back across the oceans to me, it quickly became clear that the old bonds remain formidable and will not be so easily severed. What lies behind the nationalist shenanigans in Cumberland Street is another Scotland living in exile. A vast legion, even though they may have adapted so successfully that they are sometimes difficult to recognise, but who still have Polmont or Palnackie, Unst or Ullapool graven on their hearts.

Today a steady stream of immigrants still make their way from Scotland to the Antipodes (752 to New Zealand between March 1995 and March 1996) but this represents a mere trickle compared with the exodus at its peak, a spectacular affair in which thousands of families risked everything to voyage by sailing ship across the oceans to a new life. Many of them, particularly

New arrivals from the United Kingdom including a group of relieved young Scots pictured in Sydney in 1926 after an adventurous journey during which the *Hobsons Bay* developed a bad list to port after cargo shifted. Fare from London was £34. (*John Oxley Library, Brisbane, Queensland*)

Proudly the Sim family strike a pose outside their new home at 'Pinkieburn' on the Otago Peninsula after emigrating from Glasgow in 1858.

the young, as we'll see, did not complete this voyage. Conditions were just too arduous. Even the long-awaited landfall after months at sea could simply mean swapping one hell for another.

In subsequent chapters we'll encounter families in both countries with such stories to relate. They tell of a struggle against the unforgiving elements – desert heat which burned into your soul, unfriendly native tribes wondering where all the white folk were coming from (and more importantly where they were going), dripping, impenetrable forests, vast empty plains, raging rivers and dangerous coasts where the seamanship of the Scots was tested to the full. Battlers aplenty were needed.

Sadly, the bulk of these folk were, and will remain, anonymous pioneers, unrecognised as they got the head down and proceeded to carve new lives for themselves in the Antipodes in what would be seen as a typically unfussy Scots manner. Naturally, the temptation is to dwell on the successes but as Professor Ted Cowan of the University of Glasgow has observed, much of what has been written about the Scots in the Commonwealth has been 'philo-pietistic drivel' with a huge history of failures waiting to be unearthed.

It's true that for every success story there may be a dozen depressing tales of failure and hardship to be uncovered. But even these can throw up some wonderful wee anecdotes. David Barker from Dumfries-shire travelled to New Zealand with his eldest brother John to seek their fortune and were on the central Otago goldfield in 1856. The family history tells us that David did not fare well, times were hard, so he moved to Australia. Before journeying to Queensland in search of work he purchased a gold first-day sovereign in Sydney. Returning to Scotland, a wiser man after his Antipodean experience, he married and gave the coin to his mother-in-law as a present. However, it lay in a tin for a century before being rediscovered in 1978. Inquiries revealed that it was one of only three in the world and it eventually fetched $12,000 at auction in Sydney. Back in Scotland David settled for a much more practical way of accumulating capital – he became a bank manager.

Generally though, did the Scots fare better than other ethnic groups, as some of the literature would suggest? It's impossible to say; it's a topic which does not lend itself easily to analysis. My guess is that many Scots who regarded themselves as less than successful simply because they had not made their fortune had, in fact, established comfortable lives for themselves.

The scale of these new lands is sometimes also difficult to visualise but is well illustrated by the story of Thomas Kidd from Elie in Fife who went to Victoria with his parents before moving in the pioneering days to Western Australia where, as an esteemed member of the community, he was appointed a justice of the peace for the colony. His vast but sparsely populated bailiwick covered an area which would have swallowed up the US states of California, Oregon, Washington and Idaho – or the whole of mainland Europe.

I SHALL RETURN NO MORE

For the purposes of this book I've looked for settlers' stories from the earliest days of the New South Wales penal colony (1788) up until World War II, a span of years during which the vast majority of immigrants could have no reasonable expectation of ever seeing their homeland again. The commitment was final and irrevocable.

In no sense is this book a comprehensive survey, more a series of snapshots homing in on anecdotes which I found appealing, and hope you do too, and which seemed to me to illustrate the dimensions of the Scottish experience. There are so many stories of determination and quiet bravery as the Scots helped provide the bricks and mortar, the solid foundation for the two nations. The stories which appear must speak for the millions of Scots and their descendants over six and seven generations who became complete New Zealanders or Australians.

Some cherished their Scottishness, others forgot it – but just as they helped mould the new nations, they too were unquestionably shaped and steeled by their Caledonian heritage, unwittingly or otherwise.

Tom Johnston, the Scots Secretary of State who in the late 1940s put into motion a tourist board initiative to persuade exiled Scots to return and visit their homeland (something which has, because of growing affluence and ease of communications, been successful beyond his wildest imaginings), sensed

Look out, the genealogists are about! Paddy Clark, a veteran Macnab descendant from the Bay of Plenty in New Zealand, climbs through the window of the clan burial ground at Killin, Perthshire, in search of information on his forebears. (*Paddy Clark*)

that this desire, this mysterious passion for the auld country, was very real, a resource to be tapped and a kinship to be shared. He once observed:

> Who having experienced it can ever forget the overpowering intensity of the Scottish in gatherings of our folk from Calcutta to Chicago.

On the threshold of a new century this zeal, if anything, seems more tangible and vibrant than ever, and although it is the Celtic trappings of pipe bands, Highland Games and tartan which form its most public face, it is much more a sense of shared nationhood which draws together Highlander, Islander, Lowlander and Borderer under the Saltire.

Multiculturalism is blossoming the world over and with it, in the past decade or two, a reawakening within the Scottish communities in Australia and New Zealand. A crowd of 1,200 gathered in Rawson Park, Sydney, on St Andrews Day 1988 when the Scottish-Australian bi-centenary cairn constructed from stones from every parish and district in Scotland was unveiled by the Duke of Argyll.

This burgeoning interest does not always manifest itself in a flamboyant, organised way such as through Scots-interest groups and pipe bands but is often, more genuinely, a private exploration seeking roots in the old country, a chance to see the countryside and meet the sort of folk grandparents spoke of so fondly, the chance to track down blood relations.

This development, the fulfilment of Tom Johnston's ambition, will hopefully mean that the image of Scotland Down Under will not remain static and sentimentalised, powered only by the great Celtic/tartan myth created by Sir Walter Scott, but will be adjusted to take into account the realities of Scotland today with all its challenges and problems.

Scots are to be found in significant numbers in every state of Australia and every province of New Zealand. Among the busy and overtly Scots folk we can find a staggering range of activity. The latest directory of Scottish organisations in South Australia, for example, lists dozens of Scots clubs and societies – twenty-four Highland dance schools, Scots radio stations, country dance groups, twenty pipe bands, lists of Burns clubs and entertainers, Scottish shops and even breeders of West Highland and Scottie terriers and Clydesdale horses.

THE SUBTLE SCOTS CONTRIBUTION

This book is neither an academic nor a genealogical work but more in the way of a popular history. The works of Prentis, Richards and Watson in Australia and Pearce and Brooking in New Zealand provide the bedrock. If this book sprinkles just a little insight into the sort of lives and challenges faced by our kinsfolk over a century and a half of immigration then the effort will have been worthwhile.

At a genealogy conference in Invercargill in 1996, Dr Thomas Brooking of the University of Otago confirmed the input of the first Scots pioneers and their descendants to the shaping of New Zealand and his comment that the Scots operated in 'subtle and nuanced rather than obvious and spectacular ways' applies equally to their contribution in Australia. It was, as Dr Brooking indicates, a thoroughly Scottish contribution.

One old lady who corresponded with me from Auckland in New Zealand boasted proudly in her despatches of her Scots background, the achievements of her forebears, her love of the pipes, memories of oatcakes and porridge, of reading the Psalms and the 'sough o' hame'. By chance I also exchanged letters with her daughter who discretely mentioned that I should bear in mind that, despite her obvious enthusiasm, the old lady was at most *one-eighth* Scottish.

Suchlike stories bear out the special pride which so many have in their Scottish connections in both countries, no matter how much the blood may have thinned over the generations. It seems that pursuing a Polish, English or Irish heritage just doesn't have the same sparkle.

And naturally it is these older folk, perhaps Scots-born or first-generation Antipodeans, who cling most tenaciously to the Scottish heritage. In my correspondence I have detected some resentment about the way in which they see new trade and cultural ties being forged with Japan, China, Korea, Taiwan and Malaysia at the expense of the old connections with the United Kingdom. 'They are asking us to think of ourselves now as Asians,' one lady in Wellington confided. 'Whit cheek. Not while I'm alive!'

It's not within my ability or the scope of this book to examine in detail or to give an accurate breakdown of the motives for the vast migration of the Scottish people from what was a relatively small nation but it is worthwhile looking at them in summary. Of course, the Scots had been on the

A replica of Cook's *Endeavour*, which was sent to the South Pacific in 1769 and spent many months mapping the New Zealand coast and eastern Australia, where he landed at the site later named Botany Bay. (*National Philatelic Collection: Australia Post*)

move for centuries, first in Europe as mercenaries and traders and then to North America. The exodus of Scots to Australia and New Zealand started slowly in the late 1700s with army officers, convicts and administrators heading for Botany Bay.

When immigration proper got under way with the first shipload of free immigrants reaching Australia in 1839 the movement of the Scots had for its dynamic what the social historians call the 'push-pull' effect. The immigrants were 'pushed' away from their home ground by a whole series of economic changes which were affecting Scotland, commencing even before the defeat of the Jacobite clans at Culloden, the Clearances which saw crofters pushed off the land to make way for sheep, the loss of the American colonies, the end of the Napoleonic Wars and the growth of industrial Clydeside where families could find themselves simply swapping rural deprivation for urban squalor.

Some, on the other hand, were 'pulled' by the possibility of something better, of having a greater say in their own destiny, owning some land, having a degree of job security and, yes, adventure aplenty. It's a noteworthy fact that the year Bonnie Prince Charlie died, 1788, the prison colony at Botany Bay was opened for business. The times were indeed a' changing.

It is reckoned today that the Scottish element of the eighteen-million strong Australian population (those from a Scots background rather than Scots-born) might be as high as thirteen per cent, while in New Zealand it has been estimated that because of the willingness of the Scots to inter-marry around fifty per cent of the three and a half million New Zealanders can claim some degree of Scottishness – and maybe the other fifty per cent would like to be able to make such a claim. But many ethnic groups have contributed over the past two centuries to the peopling and development of Australia and New Zealand. What exactly did the Scots bring to the emergent nations, what were the special qualities they offered?

THE CLAN AND CROCODILE DUNDEE

Distinctive characteristics which have been noted by historians on the plus side over the years included a capacity for hard work, perseverance, shrewdness, a sense of adventure fuelled by our traditional wanderlust, opportunism, resourcefulness and honesty. On the down side the critics have detected a clannishness which we Scots might be tempted to describe more accurately as family-mindedness; a dourness or killjoy attitude often seen in a religious context, known colloquially in Australia as 'wowserism'; that old standby with which the Scots are pummelled relentlessly – tight-fistedness; a pawky sense of humour often misunderstood by other ethnic groups (particularly the English); and as a result of the open celebration of their Scoto-Celtic heritage, a hopeless romanticism.

On a more upbeat note it has also been observed that the Scots seemed to be able to strike a balance between what has been described as rugged individualism and the abovementioned clannishness. Some have argued that the latter has been the moving force behind the Australian idea of 'mateyness' and appears to sit quite comfortably with the image of the bush-wise loner pitting his wits against the environment à la Crocodile Dundee. Put all these together and you have created the stereotype of the Scot. I can confirm we will not meet this mythical creature on our travels.

As well as the stories of the great and good, the low-lifes, guttersnipes and grovellers, this book tries to relate tales of the great wedge of ordinary folk who would be astonished to learn that after a century and a half their joys and heartaches in a new land would be of interest to anyone but immediate family. However, history tells us that these people were extra-ordinary, even if at most they simply thought of themselves as survivors. Professor Geoffrey Blainey, an immigration specialist, suggested at a book launch in bi-centenary year (1988) that if Australia was an empty land, in need of an instant population and economic growth, he would choose main-land Chinese, overseas Jews of the 19th and 20th centuries and the up-and-at-'em 18th-century Scots. Part Welsh, part Cornish and part Irish himself, the Prof admitted some personal grief at having to select the Scots among the most enterprising minorities in the world.

Over the past two hundred years, as Professor Malcolm Prentis of the Catholic University in Sydney and leading authority on the Scots settlement of Australia has written, the Scots were to be found in every corner of the new lands, working at every conceivable craft and involved in every facet of these developing societies. Because of this ubiquitous nature displayed by the Scot, it has been my contention in this book and in its predecessor, *Tam Blake & Co. - The Story of the Scots in America* (Canongate, 1993), that Scots left from every corner of our land and that no clachan or tenement building has remained untouched by the immigration fever. If you don't have family in Australia and/or New Zealand, it's a safe bet that you'll know someone along your street or round the corner who left to seek a more fulfilling life Down Under. To make that point I have, first of all, looked again for stories of success and failure, glory and disgrace, among the migrants who left from the places in Scotland with which I am most familiar, Clyde-bank, North Berwick and Papa Westray – the locations of my last three homes.

THE GREATEST IRONY OF ALL

A surprisingly high number of Scots must have set off for Australia and New Zealand with the unspoken dream of becoming a laird in their own right; what is equally surprising is the high number who went on to fulfil that ambition. The means by which this was achieved does not always stand up to scrutiny and could occasionally involve land-grabbing for its own sake, dispossessing the native peoples from their traditional territories (ironic this, when you consider how many of the Scots were victims of Clearances of a very similar stamp in their own land) without, apparently, a second thought about the consequences.

Few, however, could have accomplished what David Syme did as proprietor and editor of the *Age* newspaper in Melbourne in the second half of the 19th century. To all intents he was nothing less than the uncrowned ruler of the colony, later State, of Victoria. Syme was a schoolmaster's son from North Berwick in East Lothian who toyed with the idea of joining the ministry then took off in a totally different direction, heading in 1851 for the California goldfields.

Hard times lay ahead both in the States and at the Australian diggings,

The principal street of the goldrush town of Clyde in Otago in 1868. Local celebrities in the photograph include James Samson, the auctioneer and Ned Ryan, the hotelkeeper. (*Otago Settlers Museum, Dunedin*)

Gold fever saw men endure the most rugged of conditions whether in
California, Victoria, Otago, or here in the Queensland backwoods in the 1890s.
(*John Oxley Library, Brisbane, Queensland*)

where Syme and his partner, after successfully identifying a rich vein of gold
at Mount Egerton, found themselves the victims of a claim jumper. Syme's
brother Ebenezer was editing the *Age* newspaper and together, in 1856, they
bought the ailing journal for £2,000. On his brother's death David decided
to try to continue the paper although he was forced to work punishingly
long hours to make the enterprise a success. The newspaper's declared
editorial policies included manhood suffrage, the opening of the lands to
selection to would-be farmers without compensation to squatters and compulsory, free secular education. To those was added the controversial notion
of protection, a heavy taxation on imported goods, which Syme believed
would help foster Victoria's self-sufficiency.

He also took a keen interest in farming and was a constant advocate of
improved irrigation; for fifty years Syme built up the *Age* to be the most
powerful and influential newspaper in Australia. Syme is given credit, certainly by his biographers, for the introduction of protection through his
arguments. He was consulted regularly by leading figures in the colony
including Governor Sir George Brown. The general consensus is that during
this period he had the power to make or break governments and the conclusion of contemporary observers is that he virtually ruled the colony.

In a libel action arising out of allegations of mismanagement against the railway commissioners one leading counsel attempted an assessment of the power and influence of David Syme and his newspaper and concluded: 'No government could stand against the *Age* without being shaken to its centre.' With such controversial editorial policies there was always danger of advertising boycotts and Syme's answer to this was to lower the price of the paper to 1d.

Syme was remembered as a tall, stern, surprisingly reserved Scotsman who was, if anything, anti-social and could never be persuaded to make a speech or to sit on a committee. He sponsored expeditions and academic research. Some called him unscrupulous but all were agreed that the man who ran a newspaper for half a century and a colony for almost as long deserved the nickname of 'King David'. The *Age* remains a force in the land to this day.

THE PAPA WESTRAY CONNECTION

Round the firesides of Charleston, Hundland and Daybreak that cold winter of 1883/84 all the talk was of New Zealand. In the humble little crofts scattered around the island of Papa Westray preparations were well under way for a mini-exodus to the Antipodes.

Robert Seatter, a carpenter (b. 1852), and his neighbour William Rendall would go first in July 1884, followed within a few weeks by his sister May and her husband Thomas Miller. The sad farewells, the hopes for a brighter future particularly for the children were enacted all across Orkney and the rest of Scotland around this time as folk traded everything familiar for a fresh start in New Zealand, Australia, Canada or the United States. The Papa Westray colony made its base in the little town of Waikouaiti north of Dunedin, an area much favoured by Orcadian emigrants.

Robert was an experienced carpenter and joiner as well as having put in several years at the herring fishing. He sailed with William Rendall from the croft of Daybreak on the maiden voyage of the clipper *Invercargill* out of Greenock but because of unfavourable winds the voyage took ninety-one days. When Thomas and May followed them the *Auckland* made a dashing voyage averaging 270 miles per day. The *Otago Daily Times* reported that measles and bronchitis had run through the *Invercargill* en route, the measles having been brought aboard, apparently, by a contingent of Shetlanders. Robert, according to family records, was an assisted emigrant, his contribution to his passage being thirteen pounds, ten shillings.

He plied his woodworking trade at Waikouaiti until his bride-to-be Christina from Clestrain on Papa Westray arrived in 1888. They were married within a few days of her arrival and her younger brother John and his wife

Newhoose, Papa Westray: from this tiny croft by the east shore Orcadian George Burgher left for a new life in South Australia. (*Bill Irvine, Links, Papa Westray*)

Janet Harcus also settled in the Otago township, living there for the rest of their lives.

Robert and his family moved eventually to Southland where he gave thirty-six years of unbroken service to the local council at Otautau and was chairman of the Town Board during a visit by the Governor-General who, poignantly, was Lord Jellicoe of Scapa, commander in chief of the Grand Fleet during World War I.

But the Papa Westray folk also found their way to Australia. George Burgher of Newhoose, a tiny croft now called Bayview, overlooking the island's South Wick, was born in 1807. His first wife died in 1835 and George, a fisherman, was finding life increasingly hard in the North Isles of Orkney and was considering emigration. George is reported to have said that if he could have made a shilling a day he would not have left.

Their journey to Adelaide in 1854 on the *Joseph Rowan* out of Liverpool was a tedious one, becalmed rounding the Cape of Good Hope they had to wait for weeks for the trade winds. In South Australia George went to work for a Colonel Higgins at Currency Creek where he was paid the princely sum of £1 a week with double rations. The Colonel held extensive pastureland but eventually the government decided to break up the vast runs into smaller homesteads, and anyone was free to apply for land. When George heard of this he decided to apply. Having no transport he walked around fifty miles overnight to Adelaide, arriving before Colonel Higgins who had travelled by bullock cart. His prompt arrival meant that George was able to get a parcel of well-watered land which he had had his eye on at Middleton and here, despite setbacks including a devastating fire, George spent the rest of his life until he died in 1890.

TRACKER TRAILL — BEARD PULLER

Not only among the crofts of Papa Westray had thoughts turned to far-off places. Alexander Traill, following the route taken by so many younger sons of landed families, looked to make his fortune elsewhere. He turned his back on his home, Holland House, the large crow-stepped mansion which dominates the island and which had been the seat of the Traill landlords since the early 1600s, and sailed to Victoria.

Other members of the Traill clan were already in Victoria, and Alexander, leaving behind his affluent and privileged background, followed the well-trod path of young adventurers and tried his luck on the goldfields. When he was twenty-four years of age he married a servant girl Julia Bulley who had been working with the Traills. Their union was to be a fruitful one, producing twelve children, most of whom survived to a ripe old age.

They moved into the heart of Gippsland, pioneered less than two decades before by a couple of Highlanders, Angus McMillan and Lachlan Macalister. Alexander was a carrier, making his money servicing the gold mining communities as well as dabbling in mining speculation rather than digging his own claim. By 1863 the family had settled at Waterford in the Woonangatta Valley, a remote spot where the living was hard; the first four of their dozen children had arrived by this stage. Their house, to modern eyes a ramshackle collection of add-ons, was next to the bridge which provided a lifeline to the Grant and Crooked River goldfields and by the mid-1860s the Traills were operating a bed and breakfast establishment. If anyone heading for the goldfields higher up the valley pleaded poverty then it was suggested that they pay when they had made their fortune; but no one was ever turned away.

In his family history published in 1993 Bill Traill of Wodonga (VA) tells how in his declining years Alexander, by now head of a huge Traill tribe, would sleep off his dinner and his dram by taking a nap under the grapevine. His mischievous grandsons, Bernie Hurley and the splendidly named Tracker Traill, would gently tie a strand of wool to his beard and take off around the corner before giving it a vigorous tug. The old man is said to have taken their practical joking in good humour.

Duntocher-born speedway ace Ron Johnson and his trophy-winning colleagues pictured at the New Cross track in South London with film start Christine Norden on board. (*Sport & General, London: courtesy of Cyril Hart*)

THE KING OF CLAREMONT

In 1908 at Duntocher, in the rolling hills behind the shipyard town of Clydebank, Ron Johnson was born. At the age of six he was taken to Australia by his parents and brought up on a farm at Dwellingup in Western Australia, about seventy-five miles south of Perth where, years later, he began his career as a crack speedway rider, a genuine superstar between the World Wars.

Enjoying tinkering with engines more than schoolwork, young Ron also became an expert mechanic. For his seventeenth birthday his dad bought him a Harley Davidson 'Peashooter' bike and when the Claremont track opened in 1927 he was soon in action, winning his first race from a seventeen-second handicap. When a group of young Australians went to the United Kingdom in 1928 to aid the birth of the sport in this country, Ron was among them. Within three years he had won what was later classed as the World Championship and was captain of the New Cross team in South

London until 1949 when a serious head injury heralded the beginning of the end of his career.

In 1948 the life and times of Ron Johnson were told in a smash-hit British film *Once a Jolly Swagman*, with Dirk Bogarde playing the Johnson role and Ron handling the track action. Throughout his racing career Ron was a top star, a veteran of 20,000 races most of which he won; he had friends among royalty, socialites, film stars and was the idol of millions. His lifestyle was fast in every sense, he wore Savile Row suits, enjoyed fine wines and owned a 32-foot yacht. But there was a price to pay. He lost contact with his two daughters who went to America and Australia. Refused active service because of his speedway injuries, he was a stretcher-bearer in the East End of London during the air raids of World War II and worked as an aero-engine mechanic before he and his wife Roma set off to make new lives for themselves in America.

While their father partied with stars such as Humphrey Bogart and Jean Harlow, Ron's estranged daughters eked out a meagre living. When the money ran out in Hollywood Ron and Roma parted. The once great champion returned to Australia and to his mother. Towards the end of his life Ron spent his time tinkering with old bikes, having been refused a licence by local traffic police, and died penniless and alone among his trophies 12,000 miles from his birthplace in Duntocher. His family, quite naturally bearing in mind his track record, declined to offer any cash support to mark his last resting place but a group of speedway enthusiasts in London and Australia clubbed together to buy a splendid headstone and a magnificent memento, the Ron Johnson Memorial Trophy, which has been competed for annually at Claremont since the early 1990s.

Syme, Burgher, Traill, Seatter, Johnson – all members of that amazing, worldwide Tartan Army in exile which, according to some calculations and including all direct descendants, may today be sixty million strong. Most of these, mind you, will be 'sleepers', folk who are either totally unaware of or completely indifferent to their Scottish roots.

But who's counting? This exercise is more about quality than quantity, the illustrious . . . and the unsung. First of all then, let's join the bravehearts on the extraordinary journey to the Antipodes.

Chapter Two
Chasing the Trade Winds

B Y THE MIDDLE YEARS of the 1800s immigration fever of the Antipodean strain had well and truly caught hold in Scotland. It was a subject of debate and discussion, a preoccupation for families around kitchen fires across the land. Where to go? When to go? Could mither and faither be persuaded to join the adventure? How much money could be saved towards the passage?

Immigration societies to assist Scots to find a new home abroad and channel necessary information about the new lands to them were springing up everywhere. The chance to improve their lives, to gain a little more for the daily grind, perhaps to live a healthier and longer existence, to get a fair crack of the whip was an immensely tempting prospect.

The weaving community of Fenwick in Ayrshire, for example, witnessed the formation of a society in 1839 which was widely patronised, with a constant flow of departures from the district to the immigrant destinations including Australia and New Zealand. The organisers of the Fenwick group were in no doubt of the need for their services. In their constitution we find the ominous preamble:

A fearful gloom is fast thickening over the horizon of our country. Every prospect of comfort to the working man is daily becoming darker and more dreary. Trade and manufacturers are rapidly leaving our shores and, to all appearance, a crisis is at hand in which the sufferings of the working class will form a prominent feature.

The constitution goes on to emphasise that the ordinary folk should have the means to better themselves, to escape scarcity of work and, at worst, starvation. The industrial revolution had not provided anything like all the answers and the distant lands beckoned.

One-off events such as the collapse of the City of Glasgow Bank also concentrated the thoughts of many on new lands and fresh starts. When John Waugh's experiences in New South Wales were published in Edinburgh in the 1830s he was able to confirm for potential settlers that there were Presbyterian churches dotting the landscape and a great many of his countrymen residing there 'and all very clannish'. This factor was probably seen as a great incentive to migration. Some settlers went further. J. G. Johnston was of the opinion that anyone who preferred 'cold Caledonia and a life of unrequited toil' to the prospects Down Under 'cannot be under the guidance of reason'.

One of the most noted migration groups was the Highland and Island Emigration Society which, in a five-year existence from 1852, sent twenty-nine ships with 4,910 emigrants to a new life in Australia alone. In addition, as the century progressed companies were formed in Scotland such as the Scottish Australian Investment Company which allowed Scots businesses

NEW ZEALAND COMPANY–STEERAGE DIETARY.

FOR EACH PERSON FOURTEEN YEARS OLD AND UPWARDS.

	Prime India Beef.	Prime Mess Pork.	Preserved Meat.	Biscuit.	Flour.	Rice.	Preserved Potatoes.	Peas.	Oatmeal.	Raisins.	Suet.	Butter.	Sugar.	Tea.	Coffee.	Salt.	Pepper.	Mustard.	Vinegar or Pickles.	Water.
	lb.	lb.	lb.	lb.	lb.	lb.	lb.	pint												quar
Sunday . . .	—	—	½	¾	¼	—	¼	—	One Pint Weekly.	Eight Ounces Weekly.	Four Ounces Weekly.	Eight Ounces Weekly.	Sixteen Ounces Weekly.	Two Ounces Weekly.	Two Ounces Weekly.	Two Ounces Weekly.	A Quarter-Ounce Weekly.	Half-an-Ounce Weekly.	Half-a-Pint Weekly.	3
Monday . . .	—	½	—	¾	¼	—	—	¼												3
Tuesday . . .	½	—	—	¾	¼	¼	—	—												3
Wednesday. .	—	—	½	¾	¼	—	¼	—												3
Thursday . .	—	½	—	¾	¼	—	—	¼												3
Friday . . .	—	—	½	¾	¼	—	¼	—												3
Saturday. . .	½	—	—	¾	¼	¼	—	—												3
Total Weekly	1 lb.	1 lb.	1½ lb.	5¼ lbs.	1¾ lbs.	½ lb.	¾ lb.	½ pint	1 pint	8 oz.	4 oz.	8 oz.	16 oz.	2 oz.	2 oz.	2 oz.	¼ oz.	½ oz.	½ pint	21qr

Children Seven Years old and under Fourteen receive each, of Water, Three Pints a day; of other Articles, *Five-Eighths* of the Ration of an Adult.

Children One Year old and under Seven receive each, of Water, Three Pints a day; of Preserved Milk, a Quarter-Pint a day; and of other Articles, *Three-Eighths* of an Adult's Ration; or, if directed by the Surgeon, either Four Ounces of Rice or Three Ounces of Sago, in lieu of Salt Meat, three times a week.

Infants under One Year old do not receive any Ration; but the Surgeon is empowered to direct an Allowance of Water, for their use, to be issued to their Mothers. No charge is made for their Passage.

The several Articles of Diet may be varied from time to time, under the direction of the Surgeon, so as to promote the health and comfort of the Passengers, especially of Children.

New Zealand House, 9 Broad Street Buildings,
London, 1st November, 1848.

Steerage passengers to Australia and New Zealand in the middle years of the 19th century had to travel under a strict dietary regime, as this sheet indicates. Weekly allocation of water for an adult was 21 quarts.
(*Records of the New Zealand Company*)

FIRST SCOTTISH
COLONY for
New Zealand

That Fine

FAST

SAILING

TEAK-BUILT

SHIP

BENGAL MERCHANT,

501 *Tons Register*----JOHN HEMERY, COMMANDER,

WILL POSITIVELY

SAIL FROM PORT-GLASGOW

For NEW ZEALAND,

With the first Body of Settlers

FROM SCOTLAND,

On FRIDAY, Oct. 25.

SINGLE WOMEN, going out as Servants to Cabin Passengers, or in charge of Married Emigrants, will receive a *Free Passage* on board of this Ship.

All Goods and Luggage must be forwarded by the 20th instant *at latest*, on which day the Ship will clear out.

For *Freight* (having room for dead Weight and Measurement Goods) and *Passage*, apply to

JOHN CRAWFORD,
24, QUEEN STREET.

NEW ZEALAND LAND CO.'S OFFICE,
GLASGOW, 5th Oct. 1839.

J. Clark, Printer, Argus Office.

The great New Zealand adventure begins in earnest: a poster advertising the sailing of the *Bengal Merchant* from the Clyde in 1839 for Port Nicholson (Wellington). Berths were soon snapped up.
(*Glasgow Museums: The People's Palace*)

and individuals to get a piece of the action Down Under, to invest in the fast-growing economies of the new countries, and maybe also to share just a bittie in the great adventure, albeit with only a financial rather than physical risk.

PLUNGING OFF THE OTHER END

Historian James Belich tells us New Zealand was shamelessly promoted as a settlers' paradise, the perfect place for Britons to go and grow. By the 1870s the New Zealand government had seventy-three immigration agents at work in Scotland, holding meetings, distributing literature and helping folk on their way. It's said that advertisements were carried in 288 newspapers. Scores of books and pamphlets were published. Visions of a promised land, says Belich, diminished the trauma, the reality of what they were actually doing – 'plunging off the other end of the world'.

Difficulties and dangers ahead there may have been but there was no shortage of Scots ready to take the chance, often encouraged by letters from relatives who had already made the great journey. Although the statistics can be confusing it does seem that Scotland offered up a higher proportion of her people for immigration than any other part of the United Kingdom or Ireland.

Of course, all sorts of factors came into play when people finally plumped for immigration. Occasionally health was a consideration. Annie McDonald took her five children to Victoria in 1912 hoping the warmer climate might benefit her son John's health. He was a weakly lad. In fact, as his mother established a successful fruit growing business in Shepparton, young John thrived. So much so that he went on to become Sir John McDonald, Premier of Victoria.

After being gassed in World War I Jock Shaw's doctor in Scotland suggested that the young man go to New Zealand to get some sunshine for a few years. Jock arrived on the *Waimana* in 1919 and never went back. Despite the ordeal of the trenches the new country suited Jock and he lived to the ripe old age of eighty-seven.

Large family groups heading for Australia and New Zealand were common. Widow Helen Chisholm immigrated from Crichton in Midlothian to Geelong (VA) in 1851 with her extended family – daughter Helen and her husband Robert and three children; son Walter and his wife Eliza; son William with his wife Isabella and three children; and her son John and daughter Jessie. The descendants of this branch of the Chisholms now cover a wide social strata and have included a Rhodes scholar, a cabinet minister, teachers, farmers and public servants.

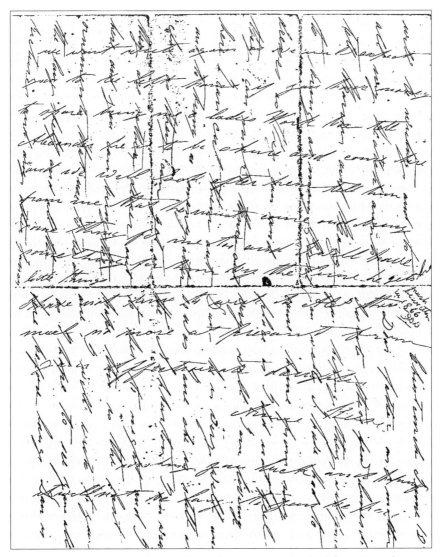

Cross-hatching – Anne Reese writes to her parents in Scotland from Canterbury before their departure for New Zealand in 1866. Shortage of writing paper is often cited for such well-filled sheets but could it have been merely Scots frugality? (*Anne Ralston, Wellington*)

Surprise has often been expressed at the numbers of old folk who were prepared to undertake the arduous trip to a new and unfamiliar land but the fact is that many willingly braved the voyage rather than be separated from their sons and daughters for ever.

The day the entire Gillies family from Rothesay on the Isle of Bute sat down to pray for divine guidance is one instance of how these momentous decisions were reached. John Gillies, the son of a crofter and handloom weaver, had risen after qualifying as a solicitor to become town clerk of his home burgh and stood square with his minister when he left the established church at the Disruption in 1843. One son John had already gone to Australia and more and more the father became convinced that immigration was the destiny of the Gillies clan. Without telling his family his thoughts he simply asked them to join in a day of prolonged prayer for guidance. By the evening it appears that a decision to immigrate arose spontaneously and was agreed unanimously.

In Otago John Gillies continued his career as public administrator including the role of registrar of births, deaths and marriages. Son John had tried his hand at sheep farming and gold mining in Australia and moved into journalism and politics when he joined his family in New Zealand. Another son Robert was said to have driven the first pair of horses seen in the Tokomairiro Plain south of Dunedin and the straightest furrow in Otago. Thomas, like his father, a lawyer, rode the length of both the South and North Islands when he decided to move from Dunedin to Auckland, a journey invariably taken by sea in those days. Thomas Gillies was one of New Zealand's first conchologists – his shell collection being supplemented on various expeditions.

WHO LEFT THE KITCHEN SINK?

When James and Anne Sinclair from Caithness left for New Zealand in 1857 their list of 'necessities' give an interesting insight into what the better-off immigrant might consider important and includes tableware, linen, silver, a sea chest each of clothes and books, grain, seeds, food, young Walter's horse and two rose bushes from Anne's old home at the Castle of Mey. The family tradition suggests that Anne, whose maiden name was Sinclair, had been promised to a future Earl of Caithness but had eloped with James instead.

Even into the 1920s the actual departure of the Scots on the great immigration adventure was an emotional occasion. The likelihood was still that the voyagers would never see their homeland again. A family history of the Lumsdens – mother, father and six children – from Kinross-shire, tells of a triumphal march to the railway station at Rumbling Bridge on the Perthshire-Kinross boundary. Thomas and Betty Lumsden were on their way to Invercargill at the southern tip of New Zealand's South Island and left Scotland for ever on 9 January 1925. The emotion of the departure must have been heightened by the fact that Thomas was leaving behind eleven brothers and sisters. This was a classic 20th-century case of 'connections'.

An affluent departure – the Mackay family leave Sutherland for a new life in the Nelson district of New Zealand in 1844. Young James, the eldest son, who was to gain fame on the gold diggings and during the Maori Wars is pictured sitting confidently on the family's gold chest. (*'The Emigrants' by Elizabeth Walker, National Library of Australia: accession no. U2582*)

Betty's sister Christina was already settled in Southland and had written regularly to tell just what a wonderful life was to be had in New Zealand.

The procession left Craigend house and walked to the station with Peter Keir playing the bagpipes and a throng of friends and relatives gathering to see them off on the first leg of their journey – by rail to Southampton. A cousin, Nan Inglis, travelled with the Lumsdens as far as Carlisle and there yet another sad farewell was enacted. The Lumsdens also had their own ideas about 'necessities' for their new home. Their baggage included three bicycles in a crate and a Singer sewing machine. Even in the 1920s there was still a distinct sense of the pioneering experience – the Lumsdens' first pillow cases were flour bags.

As with the Gillies family from Rothesay the final commitment to immigration could follow months or even years of deliberation, reading, prayer and heart-searching or it could be the decision of a moment. Here in Orkney the story is told of a couple picking tatties in the parish of Deerness last century, a backbreaking job as I can personally testify and definitely one to make you consider life's other possibilities. 'Let's go to Australia,' says the husband with the rain dripping off the end of his nose. 'Aye, why not?' says the guidwife. 'But we'd better finish this dreel first.' Early impressions in Australia were not favourable but they persevered in their new home – the only concession to the old life was to name their house Orkney.

THE PROPHET OF DOOM

They do breed a hardy crew among Orkney's green isles and in general terms the folk from Orkney, Shetland and the Western Isles made good immigrants. However, every bit of northern resilience was needed when the Flett and Linklater families from Kirkwall set off for Adelaide in 1840 with the intention of opening a grocery business.

James Linklater and his brother-in-law W. Flett departed from Leith on the barque *Indus* (Captain – John MacFarlane) but off Montrose 'ran aboard' a schooner with the result that the bowsprit and figurehead of the *Indus* were carried away. She was forced to put back for repairs. She eventually arrived at Glenelg – the port for Adelaide – five months to a day after the original departure date, a long haul by any standards.

Linklater was faced with a long walk to Adelaide at a time when the local press was appealing to newcomers not to judge the colony's possibilities by the discomfort of a tramp from Glenelg in the middle of a hot day. This public relations problem apparently developed after a 'scampish broken-down attorney's clerk' had got on board an immigrant ship in the bay and so stunned the prospective settlers with his grim accounts of conditions on shore that some of them made up their mind on the spot to go elsewhere.

Orcadians, as I say, are made of sterner stuff, but they did find conditions primitive. Mrs Linklater had to be carried ashore and the little Orkney group had to live for a time on the sandhills with only umbrellas to keep off the rain, the men taking watch duty in order to protect their pile of baggage from pilferers. After successfully operating a grocer's shop Linklater went into sheep farming in Streaky Bay, operating a station called Kirkala, sounding uncannily like his home town of Kirkwall, but in fact the Aborigine phrase for 'pig-face'.

The loss of a figurehead in the busy immigration lanes was clearly not a one-off occurrence. The *Strathallan* – out of Leith in October 1857 – was almost run down by a steamer travelling, so it was said, without lights. The figurehead, a kilted Highlander, was broken in the rigging of the other vessel and had to be chopped away. A bad omen, you might have thought, but according to the diary of young William Smaill, it was an agreeable enough voyage although one young man died of pneumonia after getting a soaking

Immigrants at dinner below decks en route to Australia from the *Illustrated London News* of 13 April 1844.
(*General Reference Library, State Library of New South Wales, Sydney*)

in horseplay while crossing the Equator. The captain, who possibly did not need an excuse, took to the comforts of the bottle after this incident, the first officer providing a more than capable substitute. Having sighted Otago Heads on the ninety-seventh day the boozy captain proceeded to take the vessel, inexplicably, back out to sea, but was restrained. Despite a series of groundings involving the tenders which held up disembarkation, the immigrants finally landed. The *Strathallan* sailed back to London within a few months with a cargo of wool – and a new captain.

In the second half of the 19th century great incentives were being given to encourage Scots to move Down Under. A brisk trade developed between Glasgow and Dunedin with the Albion Line of fast sailing ships. Some completed the voyage in as little as seventy-five days, venturing as near as they dared to the great southern ice cap to take advantage of the trade winds. The average was around ninety days and in exceptionally adverse weather conditions the trip could take upwards of four months.

Sometimes there would be experiences on the voyage which would stay with travellers for the rest of their lives. Isabella Bonthron kept a detailed log of the passage made by the *Helenslee* in 1863. Early one Saturday morning near the end of the voyage a commotion brought everyone on deck. A huge rock, 'not unlike the Bass in the German Ocean', had appeared out of the mist and there was difficulty due to stormy conditions in getting the helm to respond.

In an instant both captain and first mate had cast their coats on the deck and were pulling at the ropes of the jib by the hoisting of which sail the vessel got round the rock when so near that a stone might have been thrown at it.

Within a few hours they had sighted Southland which Isabella said reminded her of the Cheviot Hills seen from the highest part of Roxburghshire.

John McFarlane from Auchterarder sailed on the *Lady Egidia* which left Greenock on 12 October 1860 on her maiden voyage to New Zealand. It was an ill-starred trip with thirty children dying en route.

The Perthshire man's diary of the voyage is, however, filled with smashing anecdotes such as the woman wandering the deck who slipped and fell on her bottom. Blaming her carpet slippers, she threw them angrily overboard. Or the stowaway who gave himself up and was set to the 'dirty work'. There is an intriguing entry on 3 November – 'Some word of the young women misbehaving on Sunday night'; also, two young men convicted of stealing a bottle of brandy were fastened to the stays of the mizzen mast; and a prank by the young men to strip and tie up the cook failed when he threatened to let daylight into them with a carving knife. Generally conditions seem to have been hard on board and John concluded towards the end of the voyage, rather ominously, that 'None of my relations shall come out on a Scottish ship if I can help it.' There were moments too, after his arrival in New Zealand, when he must have questioned his decision to emigrate. After working on the goldfields he had to survive for days on a diet of raisins until supplies arrived.

Valued migrants were given free or assisted passage. For example in 1873 those receiving assisted passage to New Zealand included married agricultural labourers, navvies, ploughmen and shepherds. They were required to give a promissory note for £10, payable in the colony by instalment; or by paying £5 cash and the rest later. Free passages were given to single female domestic servants and to children under twelve travelling with their parents, no small consideration in the days of vast Victorian families. On arrival the immigrants would normally stay in migrant hostels until permanent accommodation could be secured.

ALL ABOARD THE PUDSEY DAWSON!

The names of the hundreds of vessels which brought Scots immigrants to Australia and New Zealand are remembered with fondness or dismay by descendants depending on how easy the journey had been.

In Australia, unquestionably the best remembered group of vessels were the First Fleet, the little flotilla of convict and supply ships which in 1788 began the British settlement of the great island continent. They were *Sirius*,

Supply, Alexander, Lady Penrhyn, Charlotte, Scarborough, Friendship, Prince of Wales, Fishburn, Golden Grove, and *Borrowdale.*

As for New Zealand, the names are etched into the story of the Scots: the *Rosanna* and the *Lambton*, ships of the original New Zealand Company which brought a group of settlers to Northland in 1824; the *Jane Gifford* and *Duchess of Argyle* carried the first 500 Scots immigrants to Auckland in 1842; in the early 1840s the *Blenheim* and *Bengal Merchant* carried Scots safely to Port Nicholson (which was to become Wellington), and the *John Wickcliffe* and *Philip Laing* carried the Free Church settlers to a new life at their Otago settlement in 1848.

Of all the hundreds of sailing ships, schooners, barques, clippers and steamships, unquestionably my own favourite is the splendidly titled *Pudsey Dawson*. Surely they were queuing for a berth on the *Pudsey*?

It was normal practice to hold a religious service on the immigrant ships before they left on the great voyage. One such sermon was given by the Rev. Thomas Fraser on board the *Duntrune* at Dundee in 1883, just before she sailed for Queensland. After singing the poignantly appropriate hymn 'There's a Home Over There', the Rev. Fraser told the assembled company that they should be proud of the Scottish stock from which they came and should endeavour to be worthy of it. Honesty, industry, thrift and the Fear of God, he suggested, would be the key to success in their new home and if they wished to make themselves rich they would do well to spend little or nothing at all on drink and tobacco.

This voyage of the *Duntrune* turned out to be something of an epic. For a start, she was the last immigrant ship to leave Dundee for Australia. She was an iron clipper of the Dundee Clipper Line and had 450 assisted migrants on board. Nearly four months later and after many trials and tribulations she finally anchored off Brisbane (QD). Eighteen children and one adult had died during the voyage. From the start she seems to have been dogged by difficulties, battered by storms as she rounded Scotland. Between Orkney and Shetland in the Fair Isle Channel some of the passengers were said to have been frightened half to death by the ferocity of the storm. This being my own current stomping ground I know exactly how they must have felt.

The first major problem which the master, John Rollo of Newport, had to deal with was the discovery that the reserve fresh water was undrinkable. Nearly 500 gallons was required daily so the water condenser carried for such emergencies was brought into action – only to break down immediately. They reached Madeira just before the supply gave out. By the time they reached the Cape of Good Hope fierce storms were raging and the conditions took a terrible toll on the wee ones. Regularly a knot of people would gather in the half light of evening to commit the body of a child to the deep.

However, if the immigrants from the *Duntrune* thought their troubles were over when they stepped ashore at Brisbane they were mistaken. Within three days of landing one of the male passengers was found laid out in a Brisbane street. Cause of death – sunstroke.

Some folks successfully avoided the crush of the immigrant fleet. Edinburgh sea captain James Meiklejohn had been involved in shipbuilding in Prince Edward Island, Canada, when he set off with his family in his own boat. His plan was to cruise the world until he discovered a location where he could happily settle. In 1857 he found his goal and acquired land at Big Omaha on New Zealand's North Island.

SEABOARD SHENANIGANS

On board the ships a daily routine was soon operating with everyone allocated tasks to keep them busy for the duration of the journey. That still left time, according to the settlers' diaries, for plenty of on-board shenanigans. Twenty-year-old Willie Hamilton from Strathearn, Perthshire, sailed to South Australia on the *British Empire* in 1850. In his journal he noted that Captain McEwen, having been informed that the first officer was making free with the unmarried females, had formed a court of inquiry with the doctor behind closed doors. Evidently the first officer was not the only randy matelot on board, and the need for the specially appointed shipboard police force soon becomes obvious. Willie notes later in the voyage:

The *Rangitata* – a typical immigrant ship which took thousands of Scots to
New Zealand in the middle years of the 20th century.

The captain has ordered one of the constables to be always on deck in the afternoon to prevent intercourse between the sailors and unmarried females.

Apparently, the boat was abuzz with all sorts of hot gossip.

On board the immigrant ship *Philip Laing* with the large Free Church of Scotland contingent was the Rev. Thomas Burns, arguably the founding father of the Otago colony. In his diary Burns reported that there was soon a busy atmosphere on the boat with much bartering of goods and deals being struck. On Saturday 12 February Rev. Burns noted that his brother Arthur had purchased the carpenter's goat which he had brought on board at Greenock for the princely sum of ten shillings.

On another occasion the Rev. Burns found himself serving on a jury of steerage passengers trying two men accused of being involved in a knife fight which, if the weapon had not been blunt, might have inflicted a fatal wound. Both men were sentenced to be rebuked before the congregation that evening after worship. One also had to carry water to the cooks for a week and the other to assist with the cleaning of the ship for a fortnight and to have his head shaved.

SCANDAL IN THE STEERAGE

Perhaps the greatest challenge faced by Rev. Burns during the voyage in this straight-laced and cramped environment was the discovery that a couple who had come aboard at Greenock were not, in fact, married. It was brewing up to be quite a scandal, with the passengers threatening to boycott the dinner table if the man and woman dined with them. The man, Carnegie by name, had taken Burns aside and explained that they had gone through a civil marriage but had not found time in the midst of frantic preparations for departure to undertake a church ceremony. He confessed, however, that they had no document to confirm the marriage, civil or otherwise. Carnegie admitted that he had lived with the woman for three months prior to sailing. As he pondered the propriety of marrying these social outcasts Burns had other matters of a delicate nature to deal with. His diary records:

> Engaged this morning investigating a most distressing report regarding Mrs Thorburn and the 3rd mate (Haddock) which turned out to my great relief to be quite untrue.

We may never know what fishy business had been hinted at. Sixty-two days out from the United Kingdom the passengers on the *Philip Laing* handed over letters to the homeward-bound sailing ship *Tenobia* which was on its way to Cape Town. The Rev. Burns had scribbled a few lines to his brother

A studio portrait of the Rev. Thomas Burns who led the Free Church expedition to settle Otago in 1848. (*Otago Settlers Museum, Dunedin*)

Gilbert saying they were all well as were the 'bull, dog and cow'. The cat had disappeared. Burns notes that he suspects 'Mrs' Carnegie of having thrown the poor creature overboard as some sort of vengeance for the delay in proceeding with the wedding. Eventually on 22 March 1848, the Otago party leader agreed to marry the Carnegies 'who had been living together as man and wife since August'. Obviously this decision had caused Burns much soul-searching.

Interestingly, two months after reaching Dunedin Rev. Burns's beautiful daughter Clementina (aged fifteen) married skipper Andrew Elles of the *Philip Laing*. Love had blossomed on the journey south.

Maritime romances did develop regularly, sometimes even before the ship had left the Clyde or Forth behind, sometimes in mid-ocean. Stuart Baillie travelled out to South Australia as an eleven-year-old on the *Loch Fyne* in 1879 with his six brothers and sisters and mother and father, the family having left behind the familiar sights and sounds of the east coast fishing port of Arbroath. They were persuaded to take the plunge by their family doctor despite rumours of fire, drought, savage natives and the very real perils of the sea journey (there were six births and ten deaths, mostly children, on what was to be the *Loch Fyne*'s last voyage to Australia). Young Stuart remembers the decks awash and the big yards dipping into the sea during the three-month voyage. The great risks they had taken became all too apparent when the Baillies learned that on the return leg to London the *Loch Fyne* had been lost with all hands.

But back to romance. In his autobiography Stuart remembers how his eldest brother Jack, who had been working as a foreman in Ireland, joined the party at the Tail of the Bank just in time for sailing. As the ship cast off and the 'goodbyes were at their tops' there was a rosy-cheeked lass called Jessie McNab on the quayside who exchanged shouted farewells with Jack, although they had never met.

> Jack must surely have put some mighty words into those last few moments, because soon after landing I learned that Jessie was also in Australia . . . and had nabbed my brother Jack.

Young Stuart had another brother on the *Loch Fyne* called George and when it emerged that a George Bailey was also travelling the scene was set for romantic intrigue. Bailey had a girlfriend in the single women's quarters and because he was illiterate he usually got Stuart's brother to pen love letters on his behalf. They were passed along by a shipboard officer who had access to all quarters. Everything was grand until brother George began to slip in a few tender words on his own behalf, with such success that he eventually cut out the original suitor. Reaching Australia, George Baillie married his girl and lived a lifetime together at Tumby Bay.

With such a mass movement of mankind across the face of the globe there was always the possibility of catastrophe – either through the loss of a loved one or indeed of almost an entire extended family as was the case with the

St Kilda immigrants of 1852. This poignant event, often cited by social historians to illustrate the hazards of the sea voyage, began when thirty-six people, a third of the population of the remote Atlantic island group, were persuaded to try their luck and a new beginning in Victoria. However, fever caught hold on the boat and only twenty islanders reached Melbourne. In the quarantine stations over the years of immigration thousands were to die, the stark dormitories all they were to see of the new home from which they had expected so much.

FOR THOSE IN PERIL

Above all it was the loss of the children which was felt most sorely. For example, the Drummonds from Fife sailed, appropriately, on the *Fifeshire* to Nelson in 1841. But little George Drummond never completed the trip. He choked to death, the family say, on the overcrowded ship when a marble was placed in his mouth by an older child.

There was another side to the coin. The Macnaughton family from Fort William sailed for Victoria in 1848 on the *Andromache*: Samuel, Catherine and their two sons Donald and Dugald. A third son had an entry to be treasured on his birth certificate – born 29 July 1848, on ship, Bay of Biscay.

When the *Philip Laing*, packed with Free Church settlers, arrived at Otago on 15 April 1848 after four months at sea, the anchor had scarcely been dropped when there was a cry of 'man overboard'. In fact, a child had clambered on to the gunwale, dropped into the sea and was being carried off by the fast-flowing tide. Without hesitation the schoolmaster, Mr Blackie, threw off his jacket, jumped overboard and held the child above the water until the rescue boat arrived. Blackie, a hero among heroes.

John Mackinnon left Raasay with the Highland and Island Emigration Society in 1852 and wrote to his brother Donald from Geelong (VA) breaking the news that his little boy Charles had died from measles 1,000 miles west of the Cape of Good Hope. He said he could not advise anyone with weak children to make the trip. He warned:

> The measles was in the ship and Charles got it and died after being ten days sick. And little Ann took it but she came safe from it. But I ought to bless God I have the rest safe, for there were plenty with me that lost all their children.

During this particularly harrowing voyage eighty-two children died.

On the other hand there were many births to report. In 1849 the Whiteside family from Carmunnock near Glasgow set off for Otago and wee Alex was born en route (the captain wanted to call him Ajax after the vessel but

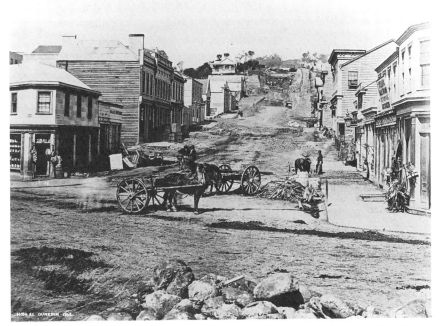

High Street, Dunedin, photographed by Coxhead in 1861 still has the hallmarks
of the frontier town thirteen years after the arrival of the first immigrant ships.
(*Otago Settlers Museum, Dunedin*)

common sense prevailed). When the family arrived in Dunedin the new
arrival caused a sensation among the Maoris who had never seen a white
baby and took him from his mother, passing him around for inspection. His
mother's anxiety was matched only by her pride.

WHAT SHALL WE DO WITH THE DRUNKEN SKIPPER

The passage of the 600-ton *Strathfieldsaye* was not the happiest in the annals
of the great migrations but it does indicate the sort of problems the innocent
voyagers often faced. James and Margaret Sim and their seven children from
Edinburgh were among 263 passengers from all over central Scotland who
gathered for the departure of the sailing ship in the spring of 1858. Unfortunately the trip was marred by the drunkenness of the skipper James Brown
which resulted in a lack of provisions for the passengers as James Sim was
later to testify at Dunedin when the ship's master was charged with a breach
of the Passengers Act; this obliged the captain to look after his charges to
the best of his ability.

James Sim had been abused by the captain for insisting on his full allowance of oatmeal. Rations of fresh water were short, occasionally foul, and on one particular day the passengers were told to gather as much rainwater as they could because it was all they would get that day.

The captain also faced a charge of shooting his second mate John McKellar on the hand after Brown had been found with one of the female passengers in a compromising position in the water closet. It seems that the crew had been regularly threatened at gunpoint. Eventually Brown was fined thirty shillings but the memory of this unhappy voyage remained in the folklore of the families who had been unfortunate enough to make the voyage with the *Strathfieldsaye*.

Letters from Scots who had made the great journey south often appeared in the Scottish Press and these were to prove invaluable for the settler planning for every eventuality. John Mackie, a gardener from Turiff in Aberdeenshire who settled in South Australia, felt that any working man would prosper in Australia but warned that for the voyage oatmeal – a Scottish staple, of course – should be brought because of the niggardly supplies available on the vessels. Mackie and his cohorts ended up swapping their flour with the English passengers for the precious oatmeal.

MERCHANT ADVENTURERS

The records of the voyage of the *Bengal Merchant* which left the Tail of the Bank on 31 October 1839 carrying 161 passengers also give some useful insights into how shipboard life was organised. Among the family groups, a number of which we encounter elsewhere in this book, we find the names of McEwen, Anderson, Buchanan, Crawford, Drummond, Forbes, Galloway, Lockie, Murray, Nisbet, Riddle, Scott and Yule.

Every migrant in steerage was given a mattress by the company plus eating utensils and a tin cup. Pots and pans for cooking were supplied. The company expected each adult to take up to half a ton of baggage but they would not have been allowed to embark without sufficient plain, strong clothing and the tools of their trade, whatever.

Women were expected to make up clothes on the passage and the travellers were warned that no fresh water would be available for washing and that they should supply themselves with marine soap. Rations for women were the same as for their menfolk except that women 'giving suck' got a pint of stout each day. The *Bengal Merchant* made no stops en route but, remarkably, there was torrential rain when she arrived at Port Nicholson on 20 February 1840 and it held up disembarkation for several days.

As well as carrying its contingent of agricultural settlers the *Bengal Merchant* brought Rev. John Macfarlane from Paisley as the first Church of

Scotland minister to New Zealand, and Francis Logan of Dunlop in Ayrshire who came to Wellington as the ship's surgeon. A graduate of Glasgow University, Logan had seen service with the Royal Navy during the Peninsular War and off North America and Africa. He made his first voyage to Australia in charge of the health of convicts on the *Fanny* in 1832 during which he had to deal with an outbreak of cholera. With every voyage down under Logan became more and more interested in the possibilities of New Zealand for settlement and joined the organisation of the *Bengal Merchant* expedition in Glasgow. He sailed with his wife and son on that historic voyage, selecting his country land at Porirua, over the hill from Wellington.

While a significant number of families travelled to Australia and New Zealand in relative comfort with their servants and enough money to make a solid start there were others, steerage passengers, who were quite simply paupers. The Scottish Records Office in Edinburgh has papers from the Highland and Island Emigration Society which give a heart-rending picture of some of the poorest. One man had lived in a gravel pit for eighteen months.

One of the first acts Kirriemuir blacksmith Alex Jones performed after the ship set sail for New Zealand was to fashion a harpoon for the mate who wanted to try his hand at spearfishing from the deck. Alex noted in his journal:

> I'm glad I can still turn my hand to my trade. I got a bottle of rum (for the favour) which is very useful and we sponge our bodies at night. It is capital prevention for vermin . . . We take a mouthful of rum inside occasionally.

Alex was interested to see how the different ethnic groups mixed below decks. He noted, perhaps a little surprisingly, that the English and the Irish mixed most together while the Scots seemed to go their own way.

> But we are not ashamed and are by far the strongest party, if not in numbers, I'm sure we are in quality.

Alex admitted to his diary that they had made a major mistake in not including a medicine chest among their belongings. Another bottle of 'medicinal' rum was coming Alex's way, however. The captain found that the main spring of his revolver had broken and Alex offered to attempt a repair. Working at the engineer's furnace and on a small anvil he soon had the revolver in working order. That same night the Jones family found a couple of bugs in their bed and speculated if they had travelled all the way from London with them.

ALBERT ROSS – WHO HE?

Some of Alex's entries range from the sublime to the truly comic. Witness his expectation of a favourable wind the following day because lots of very large birds were flying about the ship – 'Albert-Rosses, they name them'. And on the adjacent page:

> Making good progress today till a little Irish girl beside us vomited a long-worm! This caused great consternation.

Crofter and stonemason George Munro left Bonar Bridge in Sutherland with his wife and six children in October 1857 and by mid-February they were in Otago. The boat which carried them, the *Palmyra*, had a passenger list of 300 people from all over the UK, the Scots being mainly from the shires of Perth, Aberdeen, Inverness, Fife and Sutherland. Sadly George's young daughter Sara was among nine deaths (seven children) which occurred during the voyage.

Off the Canaries the ship was almost wrecked when the lookout went to sleep, the alarm being raised when one of the passengers had gone on deck in the early hours for a smoke. In addition, the chief mate who had been helping some of the passengers 'broach the rum' threatened to blow up the ship at one point and, in the absence of a cell, he was arrested and locked in one of the passengers' WCs.

Scots descendants today read and wonder about these epic adventures. One confided in me:

> Looking at the conditions some of these people were asked to endure,
> most of them displayed a staggering level of courage. I'd like to think that
> if called upon my own children would be equal to such adventures but
> you never know till the time arrives.

From time to time the Antipodes were a second option when migration was considered. James Roy and his wife Margaret of the parish of Forgue in Aberdeenshire had no house of their own and had convinced themselves that life in Scotland was set to be a 'hard grind throughout'. James had learned a little of the United States from letters sent by a neighbour's sons but as the Roys began to get down to detailed planning, the American Civil War broke out. New Zealand came into the equation.

Their voyage to Otago on the *Grassmere* in 1862 was one of the less eventful trips in the records, no deaths and two births was an unusually positive tally. Health of the passengers was generally good, says James in his journal, but one case of lunacy occupied much of the doctor's attention. The voyage of the *Grassmere* was also one of the longer on record, lasting four months and one week. And working with faulty chronometers they missed their way and sighted land to the north – it was the Canterbury coast. This meant turning southwest into the teeth of the wind. Ironically this forced them further out to sea and before reaching Dunedin they experienced the worst storm of the entire trip.

Isabella Bonthron travelled with her husband David and four children on the *Helenslee* out of the Clyde in 1863 bound for Bluff in New Zealand's Southland. She kept a splendidly detailed diary and within a few hours of setting sail she was recording a run-in with an unco-operative governess while Isabella attempted to set up a 'Sabbath class' for the children.

She wrote of gazing at the distant Galloway coast and retiring to her bed, her head spinning with memories of the life she was leaving behind, so much so that, as the other passengers burst into a heart-rending chorus of 'Auld Lang Syne', Isabella found some relief for her heavy heart in a 'torrent of tears'. Describing the daily routine Isabella said that six 'policemen' had been appointed to enforce cleanliness rules and general order. Rising at six, breakfast at eight and worship at nine-thirty a.m., school was held in the morning, tea was at six p.m. and everyone had to be abed by ten.

Gaelic was spoken by the shepherds who were travelling and this intrigued Isabella; swearing was not heard among the officers but was rife among the passengers and this dismayed her. They were quickly becoming accustomed to the ocean although every day held surprises – porpoises, huge barnacle-encrusted tree trunks which looked like sea serpents, flying fish, phosphorescence clinging to the side of the ship. All of these were greeted with excitement.

Nearing Madeira a young man was very poorly with consumption (tuberculosis) and plans were made to land him; the God-fearing folk like the Bonthrons were much angered by a young man who gathered a crowd of his contemporaries around him on the deck by singing an obscene song.

As for entertainment Isabella notes:

There is generally a dance on board every night to the music of the bagpipes occasionally a concert is got up among the young people.

An outbreak of measles is reported eight days out of port and the weather had become noticeably warmer when Isabella decided to crop the boys' hair. Other brief entries:

July 21 – Passed Cape Verde Islands

July 25 – Exchanged greetings with a Portuguese vessel; seven foot long shark landed.

July 27 – Becalmed but managed to pass letters from home to an Aberdeen bound ship.

July 29 – Isabella bemoaned the large numbers of smokers on board and records the first death, a little girl.

August 6 – Crossed line on young David's birthday.

August 10 – Young James fell out of his bunk and was discovered, bewildered at the door of Isabella's berth. Asked what was wrong, James said: 'Ah dinna ken, ah've cracked me crown.'

The arrival of immigrant ships at Australian and New Zealand ports was mostly an occasion for civic welcome. One city in particular, Bundaberg (QD), which witnessed the arrival of a series of vessels in the 1880s, seems to have got the reception business down to a fine art.

The barque *Renfrewshire* with 305 passengers on board, most of them Scots and many from Aberdeen, arrived off Burnett Heads in September 1882. Mayor Walter Adams who had been in the fast-developing township for a decade, organised a craft with a party of local notables, including the Presbyterian minister the Rev. J. G. Stirling, accompanying immigration and health officials on board to greet the waiting ship outside the river entrance.

The city of Brisbane (QD), originally the penal colony of Moreton Bay is now a thriving commercial centre with many Scots connections.
(*Australian Tourist Commission*)

The *Renfrewshire* under the command of Captain Cummings had sailed from the Tail of the Bank on 6 June.

Many of these Scots moved further afield but others remained to settle in and around Bundaberg including Miss Donaldson, who had been the ship's nurse and went to work in the local hospital and marry locally. Thomas Garland established a furniture and undertaking business; John Norval became a butcher/grazier; William Dunn, a master builder, became mayor; and a Mr Patterson, who had been in charge of the ship's stores, set up a grocery business in the town.

REGULAR AS CLOCKWORK

Five years later the Rev. Stirling was involved in another reception party at Bundaberg, this time for the passengers on the *Earl Granville*, an iron-hulled sailing ship which had left the Clyde in March 1887 taking 119 days for the voyage.

The arrival was described by Bundaberg historian Henry Marks. Over 500 residents gathered to greet the immigrants as they disembarked from the tender before they were treated to a sumptuous tea organised by the ladies' committee. The Rev. Stirling pops up with some sage advice for the newcomers. He advised them that the keys to success were in reading the Bible, avoiding drink, accepting any decent work offered to them . . . and keeping their bowels open.

Occasionally there was confusion over the terms of assisted immigration. In December 1837 the *Midlothian* arrived at Sydney with a group of 282 immigrants from Skye. These people believed that the colonial government was not only committed to give them free passage but also to settle them together, with their minister. They felt no obligation or desire to take up work with potential employers who had helped with the cost of their voyage. They were eventually settled as a group on the Hunter River.

WHEN THE FEVER SHIPS SAILED IN

But every arrival had its unusual aspects. One old worthy at the Scottish Gaelic Society in Melbourne never forgot coming to the city in 1923 to find himself in the midst of a strike by police officers – a case, he felt, of jumping out the Scottish frying pan and into the Australian fire.

Not every welcome, however, was as enthusiastic as that offered by the good citizens of Bundaberg. The so-called 'fever' ships had a very different reception. The McDougall family from the island of Coll – Alexander, his wife Mary (née MacKinnon) and their three small sons, John, Malcolm and

James, Mary's brother Donald and his family, as well as Flora who was Mary and Donald's mother – were one group of crofters who sailed on the *Persian* which arrived in Tasmania in November 1857.

Anchored in Impression Bay health officials quickly assessed the situation and as the passengers were rowed ashore to the quarantine station, the folk from Coll joined in the singing of some of the old favourite Scots hymns. This arrival left a strong impression on the young McDougall boys. Old Flora, the granny, had died at sea. Both Alexander and Mary were seriously ill and hospitalised, according to family recollections, for a lengthy period. Alexander was the last *Persian* migrant to leave the depot fully six months later.

Slowly, despite this early setback, the McDougalls found their feet in the farming business, the boys working as drovers, until they were able to purchase land in the Shepparton area (VA). Despite the traumatic start to his new life in Australia, Alex McDougall from Coll lived to be ninety.

When passengers who had survived the ordeal of the ocean voyage were told they were to be put into quarantine it was occasionally greeted with something akin to a mutiny. A Dunbartonshire coal miner who had travelled on the *Victory* to Port Chalmers (Dunedin) noted that there had been smallpox and measles outbreaks on board resulting in a total of six deaths, and when news of the delay in landing passed around the ship many of the young men refused to disembark to go into the quarantine stations. Most of the passengers though seemed quite untroubled by this problem and enjoyed their weeks of isolation on Goat Island in the harbour, declaring it the 'most lovely place on earth'.

For some of the earliest Scottish would-be immigrants conditions did sometimes appear impossible. The New Zealand Company which took so many Scots down under from 1839 onwards was actually the second company of that name. In 1824 the first expedition, with a tiny contingent of sixty Scots and Cumbrian pioneers in the *Rosanna* and the *Lambton*, arrived off the New Zealand coast filled with expectation. The hope was that they would be the vanguard of a colonising fleet.

At Hokianga in the far north the immigrants tried to establish a settlement cultivating flax, retiring to the security of their ship by night; but the constant threat of Maori unrest undermined their initial confidence and they were returned to Sydney. Several of these bold colonists found their way back to New Zealand as the immigrant bandwagon gained momentum and they became involved in both house and shipbuilding.

THE HILLS ARE ABLAZE

When William McGregor and his wife Nancy from Latheronwheel in Caithness sailed in to Port Phillip Bay (Melbourne) on the *Carrier Dove* on 3 November 1857, the hills was ablaze in a vast bushfire which later became known as 'Ash Friday'. It was an awesome sight and the McGregors actually debated whether they should disembark or go straight back to Scotland. In fact, they settled successfully to a farming life near Elmore (VA).

Sometimes the Scots arrived by the most roundabout of means. The Amos family came from Heriot Mill Farm near Galashiels but had moved in 1816 to Haverford West in Pembrokeshire. In 1820 a group of their Welsh neighbours purchased a boat called the *Emerald* to sail to Van Diemen's Land (TA) and some of the Amos clan were persuaded to join the expedition. Arriving first of all at Hobart Town they sailed up the east coast until they found suitable land at Oyster Bay, an area which by the 1860s had been named Swansea – in honour of the Welsh settlers. The Amos families settled at Cranbrook House and Glen Gala and the village of Cranbrook developed. They built Gala Kirk in 1845 to which was attached a vestry and a schoolroom, the building still being used for services and quite recently undergoing a major restoration.

ORDEAL ON THE THANE OF FIFE

Sailing from the Clyde on 14 March 1865, the clipper *Resolute* brought 354 immigrants destined for the Franklin district to the south of Auckland. If the hardy Scots folk thought that having reached Auckland their trials and tribulations after the sea voyage were over they were mistaken. Yet there remained only thirty miles to their final destination at Port Waikato from where they were to go overland to the Taukau block.

On 28 June at Auckland they were put aboard the 121-ton brig *Thane of Fife* but the little ship ran straight into a storm – a fortnight later she still had not reached her destination. On 13 July a correspondent at Port Waikato reported that the vessel had been sighted but she was unable to come in because of light offshore winds. Eighteen days after her departure the same observer was reporting the *Thane of Fife* still lying off the harbour.

> It is a pity for the poor Taukau settlers who are thus no doubt put to much suffering. We have had violent easterly winds with rain and great cold all the time. Whatever may be said in defence of sending passengers here in a sailing vessel at this time of year cannot apply to such an incompetent sailor as the 'Thane of Fife'.

Later that day the ship made port and the settlers eventually reached their upriver destination three weeks after sailing from nearby Auckland. Today the journey by road can be accomplished in less than an hour.

First impressions for these settlers from the Clyde could not have been very positive. Another batch, faced with a shorter boat journey to Papakura were reported to have been woken at one a.m. and in the midst of pouring rain, men, women and children were marched down from the Barracks (temporary accommodation) to two open boats and in these miserable conditions were put aboard . . . A far from perfect start to the new life.

Chapter Three
Kangaroo-Tail Soup and Parrot Pie

LIFE IN THE FIRST MONTHS and years after migration tended to be a routine of punishingly hard work and sleep, particularly for the rural settlers. There was hardly time for nostalgia, although after a long, often difficult day homesickness would have been a common enough phenomenon. All the special qualities which had lain dormant and which we've already catalogued had to be brought to surface and of them all, sheer staying power was probably the most vital in those early days.

Clannishness, if not Scottishness, soon disappeared for the immigrants drawn to the towns and busy industrial sites like goldfields where they were soon mixing with a broth of ethnic groups and making a grand job of assimilation. Many would lose their interest in Scotland and things Scottish within a generation or two, perhaps only their name giving any clue to their nation of origin. Others would remain regulars at Burns Suppers and St Andrews Night celebrations for the rest of their lives. It was in the small country towns and the widely spread farming communities where Scottish consciousness seemed merely to be sleeping. The re-awakening of the Scottish spirit after the essential settling-in period took many forms and could occasionally be an almost religious experience.

Old Sam McCluskey in Ayr (QD) related a lovely tale of the day his family from the southwest of Scotland rekindled the Caledonian flame. Jack Vass was a young Scot who had found work with the McCluskeys at their farm on the northern bank of the Burdekin River in the 1880s. Jack was a piper who spent a lot of his spare time making reeds for his pipes from canes growing wild in the bush. One clear, still Saturday evening after the week's work was done the family relaxed on the verandah with some of the farm hands when the skirl of the pipes sounded out as Jack gave them a bla'.

'The Wild Bunch'– a gathering of colourful Caledonians from the town of Ayr
(QD) and its surrounding district, the Lower Burdekin, *c.* 1912.
(*Laura Scott, Queensland*)

He went through his repertoire, all the old favourites, and the Gibsons,
their Scots neighbours from down the road – mother, father and two teenage
daughters – attracted by the pipes, called by. To this day no one knows who
made the suggestion but the barn was cleared and the floor swept and soon
they were dancing. In the old parlance, Jack gave it laldy. Trying to conjure
up that magical evening again Sam wrote:

> Gone was the loneliness of the migrants, forgotten the muscles that a few
> minutes before were still aching from the labours of the day, unnoticed
> the hard cement floor below their feet. The spirit of their homeland was
> alive in the new country.

When the dancing took its toll on their legs, the piper called a halt and they
collapsed in a heap. This time granny took over with her soft lilting soprano
voice and went through a medley of Scots songs. There wasn't a dry eye in
the barn. More dancing followed and the night flew past.

Word got round, even in that scattered community, during the following
week about the Saturday night ceilidh at the McCluskey place. Soon kids on
horseback were bringing messages from their parents – when would the

dancin' be on again? Could they come? And so the Saturday night dances at the McCluskey homestead became an institution on the Lower Burdekin River.

But while celebrating their Scottish heritage and wallowing from time to time in some good, old-fashioned nostalgia the Scots were also working hard at becoming Australians and New Zealanders; statisticians tell us that of all the European groups who made for the Antipodes, the Scots can claim the highest level of marriage outside their own ethnic grouping.

SCOTLAND'S CANTERBURY TALES

For the earliest arrivals at the Port Nicholson settlement (now Wellington), including a good number of Scots, delays over settling land claims meant immediate frustration and disappointment. There was an overabundance of labour and a lack of tools. However, the Scots did not sit on their thumbs. The Sinclair expeditions to Canterbury, which installed a Scots presence in what was eventually to become a conspicuously English settlement, illustrates the initiative – and courage – which often gave the Scots a head start.

Captain Francis Sinclair from East Lothian, a *Blenheim* immigrant from 1841, was unimpressed by the Wellington area and began, at a yard on the Hutt River, to build a 45-ton schooner the *Richmond*, cutting the wood in the bush and using iron plates and hoops for nails and bolts. An old musket and a sheep's bladder became a very serviceable blacksmith's bellows. It was improvisation of the first order.

On a reconnaissance expedition with his friend Ebenezer Hay who had been a merchant in Glasgow, Sinclair had been impressed by a site at Pigeon Bay on the Banks Peninsula near where Christchurch stands today. Back in Wellington they discovered that the Deans brothers had explored plains north of the Banks Peninsula on a similar expedition around the same time.

As usual the point should be made here that while it was a discovery in terms of the white settlers, the Maori races had made the place their stomping ground for centuries. This is the European chauvinism which we encounter all too frequently in relation to the opening up of the two nations.

William and John Deans from Kirkstyle in Ayrshire had experienced similar problems, delays in allocating country sections around Wellington, and they were determined to move on, confident that they would be able to exchange their land allocations in Wellington and Nelson. The *Richmond* left Wellington on 11 February 1843 with the Sinclair, Deans, Manson and Gebbie families on board. They were all Scots, most of them from Ayrshire, and all determined that this time they would put down roots further south. As cargo they carried livestock, provisions and even the timbers for a house.

The bulk of the party disembarked at Port Levy on the north side of the

Banks Peninsula while Deans, with Manson and a few others, took a whale boat up the River Avon as far as they could navigate then carried their goods on and unloaded the bricks. In a small canoe they penetrated further upriver and at a spot they named Riccarton in honour of their Ayrshire home ground, built a three-roomed house – one room for the Mansons, one for the Gebbies and the sitting room for the Deans. Soon they were growing vegetables and fruit and exporting butter to Sydney. As A. H. Reid tells us in *The Story of New Zealand*:

> When the Pilgrims (The English settlers) first set foot on these plains, mon-otonously spread with tussock and flax, swampy and treeless, some of them felt their hearts sink with despair. It was then that the little Deans homestead with its cattle and sheep, cornfields, fruit and vegetable gardens, gave them a vision of what might be done by hard work, and inspired them in their resolve to transform the wilderness into a fruitful land.

The district of Riccarton which provided such an inspiration for the weary English settlers now stands at the heart of the beautiful city of Christchurch.

This remarkable photograph of rural tranquility on the River Avon in the heart of what is now Christchurch (CY) was taken in 1860 only a few years after the arrival of the first pioneers – a group of Scots – in the district.
(*Alexander Turnbull Library, Wellington*)

WHEN IS A BUSH NOT A BUSH?

Thankfully members of these Scots communities in Australia and New Zealand recorded details of their new and unfamiliar lifestyles and shining through many of the journals is that valuable Scottish trait – adaptability.

Mrs K. W. Kirkland travelled up country in Victoria to join her husband in the bush (more than a few Scots sizing up the bare landscape have wondered just exactly where the bush is located). This lady kept detailed notes on her early years in the bush, so much so that in the mid-1840s she contributed an account of her life as a frontier wife for publication.

Her neighbours from the scattered homesteads were invited along to the Kirkland house for New Year's dinner 1841, and were treated to a feast which for the stay-at-home Scots reading of these adventures must have seemed like a bizarre mixture of the familiar and the exotic. On what was described as a boiling day Mrs Kirkland served up 'kangaroo tail soup, roasted turkey, well-stuffed, boiled leg of mutton, parrot pie, potatoes and peas followed by a plum pudding and strawberry tart, with plenty of cream'.

The menfolk may also have experienced the problem touched on by Scots in the hotter parts of Australia – how to keep your whisky cool. Everyone had their own technique but one wit suggested that simply drinking it quicker provided the easiest solution.

Across the Tasman Sea pioneer homemakers faced times of dearth with a gritty fortitude, the Clearances having steeled them for such eventualities. The Scots showed amazing skills at 'making do'. They might often be called to live off the land. It's not uncommon to find family journals mentioning that food supplies had become almost exhausted, perhaps because of the failure of fresh supplies to arrive in the remote corners. In such crises, in the North Island of New Zealand, for example, the pith of the nikau palms might be eaten and there was plentiful flesh provided by the large number of native pigeons to be found in the nearby bush.

Everywhere among the Scots settlers it was said that there was no greater luxury to offer a visitor than a 'jeely piece' made with fresh-baked bread and home-made jam. Many of the old Scots habits just refused to go away.

One of the first tasks was to let friends and family back home know as much as possible about the new home. Isobel Brand and Charlie Robertson migrated independently from Aberdeenshire in 1912, met and married during the Depression years and applied the Scots principles of perseverance, courage and quiet optimism to their lives. Their daughter Belle Avery of Auckland recalls that when her mother was asked how a city girl (she was from Marywell Street in the Granite City) coped with suddenly having to learn farm work in those difficult years, her reply was pragmatically Scottish: 'Weel, it had to be done, so we just deed it.'

Two months after her arrival in Otago in 1856 Margaret Nicol glossed over the tribulations of the voyage (apart from the poor quality of the tea due to the foul water) and wrote telling the family of her new home. David Nicol, her husband, had been a gardener in Edinburgh and was able to resume his profession on reaching New Zealand. The tone of the letter was positive.

> David says he finds this place better than he expected . . . it is a place for the working man. If labour men and ploughmen knew the way they are treated here they would not stop another day in Scotland.

Isobel went on to explain that they worked a nine-hour day – eight a.m. to five p.m., a fell difference from home, she remarked. Servant girls were in great demand, earning five or six times what they could expect in Scotland. The ladies were as gaily dressed in Dunedin as in old Edinburgh.

Margaret was impressed with the honesty of the folk; clothes could be safely left on the bleaching green and their door had never been locked, just 'ca'ed tae'. One minor hiccup that would quickly be overcome – the family

From the village of Kirriemuir blacksmith Alex Jones and his wife Jessie built a new life for themselves in Henry Russell's model community at Waipukurau (HB). Pictured here outside Mount Airlie, their big house on the hill, they are every inch the successful Scots. (*Alastair Jones, Waipukurau*)

For the early Scots pioneers travel in the New Zealand interior would have been impossible without the doughty bullock teams seen here chest deep in mud on an Auckland backtrack (1850). (*Alexander Turnbull Library, Wellington*)

were having difficulty adjusting to the idea of strawberries and black and red currants in December.

A few years later at Napier on North Island the Jones family from Kirriemuir, led by blacksmith and wheelwright Alexander Jones, were rowed ashore in an open boat through heavy surf; the eldest boy aged five was thrown into the sea and had to be dragged out.

Their destination was Henry Russell of Kinross's planned model village at Mount Herbert, Waipukurau. Russell – who possibly saw himself as part of the new breed of Antipodean lairds – had taken up 12,000 acres in Hawkes Bay in 1860 and was one of the first to commence farming. He then advertised in the Scottish papers for farm workers and tradesmen, his Utopian ideal being to have one exponent of every trade practising in his community.

The Jones family had to ford rivers to reach their new home but with only a few miles to go the bullocks foundered in a river hole and the water began to rise into the wagon where Jessie Jones and the children were perched. Awaiting rescue Jessie's cry of Caledonian defiance is remembered with affection by the family to this day – 'I've nae travelled thirteen thousand miles to be drooned in a burn.'

These bullock carts were a feature of early pioneer life in both New Zealand and Australia. Some of the conditions in which they were expected to operate were well nigh impossible. Schoolboy Andrew Miller from Fife remarked in a letter how strange it was for the Scots to see cattle – two abreast – hauling carts just like the horses did at home. For the benefit of

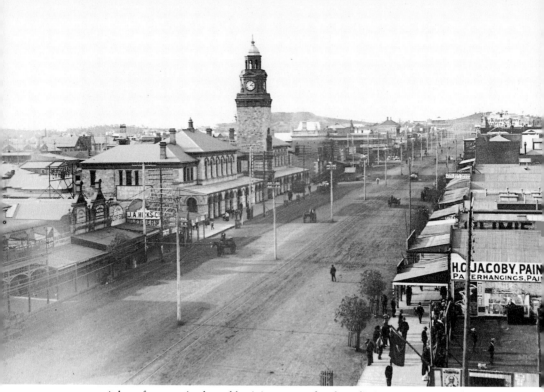

A hot afternoon in the gold mining town of Kalgoorlie in Western Australia
which grew spectacularly in its heyday in the 1890s.
(Battye Library, Perth, Western Australia: 6074P)

his little cousin back home Andrew also offered a junior naturalist's thumb-
nail sketch of Dunedin in 1862:

> There are a great many hills in New Zealand . . . something like the Fal-
> kland Hills . . . no wild rabbits or hairs [sic] here but plenty of beautiful
> birds. The Robin is here but is quite black with a white breast.

His only comment on the burgeoning frontier town of Dunedin – 'How
pretty it is to see about a hundred tents all set on the side of a hill.'

SPICK AND SPAN

How different the world must have seemed for those settlers. The truth is
that despite all the information and briefings received before departure they
did not know what to expect. For homemakers, adjusting to a dramatic
change in circumstances was the first major hurdle.

When Cecilia Gunn from Caithness arrived in Victoria in 1857 to join her
husband William who had become a successful pastoralist (sheep farmer) she
brought with her a collection of fine clothing for afternoon and evening

wear. Within days of her arrival on the station, however, seeing the scorching heat of the day and the absence of any sort of social activity such as she had been accustomed to at home, Cecilia cut up her fine garments to make clothes for the children. A different reality was making itself known.

Weekly dust storms would be a challenge for any houseproud Scottish mother but Sabina McLeod took them in her stride. Sabina came with her family to Australia from Girvan in Ayrshire in 1876 and after marrying a Cornish miner began moving around Australia from the big mining centre of Broken Hill (NSW) to Kalgoorlie (WA) before settling in the community of Gundaga (WA). There she and her husband, by this time an underground manager, raised nine children.

Sabina's granddaughter Marjory Johnston remembers the house being spotlessly clean. Despite the dust storms, the floors of white pine were kept scrubbed and pristine. Lace curtains hung in the windows and these also received regular attention, being washed, starched and ironed.

In order that her brood should always have fresh meat and milk Sabina purchased a flock of goats which, in the absence of fences, wandered out into the surrounding bush to browse, returning at nightfall for her secret food mix – chaff, bran, pollard – and stale bread. Unwittingly Sabina became a trendsetter in the district because her success with the goats prompted several of her neighbours to invest in a flock; and a century on Marjory Johnston has inherited her grandmother's love of goats and runs a flock at the splendidly named Niliamongup Angora Stud at Gnowangerup. Wool, rather than meat or milk, is the incentive these days.

THE HOUSE THAT GREW

From the Seaforth Highlanders to the West Australian bush was the challenge that John Forbes from Ross-shire and his wife Elizabeth faced when they immigrated in 1923 to a block of land near the community of Harrismith.

Jessie Duckworth, their daughter, recalls the arrival at their allocation in a horse and cart, how a large lined tent was erected and how gradually over the months a corrugated iron roof was placed over the tent and extended to form an eating area. In this piecemeal manner a house grew. In building the house, Jessie recalls that termite nests, soaked and crushed, compacted to a concrete-like finish and made a perfect floor. This was luxurious accommodation compared with the 'humpys' or rough shacks which were often simply branch and bark constructions with fertiliser bags sewn together as walling to give some semblance of domesticity.

Outside toilets came in a bewildering variety of designs but all were likely to be plagued by insects. One seasoned bushman, when asked by recent

Scots arrivals how to avoid this infestation in the loo, gave pragmatic advice worthy of the Scots themselves:

Go at lunchtime. They'll be in the kitchen then!

During the Depression, as neighbours were forced off the land and into the cities, the Forbes family hung on thanks to John's military pension. The local community, led by the Scots, worked co-operatively with equipment and labour-sharing, an imaginative, even revolutionary concept which raised as many eyebrows and questions in Wyoming as it did in Western Australia.

Before settlers were allocated land, dams were constructed and until the advent of tanks this was the only source of water. Rainwater was carefully rationed but few had sufficient for the summer. After dam water had been carted to the houses, Jessie Duckworth recalls, epsom salts was placed in the water supply to help the sediment settle. Such procedures were indeed a world away from the weeping glens of Ross-shire.

STRANGER IN A STRANGE LAND

John William Reid was brought up on the Orkney island of Westray and immigrated to Australia in 1910. These were the days when even a trip into Kirkwall could be a bit of an adventure but John, the eldest of five sons, was following in a long-established island tradition of service in distant parts. He worked in several farms in northeast Victoria before enlisting in the Australian forces during World War I. In 1922 with £100 from the Soldier Settlement Scheme he bought a farm near Benalla and despite the Depression he married and made a success of his life on the land.

His family remember him telling of his first few weeks in Australia. He wasn't slow in going along to the service in the local kirk. His total wordly wealth was eight gold sovereigns tied on a string round his neck and not knowing what was expected of him by way of an offering he put one of the gold coins on the plate. Quietly, at the end of the service, it was returned to him with some friendly advice about a more appropriate level of giving.

Generally life was tough for all but the monied immigrants. And if anything it was even more demanding for the women than the men. They accompanied their partners out into the undeveloped areas and coped with all sorts of difficulties, principally isolation and the ever-present fear of accident or illness so far from medical attention. The number of lonely graves – mostly babies and children – which are found scattered across the vast settlement areas bear witness to that. Such conditions honed the Scots sense of innovation and independence to a remarkable degree and the settlers found new depths in themselves with every passing day. This resilience can be seen in the country folk to this day and the Scottish contribution to this no small matter.

COMELY, HEALTHY AND ROBUST

Scots lasses were always popular arrivals at the immigrant ports. The *Canterbury Times* reporting the safe landing of the latest group of immigrants in 1874 said that among them was a group of females, Scots girls destined mostly to be domestic servants, 'all good, comely, healthy and robust lasses'. Just what the doctor and the lonely gold digger or sheep farmer ordered.

The Spence family from Melrose decided to make a new start in South Australia in 1839 when David Spence, a lawyer, got into financial difficulties. From a life of relative comfort in the Borders, they found themselves living like refugees on the outskirts of Adelaide – all in the space of a few months.

A member of this family was fourteen-year-old Catherine Spence who went on to become a novelist, journalist and staunch advocate of proportional representation. Initially the Spences lived in a tent, bought some cows and started a milk supply to the townsfolk of Adelaide. They stuck to the task and their fortunes changed. David Spence was appointed town clerk and Catherine found her way into teaching by way of a post as a governess.

So many stories of quiet endurance can be found in the pioneer annals of both Australia and New Zealand and it would be wrong to suggest that the Scots had it tougher than the norm. However, the saga of Elizabeth Adams, daughter-in-law of a Portsoy, Banffshire, man is almost without parallel. She arrived in Timaru (CY) in 1880 with her mother and father, landing in a surfboat. In a few short years the family had grown to six but then the father died and within eighteen months a typhoid outbreak took the mother, leaving Elizabeth and her five brothers and sisters as orphans. The church did what it could to find a home for the children but Elizabeth, being the oldest at just over twelve, was put to work as a kitchen maid at the Levels sheep station. She was given her meals on a bench outside the back door, winter and summer, regardless of weather. She was allowed one half-day off fortnightly which she used to walk the dozen miles to Timaru and go round all the family members in their new homes so that contact would not be

Catherine Spence, Melrose-born wordsmith, whose family settled in Adelaide (SA). (*National Philatelic Collection: Australia Post*)

lost. When Forrester Adams, a young baker, offered her marriage and long hours by the ovens, the prospect must have seemed like a little paradise.

While it's noted that there were very few genuinely Scottish enclaves in Australia and the immigrants spread widely and seemingly assimilated easily, one interesting phenomenon is encountered from time to time. That is the way in which the Scots could dominate in one particular trade or profession in a community. The Scots blacksmiths of Leongatha (VA) – Campbell, Munro and McFarlane – are fondly remembered.

In a sense being Scottish and British at one and the same time may have been the key to the ready assimilation of the Scots in the new societies of the Antipodes. This dual nationality, if you like, appears to have made it less difficult for many Scots to take on an additional persona, when effectively they were already citizens of two countries.

THE NEW LAIRD AND HIS CASTLE

The Scots, as they found their feet in their new surroundings, were constantly on the lookout for ways to supplement what was often a meagre income, to put a few extra pennies in their pooch. For example, during the Depression in Taranaki they were able to provide a boost to their tiny income by collecting mushrooms for export to China. More often than not scratching a living was the lot for the immigrant Scot but sometimes, just sometimes, the dream of success, money and power came spectacularly to reality. So it was for Thomas and Andrew Chirnside from Berwickshire who had taken up land in Victoria in 1842.

When Thomas reached Adelaide he had in his possession a bible, a gift from his mother, and a few hundred pounds from his father, a good start in those days. Thomas, on leaving, had told his parents he would return from Australia a rich and respected man or he would not return at all. Through a combination of business acumen, hard work and an uncanny Scots ability to read the runes, the brothers built up vast pastoral land holdings, getting land at rock-bottom prices in the pre-gold rush days.

For a number of years the Berwickshire boys led a nomadic existence but were always on the lookout for a base near Melbourne. It's said that when Thomas saw the Werribee with its gum-populated swamp lands it reminded him of Scotland. We wonder where, the Tweed perhaps? From then on he set about acquiring every acre of land he could lay hands on and by 1855 was known in Victoria's society circles as Thomas Chirnside of Werribee. By the time of his death in 1887 he owned almost two million acres along the eastern seaboard. As soon as he was settled at Werribee Thomas set out to create the world of the well-to-do 'laird' and this aspiration produced possibly his greatest achievement, the construction of Werribee Park, a magnificent sixty-room mansion built during the 1870s with its splendid tower and coppersheathed flagpole, the symbols of a successful landowner.

Thomas, who was also an excellent judge of horse flesh, owned a number of famous horses, including Harricot which won the prestigious Melbourne Cup in 1874.

One dark cloud hovered over Thomas Chirnside throughout his life, despite all his worldly success. When his brother Andrew was returning to Scotland in 1849 for a visit Thomas told him to be sure to return with their first cousin Mary Begbie, and if she refused to come out and marry Thomas, Andrew should marry her himself. This is precisely what happened. What a blow for Thomas. But instead of withdrawing into a world of his own, he dedicated his life to Mary and Andrew's comfort, doing everything in his power to make their life like a fairytale. The splendour of Werribee Park, built for his brother and sister-in-law, the largest private home ever constructed in Victoria, stands testimony to his devotion to this day.

For others simply having a roof over their heads rather than canvas was considered achievement enough. When the Roy family from Forgue in Aberdeenshire landed at Dunedin they were delighted to secure a four-room house despite the town being packed with gold diggers heading for the Otago fields. James Roy hit his own modest pay-dirt. Through a letter of introduction he obtained the post of catechist to Dr Burns at First Church and took over many of the visiting duties from the rapidly ageing founding father of the colony.

BEATING THE LAND ACT

Scots clergy played an important role in the settled areas of Australia and New Zealand. It is often said that almost as soon as the Scots had picked their location for settlement, they would build a church, followed swiftly thereafter by a school. The tough existence of parish minister among the squatters in Australia was to prove a lifetime's calling for the Rev. Archibald Cameron and his wife Christina. They settled among the Scots in what had been known as New Caledonia but was officially titled New England, in northern New South Wales. Christina from Skye thankfully kept a diary which gives some marvellous insights into their lifestyle in the 1850s.

Riding back from New England to see her parents at Manning River with her new child, Christina recalled carrying the baby on a plaid in front of the saddle and whenever the child became grumpy she would play a musical box which she had brought along for precisely that purpose. The return leg to their home at Wellingrove was completed in the luxury of a newly purchased buggy.

Scots shrewdness is displayed in the aftermath of the 1861 Land Act in New South Wales which cut up the big stations. Five years later the Rev. Cameron made his 'selection' of a property, with an adjacent selection for his son. Rules at the time demanded that the selector had to live on their property so the gallus Scots built their homestead straddling the boundary line between the properties with father and son sleeping in adjoining rooms – but each living on their own land. The selection was known as Bellevue.

The Rev. Cameron was said to have been a good bushman and could find his way with ease across his vast parish. Invariably he travelled on horseback and would often arrive out of the blue at remote homesteads. On one occasion at a far-flung station he found the whole family assembled in the living room, porridge plates still on the table and this in the middle of the day. The head of this tough Scots family was seated reading from the Bible with a shotgun at his side. If a member of the family tried to rise, the gun was pointed and the command given to sit and listen. Seeing the minister the stern faither launched into a religious discussion – but keen to free the family from their obvious discomfort the minister said he hadn't eaten. When the mother moved to prepare some food the others took this as a signal to escape the table and the Rev. Cameron was almost knocked over in the rush.

A nice ecumenical note – when the Rev. Cameron's stipend was part of

The simple beauty of one of the earliest Presbyterian churches in northern New South Wales – Wellingrove kirk, which still stands today.
(*Glen Innes Historical Society*)

a haul taken by the bushranger Thunderbolt at Ben Lomond, a subscription was organised and first to put his name to a list of donations was Father McCarthy and other members of his Catholic flock.

Jimmy Fletcher from Kirkintilloch arrived in New Zealand in 1908 with a few pounds in his pocket and his precious box of carpenter's tools. Sixty years later he was Sir James Fletcher and deservedly could be called The Man Who Housed New Zealand. He set up business with his brother in Dunedin and within the decade had expanded to a national company undertaking construction work throughout his adopted homeland. He negotiated the Depression with a combination of humour and determination.

As Pearce tells us it was to Fletcher that the newly elected Labour government turned in 1935 to prepare a scheme for state housing at a time when affordable housing was at a premium. J. A. Lee, the minister responsible for housing, described Fletcher as New Zealand's building genius. His company built more than 10,000 houses erected in the first phase of the scheme. Probably his greatest achievement came in the war years when, with Japan on the offensive in the Pacific, Fletcher was appointed Commissioner of Defence Construction and Controller of Shipping, answerable only to the Prime Minister, another Scot Peter Fraser.

Christchurch (CY) is considered one of the most English-influenced cities in the southern hemisphere but few folk there will know that the first houses were built by Samuel Manson, the Ayrshire cabinetmaker who was with the Deans expedition to Canterbury. Many examples of his workmanship are still to be seen in homes and museums.

CARE IN THE COMMUNITY

The record of caring displayed by Scotswomen in New Zealand and Australia is second to none. For example, in the little town of Fairlie in South Canterbury 'Granny' McKinnon, otherwise Annie McKinnon who immigrated from Glenshee in 1869, is fondly remembered to this day – with good reason. She was married to the manager of the Three Springs sheep station and after his death came to live in town. She became famed around the district for her willingness to travel many miles to deliver babies and do the housework.

When Mary MacGregor left the Duke of Hamilton's estate in Lanarkshire in the early 1920s for a new life in the mining community of Stockton on the northwest coast of New Zealand's South Island she was already an experienced midwife and soon became a familiar figure in the community, with her black bag and the nickname of 'Dr MacGregor'. She walked everywhere or rode the coal trains up into the hills, cat-napping by the patient's

Scotswomen often performed the role of community midwife among the early settlements. 'Granny' McKinnon was an almost legendary character in the neighbourhood of Fairlie (CY). (*Mackenzie Community Library, Fairlie*)

fireside when caught away from home on a rough night. Her husband Alex, a stickler for tidiness and efficiency, was a qualified engineer in the Clydeside tradition but could not get a job on his arrival. He ended up as a bath-house manager with some of the best polished brass boiler fittings along the coast. Alex was another great Scots walker who didn't think twice about a Sunday stroll of twenty-four miles.

With Edinburgh University a world leader in its field, it was inevitable that Scots should figure in the front line of medicine and medical education in Australia and New Zealand. In the earliest days, as we've noted, it was the ships' surgeons who found their way to the new land. William Balmain, with a district of Sydney now named after him, came with the First Fleet; and Francis Logan, a farmer's son from Dunlop in Ayrshire, served all over the world as a Royal Navy surgeon and brought his wife and son to New Zealand on the *Bengal Merchant*. Alexander Thomson (1800–1866), the son of an Aberdeen ship-owner, was also medical officer on a number of convict ships before settling in the Port Phillip district where he was a pioneer of both Geelong and Melbourne.

The Victorian capital had its medical faculty by 1862 while at Dunedin, Edinburgh professor John Scott helped build the international reputation of the University of Otago's medical faculty. Edinburgh graduates also founded Sydney medical school. Nurses from a Scottish background were also highly rated and pioneers in New Zealand including Grace Neill, Hester McLean and Elizabeth Gunn. Grace Neill's unshakeable belief was that nursing formed the basis of a healthy community.

When Adam Macmorran from Newton Stewart in Wigtownshire came to Geraldton in Western Australia in 1906 to take over the local medical practice he walked straight into an outbreak of the Black Death, bubonic plague. Local histories say he had wide experience of, and interest in, the treatment of such diseases and was instrumental in persuading the community on drastic measures. Half of the town's main street, the heart of the infected area, was blitzed and rebuilt on his say-so.

Alfred Saunders was Medical Officer for Health for Orkney in the 1890s as well as being a GP and went to Dannevirke in New Zealand's North Island for a couple of years to take over a practice run by an old friend from his medical school days at Aberdeen. Having moved around Scotland to try to lessen health problems he accepted the Dannevirke offer partly because he felt it might improve his health. Although he was homesick and had decided to go without his family he did feel that New Zealand was proving beneficial and on the return of his old university buddy he moved to Cheviot in the northern reaches of South Island and sent for his family.

In a letter to his sisters back in Scotland he explained in 1904 that it was extra quiet and that it was quite an event when a new patient turned up:

> If there are two in the same day I begin to think I'm overworked. I am earning £500 a year thanks to the big fees . . . a good rattling epidemic would about make a millionaire of me straight away.

Sad, prophetic words. In 1918 the great post-war flu epidemic reached New Zealand brought in onboard a ship called *Niagara*. It was a virulent strain, people often collapsing within minutes. Dr Saunders went out in all weathers to tend the victims of the influenza and often worked to the point of exhaustion. He became unwell, never regained his strength and died in 1923.

Archibald Anderson from Stirling was one of the *Bengal Merchant* pioneers who, with the help of his father, had purchased a town acre in Port Nicholson (Wellington) and 100 acres of rural land. He took with him a ploughman and his family and found (like so many others) that the land was not yet available. He allowed his ploughman to take up alternative work while he himself opened a store and invested his capital in the business, which thrived for a year or two.

Anderson left for Otago with the legendary Johnny Jones and had his livestock – thirty cows, two horses and five hundred ewes – shipped to his new range. Later, having prospected in southern Otago, he took up land along the River Clutha and worked the Balmoral property for twenty years. The first church service and the first school lessons in the district were held in his kitchen at Inch Clutha, where he also operated a ferry service. Archie thought nothing of walking fifty miles to Dunedin for council meetings.

Chapter Four
At the Back of Beyond

IT WAS A DAY Donald Sutherland from Wick would remember for the rest of his life. He had been trekking for hours when he crossed a ridge and found himself beside one of the most spectacular sights met by any pioneer in this or any other century. It was a waterfall with an almost 2,000-foot drop, highest in New Zealand and a location in the fjord country destined to become one of the country's most splendid tourist attractions. As Donald watched the rainbows dancing in the spray and listened entranced to the falling torrent, this loner would have been surprised to know that one of the wonders of the southern hemisphere still carries his name to this day – Sutherland Falls.

Adventurer is a title which is perhaps bandied about rather too freely when discussing the exploits of the pioneers but in the case of this Caithness man (b. 1839) the shoe seems to fit perfectly. While still a young man he landed in New Zealand and took part in the Maori Wars (1863–1870) as both a soldier and sailor. He was to be found at the diggings in the Thames field and followed the golden thread to the wild back country of Westland in New Zealand's South Island. Moving even further south he was located in 1880 at Milford Sound, still gold prospecting with a Scots buddy John Mackay and sealing to earn some extra cash.

He explored the spectacular mountains and passes, discovered Lake Ada and the Falls, criss-crossing the tracks of another Scots mountain man Quinton McKinnon (drowned in Lake Te Anau). In his later years Donald settled down, married widow Elizabeth McKenzie, and ran a boarding house at Milford Sound. He still found time, however, to steal off, even as an old man, to his beloved mountains.

A descendant of Sutherland tells me that the old couple lived in isolation

Explorer Donald Sutherland from Wick surveys the scene from his camp at
'The City' at Milford Sound in the fjord country of New Zealand: at his feet
on the tree stump, his dog Johnny Groat.
(*Burton Bros. Collection, Alexander Turnbull Library, Wellington*)

throughout the freezing winter months. When Donald died in 1919, they
were snowed in. Elizabeth, yet another practical Scot, simply lifted the floor
boards, tipped him on the frozen ground below the house, pushed the bed
back over the hole and called in the doctor weeks later when the freeze lifted.

The truth is that Donald Sutherland was the exception rather than the rule
among the Scots 'explorers' in New Zealand and Australia. Certainly Scots,
often on official government business, helped to survey and map the vast new
territories, 'pure' exploration, if you like. But more often interest in the unknown lands was prompted not by the prospect of fame, or in the spirit of
adventure, nor yet in any scientific or patriotic ambition but in a very down-
to-earth quest for more productive pastureland or mineral-bearing terrain.

LAND FOR THE TAKING

As they moved out into unchartered territory, surveyors, overlanders, shepherds, pastoralists and bushmen were mostly driven by very practical
considerations like keeping body and soul together. The hunger was for
economic development rather than a place in the history books.

The great city of Melbourne (VA) on the Yarra River was a target for a large percentage of the immigrant ships and was once described as being 'almost a Scotch colony'. (*Australian Tourist Commission*)

Even for the settlers who did not wander as far into the wilderness as the likes of Donald Sutherland & Co, getting a foothold on the land was no easy matter. Edmund Smith, an Otago immigrant, worked in Dunedin until he had saved enough cash to buy a piece of land on the coast about twenty miles from town where he cleared the bush, planted potatoes and lived for a time in an abandoned fern-tree hut, making his tables and chairs from the planks of an old Maori canoe – almost a Robinson Crusoe-style existence on the Otago frontier. Of course, Smith always found the time for the long hike to the kirk every Sunday.

And once the initial hard graft had been completed it was important to put down a marker, a declaration of permanence. At the Kirkland sheep station in Victoria, the lady of the house was to recall with pride how after plastering the exterior of the house with mud they had busied themselves with the creation of a little flower garden out front of the house.

In Australia the Scottish contribution to the earliest exploration of the great island continent was a significant one, even if we have to discount Captain James Cook of *Endeavour* fame, whose connection is maybe a bittie tenuous – his father was a Borders shepherd who had settled in Yorkshire.

One of the most understated scientific achievements was surely that of Montrose-born botanist Robert Brown who, while taking part in the three-and-a-half-year Flinders expedition which eventually circumnavigated Australia, collected thousands of plant specimens. A total of some 3,400 species were gathered from December 1801, and it's said that around half of them were unknown to science. Brown, described as a 'kindly and modest' man, received a stunning setback when the *Porpoise*, captained by Flinders, was wrecked off the east coast of Australia on its way back to London. Although Flinders and his crew were saved, some of Brown's best specimens went to the bottom. Undaunted he immediately began to reassemble his collection and in 1805 travelled back with his precious plants. His nervousness is betrayed in his diary notes of the voyage in which he writes of the unseaworthiness (in his opinion) of the *Investigator*.

For the next four years he wrote up his Australian research work, publishing in 1810 the *Prodrums Flora Novae Hollandiae*, regarded by his contemporaries as the greatest botanical work yet written. His later years were spent in the austere surroundings of the British Museum, the Royal Society and the Linnean Society. He was Keeper of Botanical Collections at the British Museum until his death in 1858.

The names of two Scots naval officers – James Grant and John Murray –

Three Sisters Peaks in the Blue Mountains which in the early years of New South Wales settlement appeared to form an impenetrable barrier to the interior.
(*Australian Tourist Commission*)

are intimately linked with the *Lady Nelson*, a 60-ton sailing ship said to have been the first vessel to sail the entire length of Australia's south coast in the early 1800s. James Grant from Forres, as captain of the vessel, was also ordered to explore the coast north of Sydney and spent time at the Hunter River which within a few decades was to become a popular target for Scots settlers. On Grant's resignation the command passed to John Murray, an Edinburgh lad by his own account, whose major contribution to the seaborne exploration of the island continent came in taking formal possession in 1802 of Port Phillip Bay in Victoria, the site today of the great city of Melbourne. Murray named a prominent hill on the bay Arthur's Seat, in tribute to his home town. Again this part of the world was later to act as a magnet to the Scots – so much so that less than forty years later it was described by an Argyllshire farmer as a 'Scotch colony'.

A better botanist than an administrator – that's history's harsh but probably accurate verdict on William Paterson (1755–1810), an army officer who became Lieutenant-Governor of New South Wales. During his term of office in Australia he is remembered for having fought a duel with John Macarthur, the pioneer pastoralist (Paterson was wounded in the shoulder); for founding a new settlement in Van Diemen's Land (Tasmania) where Launceston now stands; and for operating a weak and inefficient regime. His health was damaged by his early, arduous pioneering work, he had taken to the bottle, was easily influenced and had the disconcerting habit of making land grants to anyone who cared to apply. His pride and joy was his botanical collection and he kept in touch with Sir Joseph Banks, the famous naturalist. Interestingly he hailed from the same town, Montrose in Angus, as the above-mentioned explorer/botanist Robert Brown.

MYSTERY OF THE INTERIOR

Thomas Livingstone Mitchell from Stirlingshire was Surveyor-General for New South Wales for twenty-seven years – at a time when the opening up of Australia was gaining momentum. When he arrived in 1817 he was torn between a personal desire to explore and the need to bring some order to a chaotic survey department. In 1828 a general survey of the colony was organised and in 1831 Mitchell led his first expedition in search of a mythical river flowing northwest into the wilderness, possibly to some vast inland sea. The slaying of two of his party by Aborigines forced an early return to base. Four years later he mapped 300 miles of the Darling River but was again attacked and, according to the records, was forced to shoot several Aborigines. Botanist Richard Cunningham, a brother of the more celebrated Allan Cunningham, disappeared on this survey and after a fourteen-day search it was reluctantly concluded that he had met his death, probably at the hands of the native tribes.

A third expedition took Mitchell through the Murray-Darling-Murrumbidgee river system and into a region he called Australia Felix, which was later to become Victoria's western district and an area much favoured by Scots settlers over the years and in particular by Highlanders.

THE CADELL EXPEDITION

The vast river systems of the southeast held a fascination for Francis Cadell from Cockenzie in East Lothian and he must get most of the credit for seeing the three great rivers as commercial waterways through the wilderness.

Before reaching Australia Cadell had a glamorous career, fighting in the Chinese War of 1840 and facing the challenge of river navigation on the Amazon. Prizes were being offered by the South Australian government for river exploration which might open up the vast interior utilising river trade. While he had a steamship constructed in Sydney, Cadell and a small party carried out a reconnaissance mission on the Murray in a canvas boat travelling over 1,300 miles. When his vessel the *Lady Augusta* set off it seems to have been a sort of society expedition because on board was the Governor Sir Henry Young and his wife. But it was unquestionably a success, the *Augusta* penetrating 1,500 miles upriver.

Cadell brought back large quantities of wool and a gold and silver candelabrum gifted by the settlers to mark the fact that he had opened up the Murray to steamship navigation. Alas, it was not plain sailing thereafter. A company set up by Cadell to exploit his success collapsed because of problems with inland custom houses, and the failure of Port Elliot as a commercial harbour saw him ruined. He continued his explorations in eastern Victoria, in New Zealand and in the desolate Northern Territory of Australia where he was asked to pick the site for the capital of the Territory, his selection on the Liverpool River being widely condemned then rejected. As befits the restless, courageous adventurer, Cadell died a dramatic death, murdered by one of his crew in the East Indies.

We've learned how David and Jean Drummond from Fife lost a son, just a toddler, in a tragic accident at sea but the wheel keeps on turning and just before the *Fifeshire* docked at Wellington Jean gave birth to Peter, on 26 January 1842. She was eventually to have five surviving sons. Without a second thought the family headed off for the frontier settlement which they had dreamt about during the long, sad voyage. Nelson Haven, a new settlement across Cook Strait on North Island, was their destination and infant Peter had the distinction of being the first baby carried ashore through the

A section of the mighty Murray River in South Australia, part of the great southeastern Australian river system. (*Australian Tourist Commission*)

surf and his mother was the first white woman seen in the vicinity. Moving round the coast to settle, Jean became known as the 'Queen of Te Matu' because of her unique status. For the Drummonds a whole new magical, yet severely demanding, life was opening up. Having tried farming, David Drummond moved into the flour milling business.

The family told me a marvellous tale of the Scots ingenuity, making the best use of what's to hand, which we encounter so often in the most far-flung places. David had to improvise when a crucial piece of the mechanism for the mill was found to be missing. He dismantled an enormous grandfather clock which they had brought from Scotland and cannibalised a piece for use in the mill mechanism. It worked a treat.

The youngsters in the family remembered huge Maori canoes, some sixty or seventy feet long, perhaps with seventeen paddles on each side, bringing the wheat to be milled. It was also noted that the Maori women did all the heavy carrying. In the late 1860s the family moved, mill and all, round Tasman Bay to Marahau and over the years a little community – this time devoted to timber processing – developed, with first of all seven homes being built, one for David and Jean, one for each of their five sons and one for the hired hand.

They seem to have been a smashing couple. David was a bit of a practical joker and owner of a large Jew's-harp which, at the end of a hard and dangerous day's work in the forest, he would use to entertain the company by 'playing the instrument lustily'. And David would dance a jig with the best of them. Jean, on the other hand, was of a serious, pious disposition, regularly quoting scripture and was a pillar of strength within the family – a formidable pairing. In February 1967, hundreds of Drummonds, descendants of David and Jean, gathered to mark the anniversary of that famous day when the Drummonds came to Nelson Haven.

MAKING HEAVY WEATHER OF IT

Climate was a factor which few Scots seem to have taken into account when they weighed up the pros and cons of immigration but its importance very quickly became apparent. Family journals and diaries occasionally indicate that the Scots were dismayed to find Australia too hot – and headed for New Zealand. People such as Argyllshire farmer Hugh Buchanan who left Melbourne for New Zealand as soon as he could arrange it after experiencing temperatures which soared above 100 deg. F. He was to settle eventually in Canterbury.

The first autumn and winter for the Free Church settlers in Otago was so exceptionally wet and unpleasant that a frequent comment was that they must have imported the dreich Scottish weather along with their other baggage.

Drought – a distinctly un-Scottish phenomenon – was particularly testing

For the early explorers of New Zealand's West Coast dense bush provided a testing obstacle. (*New Zealand Tourism*)

The Indian-Pacific service makes its spectacular run across the desert wilderness of Australia. (*Australian Tourist Commission*)

Scots immigrants quickly learned about the ferocity of the Antipodean climate. Scenes of devastation in the frontier town of Darwin after the cyclone in 1897. (*Price Collection, Northern Territory Library, Darwin*)

for the Scots in the Australian bush. Effects of prolonged dry spells often lasting years could be devastating. The drought of 1894–9, for example, saw the sheep population of New South Wales drop by twenty million to just over thirty million. Then there was flood, devastating whole communities as it did in the Clutha (Clyde) district of southern Otago in 1878.

Explorer John McKinlay (1819–1872) was born at Sandbank on the Clyde and migrated to Australia as a teenager. In South Australia he ventured into the bush and befriended the Aborigines. In what is now Northern Territory, 1865 saw a particularly severe rainy season and while on the Alligator River his party was surrounded by floodwater. Improvisation came to the fore again as McKinlay and his team, having killed their horses constructed a raft with their hides and made a perilous floating journey to the coast.

Dry season desert conditions were equally extreme and shade temperatures of over 130 deg. F. are not uncommon. Explorers reported the skin burning off their dogs' paws and ink drying on a pen in the fierce heat before it could be used.

Soil erosion was a common problem and numbers of Scots were forced to abandon their new homes in South Australia. Many made the hazardous journey to a second chance in Western Australia. However, it could be equally punishing there. Bookbinder Arabella Smyth from Perthshire had some harrowing experiences as a Western Australian settler. She also suffered eye complaints as a result of whirling airborne dust and the piercing, relentless brightness of the Australian sunlight.

The McNabs from Girvan in Ayrshire were struggling to get a start in South Australia in the 1870s. Helped by their three daughters, Jessie, Sabina and Virginia, they cleared the bush, months of backbreaking work, but once exposed the wind tore away the topsoil. This family left for a fresh start at Donnybrook, near the southwest coast (WA). Cyclones, bush fires, earthquakes, insect plagues, volcanic eruptions all made for an interesting if testing, settler experience.

CABBAGE GROWER TO THE NOBS

The Darling Downs, a vast, fertile region of southern Queensland extending to some 21,000 square kilometres, was first explored by Renfrewshire botanist Allan Cunningham in 1827 and pioneered to a large extent by his fellow Scots. When Cunningham landed at Sydney it was as botanist to the New South Wales government and he was soon leading the push northwards prompted by the success of John Macarthur's sheep-breeding experiments and the need for vast new pastures. In 1824 he was at Moreton Bay (Brisbane) for the founding of the new penal colony and within a few years he had reached an area of extensive plains, the Downs. He wrote in his diary of excellent pasture for cattle and sheep and grass and herbiage, extensive tracts of open country which even in the depths of winter showed extraordinary luxuriance of growth.

Cunningham is accorded an important place in the annals of Australian exploration not just because of his treks to the Darling Downs but also

The Lammermoor sheep station in Queensland which was the home ground of Berwickshire pioneer Robert Christison. (*John Oxley Library, Brisbane, Queensland*)

Sheep farming provided an early mainstay for the Australian economy and remains a vital component in agriculture today. (*Australian Tourist Commission*)

because of a number of voyages around the Australian coast in the fragile 85-ton *Mermaid* during which he collected botanical specimens. In those early days expeditions were often poorly equipped and genuine courage was a requirement. His career as a government botanist ended on a sour note when, after a spell in London, he returned to Sydney only to find that one of his jobs was to grow cabbages for the dinner tables of government officials.

Because of the difficulties of access and the counter-attraction of Victoria it was fully thirteen years before the first settlers began to drift on to the Darling Downs. The government still prohibited this distant settlement but the hunger was for land and the squatters pressed on.

HERE COME THE SCOTS!

Scots names are quickly etched on the history of steady progress towards the Darling Downs – Peter McIntyre, Semphill, Alexander Campbell and John 'Tinker' Campbell who established himself in 1840 on the north bank of the Dumaresq River, earning for himself the title of first squatter in the future colony of Queensland (the term squatter did not carry the same stigma here as it did in the United States).

Within a few months Patrick Leslie, one of a group of ten Aberdonians who migrated to Australia, passed Campbell's station and halted at Toolburra to create the first station on the Downs themselves. Leslie had been offered particulars of the route by Allan Cunningham himself but the botanist had lost the original map so Leslie was simply told to 'look out for Ben Lomond'.

The Leslie brothers, Patrick, Walter and George, divided their holding and had for neighbours Colin and Archibald Campbell at Glengallan, Ernest Dalrymple at Talgai and (a few years later) George and John Gammie, also part of that intrepid bunch of Aberdonians.

Physical obstacles seemed to present no problems to these fearless Caledonians. In fact, says L. J. Jay, they treated the wild country with 'nonchalant disregard'. They were restless, mobile. Although by 1845 herds of cattle were on the Downs there were already almost quarter of a million sheep grazing there.

In the list of early sheepmen who combined their pastoral activities with exploration, the name of Glasgow's Thomas Archer figures prominently. In 1841 Archer and his brothers drove his 5,000 sheep north into uncharted lands in what is now south/central Queensland. Again this was not pure exploration but driven by the need for fresh pastures. The outback life did not suit Archer's young Scottish bride he had brought back from Europe and they both returned to Scotland. However, the Queensland landscape drew him like a magnet and he spent eight years at the Gracemere Station, some seven miles from Rockhampton, the site of which was fixed by the Archers. For most of the 1880s Archer was Agent-General for Queensland, based in London.

After 1842 Moreton Bay (Brisbane) was proclaimed a pastoral district with an indefinite northern boundary. Stations had been quickly taken up on the Downs and the advice to the stream of new arrivals was to 'Turn Right' at the swamp (Toowoomba) for unoccupied pastureland. By 1848 eighteen runs had been taken up in the Brisbane Valley itself, among them Eskdale, Kilcoy and Waverley, with a good sprinkling of Scots among the licensees including the Balfours, McConnels, Forbes, Grahams, Archers and McKenzies.

MAD HATTER'S TEA PARTY

Tantalisingly the mysteries of the centre of the continent persisted. That was until the early explorations of Fifer John McDouall Stuart, the son of an army captain. He finally shattered the belief in a great inland sea in the centre of the continent. Although this remarkable journey was to damage Stuart's health permanently its repercussions were enormous – as a result London and Adelaide were soon linked by cable.

John McDouall Stuart, pioneer of the trans-Australia south-to- north route poses against a wilderness backdrop in an Adelaide photo studio. (*Mortlock Library, Adelaide, South Australia: B500*)

However, hailed by some as the greatest epic of exploration in the history of the continent, Stuart's first south-to-north trek across Australia beginning in 1861 got off to a bizarre false start when the team were invited out to lunch. At the start of the expedition Stuart and his party of nine men had gathered at the home in North Adelaide (SA) of James Chambers, who with his brother John had provided the capital for Stuart's wanderings in the wilderness. With their loins well and truly girded they were set to take their leave when Catherine, wife of James Chambers insisted: 'I do hope you'll stay for lunch.'

Stuart, according to his journals, had hoped for a historic ten a.m. departure but courtesy demanded that they wait for the midday meal. According to the records kept by expedition members, what followed was nothing short of farce. The team, after many impressive speeches, finally got under way. Buoyed by the prolonged send-off the party stopped off for just one more toast at the Heart and Hand Inn. Within a couple of hours the leader Stuart had reappeared at the Chambers house with a bloody hand, having been kicked by a horse. It meant a lengthy delay and a stuttering start for one of the most famous cross-country explorations in Australian history.

After weeks of trekking in the searing heart and the bitter cold of night Stuart was finally able to plant the Union Jack on Australia's northern shore, about eighty miles east of the site of Darwin and returned – carried the last 600 miles on a stretcher – to a hero's welcome in Adelaide. In his diary Stuart records the dramatic moment when he knew the great crossing had been successfully negotiated:

> Coming to a plain I could hear the wash of the waters and seeing the dense bushy scrub I knew it at once to be bounding the sea . . . Thring (the second officer) got so excited at first sight of it he called out – The Sea! The Sea! At length the rest of the party understanding what was meant commenced cheering at a terrible rate.

There is a John Stuart Society which fosters his memory and a wee museum in his home village of Dysart.

In that exciting, pioneering period even the most routine roles in the community could carry the promise of adventure. Being a councillor in New Zealand's remoter corners in the early days of settlement required more than just a knowledge of standing orders. Jim Davidson, an Aberdeen man, had been part of the team which went in search of the missing Franklin expedition in the Arctic, had worked in the Victoria goldfields and operated a coastal trader in New Zealand waters, before settling down eventually at Kaikoura (NM). He represented Clarence in the Marlborough Provincial Council (1871–4) and his 150-mile round trip to council meetings was an arduous one, winter or summer, with many dangerous rivers to ford.

Even for the more gregarious Scots it was some time before towns recognisable as such developed in the interior. When Alec Mutrie got an invite to join his uncle Bob Cockburn at the new town of Masterton (WN) in 1861 he walked from Wellington. This, in his own words, is how he found Masterton:

> I reached Kuripuni and saw a woman washing clothes outside a clay
> house. I asked her where Masterton was and was told – 'This is it!' . . . it
> contained only a few settlers.

OVER THE SEA FROM SKYE

The name of Angus McMillan of Glenbrittle in Skye is etched in the annals of early exploration in Victoria and he was responsible for opening up an area today called Gippsland. Originally McMillan dubbed it 'Caledonia Australis' but the authorities, thinking that too partisan, rather unimaginatively named it after Sir George Gipps, a New South Wales governor.

From farming stock McMillan arrived in Sydney in 1838 with letters of introduction to Captain Lachlan Macalister who hired him for his station at Goulburn. As often was the case drought prompted a search for pastures new and McMillan rode south with an Aborigine called Jimmie Gibber.

The sad remains of Victoria pioneer Angus McMillan's homestead at Bushy
Park. (*Anne Fernando*)

Having returned to report progress he made another sortie and a few months later crossed the Snowy River and established a cattle station at Ensay.

Finally he penetrated to the south coast despite a hostile countryside where he found dense scrub and rivers in flood. The site where he reached the sea is called Corner Inlet and from there he built up an export trade in cattle to Tasmania, settling at Strathford on his patch which he called Bushy Park. Scots in that area today tell me it was a tradition among the settlers that Bushy Park had always been dingo-free, the story being that the scrub was so dense that the wild dogs choked to death when they tried to bark.

McMillan is described in the official biographies as a natural leader whose tact, good sense and kindliness enabled him to get on well with his men 'including the Aborigines'. The native Australians have another view on that altogether as we see elsewhere.

Across the Bass Strait from Corner Inlet Scots were also busy making their mark in Tasmania. Historically the northeast corner of the island is very much surveyor James Scott's territory, and not simply because the largest town, Scottsdale, is named in his honour.

Earlston in Berwickshire was James's home ground. He sailed for the island colony, then called Van Diemen's Land, in 1832 and began training with his older brother Thomas who had been in the Antipodes since 1820. For most of his working life James was a contract surveyor and recognised as a hardy individual gifted with what was described by his contemporaries as that peculiarly Scottish trait of 'indomitable perseverance', dogged determination to you and me. Although he explored other districts of Tasmania it is in the northeast, in areas marked on the original maps 'Land Unexplored', that he made his name. And although there were settlers on most stretches of the coast by the 1850s few had ventured into the interior.

As Scott with his team of five or six men and pack horses penetrated ever deeper into the dense scrub, conditions became extremely testing. On one occasion a member of his party asked to be left behind to die but a confident prediction from the optimistic Scott that they would reach a shepherd's hut by the next evening was enough to drag the exhausted man to his feet.

The fertile section marked on one of the first maps of the area as 'Scott's New Country' attracted only a trickle of settlers initially but soon families of Scots – McGilps, Cunninghams, Campbells, Shearers, Farquhars and Watsons among them – arrived in number, all walking to their new homes with their saddle horses. Today Scottsdale is a busy little country town with a population of 4,000, many of them proud to claim Scottish roots and of their home in 'Scott's New Country'.

But settling was not always so straightforward. There's a corner of Tasmania which has become known as Cook's Rivulet after a Dundonian

Andrew Cook who was trailblazing in southeast Tasmania in the mid-1800s. He bought a plot of land valued at £11 in the middle of nowhere but if he thought he was to be allowed to settle to a peaceful life, he was up a gum tree. His wife was a relative of the notorious bushranger Martin Cash who used the remote homestead as a hideaway from the police. Andrew and his wife had nine children but there is no happy ending to this particular settler's tale. The Scot (b. 1828) was killed in a freak accident when a tree, burnt out and seriously weakened in a bushfire, fell on him without warning.

WATER TO THE WILDERNESS

Across in Western Australia, an area developed much later than other parts of Australia, it is a touch ironic that it should be a family from Stonehaven by the name of Forrest who made the most significant Scottish contribution to the exploration of the vast, treeless expanses of Western Australia.

Lawyer William Forrest brought his family to the state in 1842 and settled near Bunbury in the far southwest. It was his sons John and Alexander who

A surveying expedition organised by Scots descendants the Forrest brothers prepares to set off for the interior from the hotel at Geraldton on the West Australian coast. (*Battye Library, Perth Western Australia: 5172P*)

gained international fame for their treks into the wilderness. As government surveyor for the district John reached Adelaide by the south coast and also crossed the heart of Australia as far as the north-south telegraph line which was nearing completion. The search for water on this latter expedition meant constant deviations and the party reached the line with only four horses between six men. Often they were in danger of dying of thirst but for the incredible bush skills of their Aborigine trackers.

John Forrest was also to figure prominently in the politics of both Western Australia and Australia generally after Federation in 1901 when he served in the national government. He encouraged rail development and was Premier of Western Australia for ten years.

One of his great successes was in seeing the completion of a 330-mile water pipeline from the west coast to the goldfields. A five-year construction programme was undertaken amid much cynicism about the outcome but in January 1903 water finally reached the gold mining townships of Coolgardie and Kalgoorlie. In 1918 John Forrest was made Baron Forrest of Bunbury, the first native-born Australian to attain the honour.

It's also interesting to find the younger sons of the Scots aristocracy among the explorers and early pastoralists in Australia. David Carnegie was fourth son of the Earl of Glenesk, and eventually died in the style of the adventurer, killed at the age of twenty-nine by a poisoned arrow during an uprising in Nigeria in 1900. His Antipodean explorations centred on the western deserts where he mapped practicable cattle routes. With four companions and nine camels he crossed the wasteland, always on the lookout of course for indications of gold deposits.

Plain Francis Grant served as a midshipman in the Royal Navy before trying the life of a farmer in Otago. Trying and failing to make a go of the homestead he lost all his money and had to settle for casual labouring. On the death of his father he inherited the title of 10th Earl of Seafield and his biographer tells us in one phrase of his dramatic change of circumstances: 'thereafter he interested himself in philanthropic movements'.

PEARL AMONG SWINE

Georgina Travers swapped the relatively peaceful surroundings of the Highland capital of Inverness for the pearl fishing town of Broome, also in Western Australia. Migrating in the early 1900s to Victoria to take up a post of housekeeper to Sir Rupert Clark she met her dashing sea captain husband-to-be and moved west. Her husband held a half-share in a pearl lugger with a German, although he was also a local government contractor and a horse importer.

Pearling luggers at Broome, Western Australia– one of the unusual occupations
the Scots found themselves working in Australia's pioneering years.
(*Battye Library, Perth, Western Australia: 6074P*)

The lugger, known as a 'black' boat because of the Malay divers, found
the famous 'Pablo Pearl'. This jewel brought nothing but bad luck to the
Travers family culminating in the disappearance of John Travers while at the
town of Carnarvon. Reported lost off the jetty, there were many who
believed he was just the latest victim of a series of murders connected with
the pearl. Georgina – prevented from returning to Scotland by World War I –
became a hotel owner and died in Western Australia in 1943.

JOCK AND THE LEGEND OF NUGGET JERKINS

Although the 19th century was the period when most of the adventuring
was undertaken we musn't lose sight of the Scots who took to the trail in
the first half of the 20th century.

Nominated as a free immigrant at the age of sixteen by his sister in western
Tasmania, Jock McNeil Inglis, a Glaswegian with his roots in the Borders,
got his first job in a railway construction gang . . . and lied about his age to
secure the work. Jock's interest in gold prospecting around the community
of Queenstown grew almost daily and he was taught the tricks of the trade

by a bush legend, 'Nugget' Jerkins, a survivor of the Mount Lyall mining disaster of 1912 who lived alone in the wilderness. By 1935 Jock was working full-time at the Comstock mine in western Tasmania, winch driving and shaft sinking were his specialities, and he continued prospecting in his spare time.

Jock's other great love is boxing and he sparred with the Tasmanian champion Les Stubbs as well as taking part in amateur contests. In one bout there were 200 spectators including Ernie Hocking whose daughter Jock was courting. Prior to the first round bell, when you could have heard a pin drop, 'Hock' stood up and shouted: 'If you don't win you Scots bastard you'll not be marrying my daughter.' The crowd roared with appreciation, delaying the start of the fight. Jock got the verdict and married Hock's daughter.

In his bush experiences with Nugget Jock learned how to deal with claim jumpers. Once, returning from Queenstown where he had placed a few bets and sunk a few beers, Nugget found two men panning his claim and putting gold into a tobacco tin. They soon found themselves staring into the barrels of a shotgun. The old prospector gave them thirty seconds to get off the claim and 'persuaded' them to leave their tin behind. The claim jumpers had paid for Nugget's weekend entertainment.

The old man's health deteriorated and his journeys into town became more infrequent. One day on his way to the afternoon shift Jock was told that Nugget had been found dead at his camp. A man who had lived his life in a totally individualistic manner was not about to cash in his chips predictably. Nugget was found stone dead, standing up, his brow resting on the edge of a shelf, his left hand leaning on the table and his right reaching up for his rum bottle. The doctor who attended confessed to having never seen the like.

SCOTS IN HIGH PLACES

A mountain range without a Scot wandering upon its slopes would be a strange place indeed. No surprise therefore to find the Scots active in the early days of climbing in New Zealand where the magnificent Southern Alps provided the most substantial challenge. Of all the many Scots and Scots descendants who looked to the hills, the love of these high places is probably best exemplified by Charlie Douglas, Edinburgh-born mountaineer and surveyor, and Malcolm Ross, the son of an immigrant Scots family based in Dunedin.

Malcolm Ross served his apprenticeship on the *Otago Daily Times*. Later he was to work in Wellington as a parliamentary reporter and New Zealand correspondent for *The Times*. An all-round sportsman, his great love was mountaineering and with his brother he took part in many epic climbs, probably the most celebrated being the first traverse and fourth ascent of

While three of the Scott children look on, Edinburgh mountaineer and surveyor
Charlie Douglas (*right*) shares a drink and a smoke with Andrew Scott outside
the barn at Karangarua about 1895.
(*A. C. Graham Collection: courtesy of Westland National Park*)

Mount Cook (New Zealand's highest at 12,349 feet) in 1906, an ascent forced
through in difficult conditions in a thirty-six-hour day. He helped found
the New Zealand Alpine Club which opened up the mountains to the people
of New Zealand. He was also the author of several books.

Charlie Douglas has been described as a diarist, philosopher, bushman,
climber, artist, naturalist and surveyor, but above all he was a mountain man.
Despite an education in the classics in Edinburgh, Charlie chose the adventurer's life and was drawn to the deep valleys and spectacular peaks of the
southwest. Douglas arrived on the West Coast of South Island in 1867 and
after trying his hand at prospecting and farming he went into the mountains
to map the last unknown pockets. The handbook of Westland National Park
tells how on these expeditions Charlie's only companions were his pipe and
his faithful dogs who were expected to round up game and wild birds. In
his diaries Douglas reflected on the circumstances which had brought him
into the high places of such a far-off land:

Had I remained at home in the Old Country I might now have been the respectable father of a family . . . a comfortably situated old Foggy . . . I know that even if I perish miserably the impulse to search the wild places of the earth is good.

Charlie completed forty years of exploring until rheumatism, the legacy of too many cold nights on the mountain, began to take its toll.

Edinburgh medical school, perhaps surprisingly, provided New Zealand and particularly Otago with a talented group of young men who turned to the natural sciences in their spectacular new home. Of these, Sir James Hector, an Edinburgh-born physician/geologist (b. 1834), is particularly intriguing. He was involved in much of the early work to find the most suitable land passages across North America between Atlantic and Pacific before, as a youthful but seasoned twenty-eight-year-old, he was appointed geologist to the province of Otago. He plunged into the mountains, surveying and producing a report on the coal potential of the interior. He tried and tested many difficult and dangerous routes in the quest for the easiest access from Dunedin to the west coast where the possibility of settlement was being considered.

Before the community of Glen Innes in northern New South Wales was established by a retired soldier from Thrumster in Caithness, Archibald Boyd from Selkirkshire reached the area with two famous guides and bushmen, Chandler and Duval, noted for their long flowing beards and nicknamed

Stonehenge – an early Scots homestead in northern New South Wales belonging to the Boyd family which later became a hotel. (*Glen Innes Historical Society*)

'The Beardies'. Another member of the family, William Boyd, established Stonehenge, a large building with slab walls and a bark roof which was held down outside by saplings. Later he also established an inn at the site.

Back at ground level new and unexpected hazards faced the Scots families as they settled the new lands. The Milroy clan were active in the hazardous business of gold mining in Victoria from the middle of the 19th century but it was in 1922, after leaving the goldfields to seek work in Queensland, that Robert Milroy was killed. As the family records starkly report, he was 'accidentally taken by a shark'. Robert was working with cattle droving teams and was attacked while crossing a river near Brisbane (QD).

THE STRANGE SWAMP CREATURE

One of the least known but most sensational encounters between the Scots and Australian wildlife happened in 1884 when Scots zoologist William Hay Caldwell was taken into a swamp by an Aborigine guide and shown an astonishing creature which seemed to defy all the rules of the natural world and which was being seen for the first time by an expert European. With its birdlike bill, webbed feet and ability as a swimmer, its fur coat and the fact that it lays eggs and suckles its young, it was unquestionably the strangest creature Caldwell had clapped eyes on. He named it the duck-billed platypus and immediately fired off a preliminary report to London. Among the top naturalists of the day Caldwell's discovery was treated first of all with great scepticism then growing astonishment and excitement.

Across in Western Australia the vanishing of old William McJannet from Ayr is almost as big a mystery. William (b. 1822) had married Agnes Nevin and the couple sailed to Australia on the *Lightning* in the middle years of the 19th century, settling on the Gascoyne River. He became a popular figure around the town of Carnarvon, renowned for his integrity. However, during a visit by Governor Broome to the town, William had been attending to a shipment when the Governor asked to 'make his farewells to that grand old Scottish gentleman'. McJannet was nowhere to be found and was never seen again. It is presumed that he drowned.

His daughter Jessie married Charles Wheelock, a legendary shepherd, tracker and bushman of the Gascoyne River who was the expert on the Aborigine peoples and their customs. For a white man Wheelock's bushlore was said to be exceptional. Family diaries also tell us a little about Jessie:

Tall, with black hair and dark brown eyes, she courageously faced the un-tamed loneliness during her husband's long absences from home, learning from him to befriend the Aborigines. When the law decreed separation of

The Darwin end of the incredible north-south Overland Telegraph while construction work was under way in 1870. The route through the vast wilderness was surveyed by adventurous Scots such as McDouall Stuart and John Ross. (*Spillet Collection Northern Territory Library, Darwin*)

Aboriginal children from their parents, frightened native mothers would seek refuge with Jessie convinced that the 'Gub'mint' man could not reach them in that sanctuary.

Apart from the high profile adventurers such as McDouall Stuart there was a throng of Scots whose contribution to the first phase of development in Australia and New Zealand is noteworthy. Take John Ross, a miller's son from Dingwall in Ross-shire who decided that life at the grindstone was not for him and immigrated, arriving in Sydney in 1837. Immediately he got himself involved in the pastoral industry and took part in the late 1830s in the first overlanding of stock from Sydney to South Australia.

As the years passed Ross, a tall, impressive figure with a full black beard, gained experience as a bushman and station overseer and seemed like so many others to be drawn into the virtually unexplored northern reaches of South Australia, right into the heart of the continent. Ross was responsible, in large part, for opening up this dry region which now successfully carries both sheep and cattle.

In 1870 he was chosen to explore the route for the Overland Telegraph, roughly along the line of McDouall Stuart's epic trek. He carried out detailed survey work in testing conditions and having finally reached the north coast he returned to Adelaide and a civic reception, by boat, having suffered badly from scurvy. Incredibly on this scientific expedition Ross had no surveyor and his meagre equipment consisted of a copy of Stuart's map, a prismatic compass, a protractor and a carpenter's lead pencil. He had no instruments to determine latitude or longitude. Almost blind, deaf and destitute Ross died in Adelaide in 1903. The local paper, the *Adelaide Register*, had carried an article about him and his distress and many offers of help were received. Sadly, it was too late. He died as a result of a fall in his home on the day following the publication of the article.

One bonus accorded occasionally to the early Scots explorers, certainly in Australia, was to select their own location to settle. Earliest pioneer to set up home in the extreme south of South Australia was Arthur Fydell Lindsay, yet another surveyor, who arrived with the first governor, Hindmarsh. During explorations on behalf of the governor, Lindsay found a site on a flat river plain set against towering mountains and perhaps, rather predictably, named his new home . . . Glen Lindsay.

THE VERSATILE NUMBER 8 FENCING WIRE

Robert and Ellen Horn from Cadder on the outskirts of Glasgow would have laughed if you had described them as frontiersfolk yet their experiences well displayed the fortitude required of immigrant tribes. They migrated in 1888 with baby son John to Bundaberg (QD) where Robert found work on bridge construction and Ellen took in washing while living in a work camp. The rewards did not match their expectations and in 1893 Robert sailed for New Zealand and walked fifty miles to secure a job in a timber mill.

Robert was joined by his family and eventually, with their eight sons and two daughters, they settled to dairy farming at Gollan's Valley near Wellington. After moving north again Robert and his son started breeding pedigree cattle and after World War I founded Allandale stud. Both became renowned show judges and successfully showed champion cattle at all the top New Zealand events.

As an old man Robert would call his grandchildren into the house on the way home from school to listen to 'Granny's Hielan' Hame' on the gramophone. Their reaction is not reported but Robert Horn is remembered by his family as a jack-of-all-trades who taught his family to build haystacks, cook potatoes in their skins over a bush fire and how to use a piece of No. 8 fencing wire to carry out a multitude of repairs. A patriarch indeed.

Using Australia as a stepping stone to New Zealand was a regular occurrence. Sir Walter Buchanan of Glendaruel, Argyllshire, went to Australia in

1856 where he spent six years as a stockman to Niel Black. His destiny was in New Zealand, however, and he crossed to the Otago goldfields in 1862, made a fine profit as a trader rather than a digger, and moved to the North Island where he pioneered many farming techniques from the eradication of rabbits to the introduction of refrigeration.

The reasons for making this leap across the Tasman Sea were many – dislike of the weather, farming failure, desire to see family, loss of a spouse, to fulfil a long-term plan or simply to answer that insistent voice which promised greener grass, just over the next hill.

Chapter Five
Sober and Upright, Mostly

THE IRISH were quaint and amusing, the English ambitious go-getters, the Welsh hard grafters and fine singers but the Scots – oh dear. The Scots have so often been accused of injecting an over-serious, almost dour element into the new societies, regularly portrayed as party-poopers and spoilsports. However, like the other ethnic portraits this is a stereotype and tells less than half the story.

Lack-lustre 'wowsers' some of the Caledonian tribe may have been but there is no doubt that it was their levelheadedness, their unswerving application to the business in hand – the creation of a nation – which kept Australia and New Zealand on an even keel in the frenetic, formative years. In business, education, medicine, banking, religion, law and politics the Scots, although small in numbers, exerted a strong and steadying influence.

Australians and New Zealanders today believe they have the best lifestyles in the world. Looking around, they may well be right. However, this prosperity and feeling of well-being has been built on a bedrock of purposefulness and duty to God which, although now considered an outmoded and stuffy approach to life, were the principles which the bulk of the Scots lived by. It was implicit that a good, rounded education was needed to 'get on' and this, combined with an unshakeable belief that they had the Lord on their side, made them a formidable immigrant group. Serious? Certainly . . . Successful, you betcha!

Malcolm Prentis has tried to explain the overabundance of Scots in politics and the media and attributes this to the fact that they were generally better educated, civic and independent-minded, ambitious, and perhaps most important of all, argumentative. Certainly civic leaders of Scottish origin have been found in abundance in both countries. This record, of course, is maintained right into the present day, for example with Robin Gray from Aberdeen, who was Speaker of the New Zealand Parliament in 1995.

Some adventurers also showed a natural flair for civic leadership. James Sutter (1818–1903) from Peterhead was a master mariner at the age of twenty-one and sailed around the world in command of trading ships including a China clipper. When he left the sea behind it was first of all for the goldfields of Otago before he settled at Timaru (CY) where he opened a store and timber business and was involved in local government to such an extent that he was six times mayor of Timaru.

THEIR STAFF AND COMFORT

For so many of these people the church – whether it was the established Church of Scotland or the Free Kirk – underpinned their lives; providing a physical core to the community, its teaching and tenets offered the foundation which allowed the pioneers to cope philosophically with whatever life flung in their direction whether it was premature death, natural disaster, fear, loneliness or occasional despair.

The Presbyterian Church with which the settlers identified so closely also carried the banner of education, of course. John Knox had wanted a school in every parish. In fact, religion and education among the Scots were almost synonymous. This emphasis on learning does seem, quite literally, to have giving the Scots a head start. It is known that the Shorter Catechism which was handed out for the children to learn by rote had the times tables on the reverse, learning and belief inextricably linked.

When the pioneer runs in New Zealand's Southland were broken up for farms and little communities began to develop in the late 1800s, according to the curator of the Historical Museum at Gore, the Scots made their first priority the setting up of a church in which to worship and a school to educate their children.

BANKING ON THE SCOTS

Behind the excitement of the great exodus from Scotland to Australia and New Zealand strong business and banking links were developing between the young nations and the auld country. Even people in Scotland who would never have considered immigration handed over their savings to the companies helping with the development of the new nations, anxious to have a share (albeit at a distance of many thousands of miles) in the great colonial adventures of the 19th century. The banking systems in Australia and New Zealand were heavily influenced by their Caledonian links and

Scots bankers and businessmen played an important role in providing stability
in the frontier communities of New Zealand. Here is the Bank of New South
Wales in the Scottish enclave of Invercargill (SD), taken in about 1860.
(*Making New Zealand Collection: Alexander Turnbull Library, Wellington*)

many of the leading colonial bankers had Scottish connections or were indeed
Scots.

Greenock-born merchant Robert Campbell (1769–1846) was appointed
treasurer of public funds in 1806 in New South Wales by Governor Bligh
(of *Mutiny on the Bounty* fame) because no bank existed. When the Savings
Bank of New South Wales finally came into existence in 1832 it emerged
that Campbell had been acting as a bank on behalf of the community and
had deposited with him £8,000 belonging to transported convicts (by far the
majority) and £2,000 belonging to free colonists – and Campbell had been
giving seven-and-a-half per cent interest.

Sir Thomas Dibbs entered the Commercial Banking Company of Sydney
as a clerk. He came from a St Andrews family who had settled in New South
Wales and his meteoric career saw him rise to general manager of the company
by the time he was thirty-five, holding that post for a remarkable forty-eight
years. His brother George was Premier of New South Wales in the 1880s.

In New Zealand Sir George McLean from Elgin managed to combine the
rigorous role of chairman of the Colonial Bank of New Zealand with his
love of horse racing and was able to produce winners in both fields. For
thirty years he was President of Dunedin Jockey Club.

During a banking crisis in New Zealand in 1894 John Murray, who was born near Dumbarton and immigrated in 1863, was asked by the directors of the Bank of New Zealand to liaise with the government over a rescue plan. The responsibility for devising a scheme of assistance fell to Murray through whose efforts the bank was re-established. However the Scotsman retired, his health broken by the stress.

Scots certainly played an important role in the development of capitalism in the two countries, their reputation for financial prudence not being entirely a music-hall myth. They were a hardheaded bunch. Malcolm Prentis records a transaction when Queensland settlers Donald and Dugald McIntyre signed a promissory note to help out their brother Malcolm; not only were they seeking guarantees about the return of the borrowed £140 – but they were looking for interest at twelve-and-a-half per cent. In addition John Dunmore Lang, the fiery minister who was responsible for encouraging thousands of Scots to Australia, met an emancipist woman (a freed prisoner) by the name of McLeod who in 1824 was lending at twenty-five per cent. This is how stereotypes are born.

During his teenage years in the 1870s James Edmond could be found poring over books in Glasgow's libraries and after migrating to Queensland he started as a newspaper proof-reader before making a name for himself on the staff of the *Sydney Bulletin* in 1886. Although he had little knowledge of finance he collected balance sheets and studied company reports, effectively pioneering financial journalism in Australia and producing witty and incisive columns. He eventually became editor of the *Bulletin* and was a great advocate of federation (the various Australian colonies came together in 1901).

If you're seeking a prime example of the imaginative, upwardly mobile Scot in the Antipodes in the 1800s then look no further than Fifer Alexander Berry, one of the most colourful – and successful – products of Cupar Grammar School. He studied medicine and signed on as ship's surgeon on a clipper on the China run. This changed his life forever because he was sickened by the brutal floggings which the sailors had to endure and the injuries sustained which he was supposed to mend.

With a part share in the *City of Edinburgh* he explored the Pacific in the early 1800s, taking part in 1809 in the rescue of a handful of survivors – a woman, two children and a cabin boy – from the *Boyd Massacre*. This ship en route from Sydney to the Cape of Good Hope had been overrun by a Maori war party while taking on fresh water at Whangaroa harbour in the north of New Zealand, an infamous incident in early Maori-settler relations.

Berry made various trading ventures but in 1812 the *City of Edinburgh* sank off the Azores. From 1819 with his partner Edward Wollstonecraft he

The first merchant prince of Sydney, Greenock-born Robert Campbell who is credited with breaking the East India Company's monopoly and getting Australian free trade up and running. (*Mitchell Library, State Library of New South Wales, Sydney*)

was based in Sydney and within months was being described as an 'eminent merchant'. Both partners received extensive land grants. One block near the Shoalhaven was extremely swampy but undaunted Berry, using convict labour, had a canal dug. His relationship with the transported prisoners was an interesting one. Berry found that many of them had been transported for relatively minor offences and if properly treated were prepared to work well.

Having survived shipwreck and the strain and stress of the early settler/trader's life Berry lived to the fine old age of ninety-two.

It's a remarkable fact that two members of the Campbell clan, the aforementioned Robert Campbell from Greenock and Sir John Logan Campbell from Edinburgh, were the first merchants who operated on any scale in Sydney and Auckland respectively.

Robert Campbell had reached Sydney by 1798 where he opened a branch of the Campbell, Clark Trading Company, built Campbell's wharf and settled to business in whaling, sealing, shipbuilding, general trading and farming. He received many land grants and was a pioneer of the district where the Australian capital Canberra now stands in the pocket of New South Wales called the Australian Capital Territory. On the site Campbell built a large property which he called Duntroon.

In 1825 he was appointed a member of the first New South Wales legislative council. He is credited with taking a lead in breaking the monopoly in the military-operated rum trade by lowering prices. As a result of this brave move he won general support and was considered the most trusted member of the pioneering community.

Sir John Logan Campbell was a doctor who came to Australia initially as a ship's surgeon but attracted by reports of the planned New Zealand colony he crossed the Tasman Sea. With his partner William Brown he went prospecting but on the foundation of Auckland was soon the leading merchant house, sending their first cargo to the United Kingdom in 1844. Campbell found time to travel widely despite his range of interests which included the *Southern Cross* newspaper. He also began to take an interest in politics and was elected superintendent of the province. He was also involved in shipping, banking and rail transport. A man of many parts, oor Johnny. His descriptions of the early days of Auckland are fascinating. He wrote of boats and canoes strung along the beach, a few white tents and improvised windbreaks amongst the scrub, beyond the shore scrub and tall tangled fern as far as the eye could see. Campbell – later called 'the Father of Auckland' – knew what he was talking about. His first home and warehouse was one of these tents.

Duntroon, Robert Campbell's residence from 1825 near the site of Australia's modern capital Canberra. (*Courtesy of the Prell and Jeffreys families and the Mitchell Library, State Library of New South Wales, Sydney*)

BOOKED FOR SUCCESS

Scots success in the world of commerce and industry was impressive in both countries – from locomotive engineers to brewers, from tobacco manufacturers to shipbuilders. And as we've seen, when it came to the money markets, the Scots were never far away. Businessman George Hunter held the important position of storekeeper general to the New Zealand Company's settlement at Wellington from 1840 and when the community was declared a borough in August 1842, he was declared first mayor. Devotion to duty killed him. After a massacre of settlers in Nelson he organised a public meeting to express sympathy with the families and caught a chill from which he died the following month.

One of the most interesting products of Glasgow's famous Andersonian Institute was Sir George Fowlds, son of a Fenwick handloom weaver. George cleaned railway carriages and laid kerbstones in Cape Town, South Africa, before going to New Zealand for his wife's health. In Auckland in the late 1800s he started at the bottom rung again working as a labourer but saved enough money to buy the stock and fixtures of a bankrupt clothier, this deft move setting him on the road to business success. He was also a noted politician and had the Scots disease – a passionate love of education.

Business acumen was also a proven attribute of Edward McGlashan (b. Edinburgh 1817) as shown by his planning for the move to Otago. Edward bought up the entire surplus stock of books from the publishers Chambers and Sons. Selling his books in Melbourne he made a good profit which he reinvested in stores and provisions and set off for New Zealand, again being able to sell on his goods at a handy profit. He ran the flour mill at the Water of Leith in the heart of Dunedin and also took an interest in paper-making. In the political arena he was an advocate of selling land cheaply to induce immigration.

AFTER THE GOLD RUSH

The Rev. Thomas Burns's son Arthur was one of the pioneer industrialists of New Zealand. The Otago provincial council offered £1,500 to the first person to produce tweed in the province and Burns, correctly predicting a glut in the labour market after the gold rush, took up the challenge.

Burns returned to Scotland in search of technical information to help set up such an industry and in 1870, after ordering the necessary plant and having engaged workers, returned to New Zealand where he bought an old flour mill and with the help of those who had travelled with him set up the Mosgiel Woollen Mills near Dunedin. He named the community after his uncle the poet Rabbie Burns's farm at Mossgiel in Ayrshire, but somewhere along the line the Otago town lost an 's'. The first cloth came off the mill in October 1871, just a year after he had signed an agreement at Innerleithen – a notable achievement. The homely Scottish nature of this mill is illustrated by the story told by a settler in Mosgiel who remembered how, around the turn of the century, the mill manager's wife would bring a big 'billy' of tea and buttered scones for the workers who had been allocated the most unpopular late summer task at the mill, cleaning out the dye creek where all the residue from the mill was tipped.

Landlocked Haddington in East Lothian is the unlikely home ground of John Macfarlane, a pioneer merchant prince of both Australia and New Zealand. He operated a schooner on the Auckland-Sydney trade route in the 1840s before settling in Auckland, visiting California and developing coastal trade in New Zealand with his steamships *Iona*, *Rowena*, and *Southern Cross*.

MISSION IMPOSSIBLE

There were many difficult tasks to be undertaken in the early days of settlement Down Under but it's arguable that Glasgow's James Busby (1800–1871) was landed with a mission doomed to failure.

Lawlessness among the Maori tribes and the hardy whalers and early traders in New Zealand prompted the authorities in Sydney, who oversaw the affairs of New Zealand in the early days, to appoint what they decided to call a Resident for New Zealand. They hoped the Resident would effectively be a troubleshooter but it was a weak title for an impossible assignment.

James Busby's first love had been wine and it's said he compiled a thesis on viticulture on board the sailing ship which carried him to Australia in 1823. There must have been many times he'd wished he'd made a career out of wine but he proved an impressive civil servant and was appointed Resident in 1832.

Among his many duties was to keep on good terms with the Maoris and missionaries alike, encouraging trade, assisting settlers, apprehending escaped convicts and generally creating a climate of law and order in what was a genuine frontier society. He was promised a British man-o-war to give him effective clout and it had been planned to give him the powers of a magistrate over the British subjects. He got neither.

Busby, according to at least one historian, seemed oblivious to all this – a young, pompous man, who felt destined for greatness but who found himself cast as the central figure in a solemn farce. The Maori chiefs paid

James Busby, a Glaswegian wine expert and the first 'Resident' of New Zealand who, as head of the colonial administration without any military or civil back-up, had the impossible task of keeping the peace between settlers and Maoris. (*Alexander Turnbull Library, Wellington*)

him no heed, he could not strike up an understanding with either the missionaries or the settlers and it seems he was the only person in New Zealand who took his job seriously. Other biographers have pointed out that Busby, whose frequent requests for increased powers went unheeded, gained an undeserved reputation for inefficiency. Sadly, he gained the nickname of 'No Authority' Busby and was to narrowly escape death when native marauders attacked his house. Meanwhile the settlers were operating their own form of lynch law.

The Gilbert and Sullivan-style comic opera reached its climax when a daft Frenchman, Charles Philip Hippolytus de Thierry, a self-styled Baron, announced in 1835 that he was to set himself up as sovereign chief of the Maori races. This forced Busby to get the chiefs' agreement that New Zealand should be a British protectorate.

The impotence of Busby's rule was fully exposed by the outbreak of tribal wars right across North Island. However, it should never be forgotten that Busby helped draft the Treaty of Waitangi which formalised the relationship between the paheka (white settlers), the Maoris and Queen Victoria, offering the tribes protection and security in exchange for their sovereign rights. A criminal act some have said subsequently but, in effect, New Zealand became a British colony. In the crowd at the signing ceremony on the lawn of government house at the Bay of Islands were a number of Scots witnesses apart from Busby. One of them was Logan Campbell's partner William Brown, from Dundee, who camped on the site of Auckland long before the arrival of the first settlers there.

But the Scots, with that inherent flexibility, were ready for any opportunities which presented themselves. Charles Traill needed a holiday from his business in Oamaru (OO). When he travelled south to Stewart Island he made an interesting discovery – extensive oyster beds which prompted him to sell up his business in the north and establish a fish-curing business on the southernmost island. The enterprise failed but Orkney-born Traill became attached to the remote location and settled on a small island which he called Ulva. Here he ran a store and kept a post office. His biography indicates an interest in natural history and concern for the welfare of the Maori people. As well as the Traills, Stewart Island is studded with Orcadian connections and names such as Pottinger, Leask, Clouston and Louttit are found.

FROM PAISLEY TO PETONE

The first Presbyterian church in Australia has been identified at Portland Head on the Hawkesbury River where a group of Borderers settled in 1802. Until the effervescent John Dunmore Lang held the first communion in the church in 1824 services were conducted by a lay preacher. However, even before the Ebenezer Church opened its doors on the Hawkesbury we know that two of the Scottish Martyrs – political transportees, Thomas Muir and William Skirving – remained faithful to the Presbyterian tradition and sang the metrical Psalms on the Sabbath in their backyard in Sydney.

Across the Tasman Sea the first Presbyterian service in New Zealand was conducted by the Rev. John Macfarlane at Petone near where Wellington stands today. This historic event took place just six days after the arrival of 120 pioneer immigrants on the *Bengal Merchant* in 1840. Until he had been selected to accompany the expedition the Rev. Macfarlane had been ministering at the Martyr's Church in Paisley. Macfarlane also preached the first Gaelic service in New Zealand the following year at Kaiwarra, for the benefit of the Highland settlers.

First minister to preach among the gold miners at Gabriel's Gully in Otago in the 1860s was Alexander Todd, who was born at St Andrews. Alex knew the ropes because in Scotland, almost as soon as he had been licensed by the

Free Church, he began preaching among the miners of Cowdenbeath in Fife and Kirkoswald in Ayrshire.

MARY – REBEL WITH A CAUSE

The people of Sydney (NSW) and Roy Bridge, Inverness-shire, were united on a January day in 1995, together though thousands of miles apart to celebrate the beatification of the woman who is set to become Australia's first saint – Mary MacKillop.

Although born in Melbourne in 1842, Mary was the daughter of Highland immigrants Alexander and Flora MacKillop. Her father had trained for the priesthood but arrived in Australia as a teacher. However, another career switch saw him go into business, a decision which landed the family with an itinerant life and condemned them to borderline poverty. To help support the family Mary worked as a shop assistant in Melbourne, governess to her young cousins at Penola (SA) and ran a boarding school. Alexander Cameron, so-called 'King of Penola' was her uncle.

Mary was called to the Order of the Sacred Heart in 1866 and when she became its leader it expanded rapidly. Today, it is the largest congregation of nuns controlling schools, hospitals and charitable organisations.

Mary MacKillop, the girl from an Inverness-shire family who is destined to become Australia's first saint. (*Mary MacKillop Place, Sydney*)

The process of beatification and canonisation was introduced in 1973 and on that southern summer's day in Sydney, the Pope beatified Mary, who died in 1909, in a ceremony incorporating, symbolically, the music of the bagpipes and the didgeridoo.

Mary's passion had been to provide an education and social welfare for all, but this found her in conflict with the conservative elements in the Roman Catholic Church hierarchy who preferred their nuns behind the convent walls. Falling out with the Catholic establishment, she was temporarily excommunicated. Undaunted, Mother Mary of the Cross, as she was known, went to Rome to seek the permission of the Pope for her work, received it and returned to found the Sisters of St Joseph. From Rome she even brought back recruits in the shape of some Irish women keen to join Mary and her Order. For Mary to finally be declared a saint, a miracle needs to be attributed to her.

NATURE'S WAY WITH NICETIES

Presbyterianism developed only slowly in New Zealand as the need and the growing population demanded. However, with poor communications and isolation, concerns of the church nationally or even regionally seemed of little moment.

The first minister of the Presbyterian Church in Auckland was Davie Bruce from Cramond on the River Forth whose vast charge embraced the whole of the northern region of the country. He sailed shortly after being ordained at Aberdeen in 1853.

Kerr Johnston in his history of the Hunter River (NSW) tells a story which indicates that the Aborigines found some strict Scottish practices amusing. J. D. Lang's brother Andrew came out to Australia and settled at Dunmore near Largs, a station which eventually housed convicts, workers and Aborigines as well as the family within its acres. Mrs Lang was a strict Scottish matron who insisted that everything was done with the proper decorum and under her personal supervision. All, including the Aboriginal girls, had to dress and behave with total modesty. Sometimes, however, the natural world makes no allowances for such niceties. Andrew Lang did some horse breeding and in the course of this activity it became necessary to take a new blood stallion to the mare. The mare, however, did not co-operate and repelled the stallion with her hooves. Andrew was not best pleased with this especially as his Aborigine helper was laughing uncontrollably. Asked the reason for this level of hilarity the helper pointed at the mare: 'That mare – she good Presbyterian.'

Of course, not everyone who came out of Scotland was drawn to the

Presbyterian tradition although social historians use the tag as a useful guide to population movements by Scots in the two countries. Henry Dewsbury from Alloa joined the Methodist Episcopal Church while serving his articles as an architect in Christchurch (CY) and became a minister of the Methodist Church, preaching widely throughout New Zealand.

John Chambers was a Quaker who married into a Presbyterian minister's family in Fife, and after being involved in early Australian explorations he moved to Hawkes Bay in New Zealand's North Island where he and his wife are credited with establishing a kirk at Havelock North.

If there seems to be an overemphasis on the role of the kirk in the areas of early Scottish settlement in the Antipodes then it's as well to remember that, unlike these largely secular days, the overwhelming majority of Scots in the heyday of immigration were active Christians, their faith an anchor in the storms of pioneer life.

Glasgow missionary James Chalmers found his calling on the remote islands of the southern Pacific. Born at Ardrishaig in Argyll in 1841, it seemed that he was not destined to reach his posting. The ship ran on to uncharted rocks and had to return to Sydney. It sailed again and was wrecked, all aboard being saved. He moved on to New Guinea where he tried to block the trade in alcohol, opium, firearms and explosives but was murdered in 1901 by a crowd of hostile natives at the Fly River.

The first settled minister at Melbourne was the Rev. James Forbes (1813–1851) who was born in the parish of Leochel-Cushie west of Aberdeen. Installed at Melbourne in 1837 he championed the Free Church cause at the Disruption, resigned his charge and was followed by many of his congregation. He brought out a Christian newspaper and built another church and school in Swanston Street, one of Melbourne's most famous thoroughfares. This became Melbourne Academy which in turn grew into Scotch College, one of the great public schools of Australia.

To the list of pioneer preachers in the wilds of New Zealand we must add the name of David Hogg, born in 1811 in Haddington, East Lothian. Hogg came to New Zealand on the *Slains Castle* and was appointed to the missionary station at Wanganui where he preached his first sermon to a congregation of thirty people in a *whare* or Maori dwelling-house in January 1853. Methodist preacher Alexander Reid worked among the Maoris. In Waikato he encouraged them in sheep farming and marketing wool but had to struggle constantly to keep the warlike tribes at peace. As opposition to British rule grew in advance of the Maori Wars he was forced to abandon his station.

TO THE PROMISED LAND

The Rev. Thomas Burns (1796–1871) is recognised as the founding father of Otago. At the time of the Disruption he was ministering to the parish of Monkton in his home county of Ayrshire but threw in his lot with the Free Church and became interested in their plan for a Scottish settlement in New Zealand, for which he accepted the post of first minister.

Even when the plan was temporarily shelved Burns remained a strong advocate of the proposal and saw his dream come to fruition when the *Philip Laing* reached Port Chalmers (Dunedin) in April 1848. He worked tirelessly both as minister and administrator, visiting his widely scattered flock, advising and cajoling them on matters both spiritual and practical until the arrival of two relief ministers in 1854. And he seems to have been a tough individual, prepared if the occasion demanded to lob a bible at a dozer in the kirk.

Throughout his great adventure in Otago Burns stressed the importance of the traditional Scottish education and although elected Lord Chancellor of the new University of Otago he did not live to see the inaugural ceremony.

Burns had always been determined that Otago should be an exclusively Free Church settlement but when the first immigrant ships sailed into Otago

Moving with the times: the Presbyterian church in the growing community of
Te Awamutu on its way to a new location in Mutu Street.
(*Te Awamutu Museum*)

Harbour only two-thirds of the settlers were actually Presbyterian; greater work opportunities back in Scotland and discouraging news of Maori attacks meant that the restrictions on outsiders had to be eased simply to make up the numbers. In fact, the *Otago Daily News* which first appeared within a few months of the arrival of the first settler ships in 1848 had to close after two years – it had been just too outspoken in its criticism of the Free Church leadership who were insisting that the colony should continue to strive for the original principles and exclusivity.

When Thomas Dick came to Dunedin in 1857 with his wife and young children, he came as a Baptist but found no Baptist congregation. Undaunted he threw himself into the activities of the Presbyterian First Church until the Baptist Church was opened in 1863. He began a Sunday school in a local sawmill in those difficult days and was superintendent until his death.

'Making do' was the basic requirement, even for the minister in the frontier days. When the scholarly Rev. Alexander Shepherd arrived in Hawkes Bay he found he had neither kirk nor manse and that the Scots congregation met in Kirriemuir blacksmith Alex Jones's front room on the Sabbath. He had a letter of introduction to the Jones family and they gave over their front room assuming it would be a temporary arrangement. The minister made the 14 × 12-foot room his bedroom, study and tackroom, storing his horse fodder and saddle in one corner. Although he would retreat up the hill to study when the Jones boys got noisy he obviously felt at home and remained there for three and a half years.

To George Stevenson, a farmer's son from Berwickshire, went the distinction of being the first newspaper editor in South Australia, having editorial control of the *Gazette and Colonial Register* when it first appeared in Adelaide in 1837. As for length of editorial service, the sixty-two years Scots-born John Watson was at the helm of the *Border Watch*, a Scots-interest newspaper in Mount Gambier (SA), looks unbeatable.

Although by dint of numbers the Presbyterians dominated the Scots contribution to religious life in Australia and New Zealand, the Roman Catholic input is not restricted to the luminous presence of Mary MacKillop.

Malcolm Prentis has listed many such as Father Colin McKee, a priest in Sydney in 1830 who was a convert to Catholicism and hailed from Tiree; two Scottish priests did important work with the Aboriginal missions and, interestingly, both were related to Mary MacKillop – her brother Donald and her cousin Duncan McNab, an outspoken individual who argued that the Aborigines should be treated as 'responsible people' and not as a problem. Their relative lack of success in making conversions may have been down, at least in part, to this philosophy. The Catholic contribution, particularly in the field of education, was out of all proportion to their numbers.

THE KISSING, CUDDLING RELIGION

By the 1820s the authorities in New South Wales and Tasmania realised that if their colonies were to develop then a better class of immigrant would be needed to provide a balance in the community, which was predominantly from a convict background. The Rev. Archibald Macarthur, the first Scots minister in Tasmania, seemed to meet all the requirements. That was until he tried to introduce the practice of 'holy kissing', a technique of the early Christians he told his elders, after having been caught hitting on the wife of the Lieutenant-Governor's secretary. The affair caused an uproar in the colony. When news of the strange goings-on leaked out into the community there was great amusement at the prospect of one of the men who had been brought to remove the convict taint from the rising population falling so spectacularly from grace.

The affair did have its sad aspect. The lady in question, a Mrs Turnbull, had visited the dying Mrs Macarthur. When the minister attempted to kiss her and was repulsed, he gave the game away by confessing to her: 'You cannot mistake me; you must often have observed how I looked down upon you from the pulpit.'

His plea that he was merely trying to introduce the loving practices of the old church fell apart when another woman testified that Macarthur had seized her with his teeth at the nape of her neck. The elders, according to one social historian, 'realised that their minister had a peculiar way of manifesting his holiness'. You can say that again! The Press had a field day and wrote of the end of the 'kissing and cuddling' religion, and when the famous Rev. Lang arrived by chance in Hobart to find the censors of public morals denouncing the Kirk minister he sought and obtained Macarthur's resignation. Sadly it seems that Macarthur, unlike the firebrand Lang, was basically a kind and gentle individual who had lost his way.

EVOLUTIONARY PROPOSALS

Far-seeing Charles Fraser of Aberdeen was the first Presbyterian minister in Christchurch but often found himself in conflict with his congregation over the fact that he was a keen naturalist – able to give a lecture on the lifestyles of seals, for example, with ideas rather too close to those of Charles Darwin for comfort.

He arrived in 1856 on the *Oriental* with his wife Jane, inducted himself to the new charge of St Andrews and then went out to found charges in the surrounding communities. Fraser took a prominent part in the early educational life of Christchurch, serving as chairman of the school board and even

Bonar Bridge's George
Munro (1801–1886) was
a kenspeckle figure
around the church of
Warepa in South Otago.
(*Ernie Munro*)

teaching *gratis* to help school funds. He took part in the great debate over
national education, being an advocate of a non-church system which, he
believed, would prevent sectarian bickering.

The Munros from Bonar Bridge who left Scotland in 1857 eventually
settled near Balclutha in South Otago where George Munro became deacon
of the church at Warepa and Gaelic precentor. The question of instrumental
music agitated the whole church, the organ being classed as inanimate and
not suitable. George refused to have anything to do with the 'kist o' whistles',
which he believed to be an invention of the devil and which he compared
to the yowling of dogs.

In his later years George would appear at church with a large red and
white spotted handkerchief round his neck. During the sermon the snuff-box
was passed around the congregation and if someone was more interested in
the sermon than passing the snuff George would speed things along by
standing up and glaring at the offender. He placed his handkerchief carefully
on his lap while taking the snuff, passed on the box then carefully folded

and tied up his handkerchief so that any spilled snuff was put to good use in the coming week.

George died in 1886 at the age of eighty-five and in a remarkable tribute the Warepa church, in celebrating its centenary in 1968, remembered the legendary George Munro thus: a local man grew a beard, wore a red and white spotted hankie and – just for a day – became George Munro.

SAVED FROM THE DROP

The Incident at the Eureka Stockade – an abortive miners' revolt in Victoria in 1854 – is said by some historians to have been the springboard for true Australian democracy. What is not so well known is that the lawyer acting for the accused miners was a Scot, James Macpherson Grant from Alvie in Inverness-shire. Grant came to Sydney with his parents in 1836 as a teenager, visited New Zealand where he served as a volunteer against the Maoris and returned to New South Wales to train as a lawyer. After chartering a vessel for a trading trip to California and trying his hand in the goldfields at Bendigo (VA) he was practising as a lawyer in Melbourne when – without a fee – he took on the miners' case.

The miners' list of grievances had been a long one. They were complaining of extortionate mining charges, police corruption, a delay in giving the miners a vote and the acquittal of a hotel owner on a charge of kicking a miner to death. A group of diggers holed up behind a stockade of slabs and raised what they called the New Australian flag – the Southern Cross on a blue background. There was talk of an Australian republic and it was all too much for the authorities. In less than quarter of an hour the rebels were overrun by troops with the loss of twenty-two miners and six soldiers. Thirty men were sent for trial on charges of high treason. Eventually all were cleared.

Elected to the legislative assembly in Victoria, Grant held a number of ministerial positions and succeeded in 1869 in passing a Land Act which formed the basis of all subsequent settlement in Victoria, insisting that the settlers should occupy their selected land and in doing so foil the various tricks for land acquisition adopted by the squatters.

The first Labour government of any significance in the world is credited to Queensland in 1899 and included William Kidston, an iron moulder from Falkirk, and miner Andrew Fisher from Crosshouse in Ayrshire, who was later to become Australia's Prime Minister.

Earliest lawyers to arrive in New South Wales from Scotland were at a disadvantage because the Scots legal system retained after the Union of the Parliaments in 1707 is based on Roman law, quite different in practice and principle from the Anglo-Irish system which was used universally in the colonies.

For thirty-three years the steely gaze of police magistrate Joseph Panton from Knockiemile, Aberdeenshire, dominated proceedings in Melbourne. Criminals, it's said, developed a quiet respect for the Scot who, it would have astonished them to learn, had absolutely no legal training. He was from an adventurous family, his father having served with the Hudson's Bay Company, but Joseph went to Australia with the intention of trying his hand at farming after studying geology at Edinburgh University. Within a year, however, he had been appointed assistant commissioner at the Bendigo goldfields. His greatest achievement was in brokering peace between the Chinese and other diggers and so avoiding a possible racial bloodbath. The royal commission appointed after the incident at the Eureka stockade also commended Panton for his work in the Bendigo district.

A RACE AGAINST TIME

Francis Ormond, another Aberdonian, was the sort of man who liked to see everyone get a fair crack of the whip. At the age of nineteen he was given the management of his father's small sheep station in Victoria and, finding that the boys employed on the station were quite uneducated, he set up his own classes giving them an elementary education.

Ormond became magistrate in 1853 and a few years later was called in to take a deposition in the case of the death of a hut-keeper. He came to the conclusion that the death had been accidental. Later he was stunned to read in his newspaper that a man called David Healy had been convicted of the supposed crime and was to be hanged in two days. Ormond ordered two of his best horses prepared and, riding one and leading the other, started on the long journey to Melbourne. Despite having to cross the Little River (which belied its name because it was in flood) he arrived in time, saw the Attorney-General and succeeded in convincing him that Healy was innocent.

It will be no surprise to learn that this seeker after truth and justice became one of Victoria's greatest philanthropists, endowing churches and colleges in-cluding a working men's college which became Melbourne's technical school.

RUNNING LATE, WITH LUCK

If you ever need confirmation that the road to success in life is paved with large slabs of luck then lend an ear to the story of young James Murray who came to Australia from Aberdeen on the *Hesperus* in 1854 at the age of six. His family had been shipbuilders. Times got tough financially for the Murray household, so at the age of fifteen James was delivering telegrams for the Sydney Telegraph Company.

Wandering along the street on one occasion he saw, in a shop window, his first mechanical train set running hypnotically round and round its track. He watched fascinated for fully fifteen minutes, forgetting all about his telegram. Realising suddenly that he would have to make tracks, he sprinted off down the street. On a corner he was stopped by a distinguished-looking gentleman who had recognised the telegraph company uniform, intercepted the messenger and identified himself as the head of the company. The boss said he was most impressed to see a lad so energetic in his duties and keen to make a prompt delivery and as a reward offered James the chance to attend night classes. Naturally, the boy did not explain the reason for his haste but attended the school as arranged and then enjoyed rapid promotion within the telegraph company until it was taken over by the Postal Department. He finally retired from the position of chief finance officer of the Australian Post Office. From message boy to high heid yin in one lucky sprint.

TRIALS OF AN UPCOUNTRY DOMINIE

Often immigration could mean lengthy separation for young, recently married or engaged couples. So it was in the case of schoolteacher Jim Wilson, descendant of Ayrshire weavers, and his colleague at Cromarty school and fiancée, Harriet McRae, of Belhelvie near Aberdeen. James immigrated in October 1890 to Australia on the SS *Orizabal* and for four years the young couple corresponded until Harriet set off for Victoria and they were married soon

Scots schoolmaster James Wilson and his pupils at Poowong East School, Victoria, around 1897. (*Stuart Wilson, Victoria*)

after her arrival. Born at Cumnock in 1862, James died in his late forties – but with Harriet's support he played a significant part in establishing an educational tradition in the rough, remote timbered country of northeast Victoria.

Soon after his arrival James passed a demonstration class lesson and began teaching. Three years later we find him at Running Creek School. Although letters took months to travel across the globe the young couple's relationship deepened and strengthened. Just occasionally, quite naturally, reassurances were sought – and given. James wrote:

> I do not know that I have any expectations with regard to you, Harriet. All I want is a loving little woman who will do her best to make for me a good wife, and I am sure that expectation will be fulfilled . . . I do not think you will find me a hard task-master, my sweetheart.

Correspondence his family has retained also gives a splendid insight into both the life of the settlers in a developing country and the problems he faced as a pioneer teacher, arguing for better conditions for his pupils against a rigid and distant bureaucracy.

At one of his schools, after addressing the problem of inadequate seating, he pointed out that when it rained the children – some thirty-five pupils – had to squeeze into one half of the schoolroom to avoid the drips. Another letter expressed anxiety about two settler families who had built their homes on a stretch of the Kiewa River which was subject to sudden disastrous flood from snowmelt. The children had to cross the river on horseback to reach the school and were often absent. He also expressed concern that because of the lack of water storage facilities the children were drinking out of a creek which they shared with pigs and cows, 'not to speak of dogs'.

Eventually Jim Wilson, as a result of poor health, was forced to leave for the less harsh surroundings of Shepparton East, where he died in 1910. After Jim's death Harriet, with children of her own to care for, returned to teaching in the remote rural areas of Victoria.

In New Zealand Thomas Fleming, who had migrated from Edinburgh to the West Coast, is given the credit for almost single-handedly getting the home reading movement off the ground; and when in 1877 a bill gave the country a uniform national system of education – free, secular and compulsory – many of the provisions were drafted by Midlothian's John Hislop.

Generally across New Zealand and Australia the Scots filled a disproportionately high number of teaching posts. One way this can be verified is through the various census forms. Most academics are prepared to equate Presbyterianism with Scottishness and on that basis Malcolm Prentis found that in 1901 over eighteen per cent of teachers in New South Wales were Scots either by birth or marriage.

The description given in the biographies of Edinburgh-born Margaret Burn, who was the first principal of Otago Girls High School (itself the first girls' high school in New Zealand), suggest she was deeply religious, charitable, yet a strict disciplinarian. This description must have equally applied to many of the stern dominies who found their way from Scotland to Australia and New Zealand. Another such individual was Alexander Morrison from Forres, headmaster of the famous Scotch College in Melbourne (VA). He helped make the college into one of Australia's leading schools.

Life for schoolchildren in New Zealand even into the early 20th century was an altogether harder slog than it is today. Many children had miles to walk to school where they were accommodated in often cold and cramped conditions. For youngsters lucky enough to have a horse, many of the rural schools had a paddock adjoining the school buildings. Country children, in particular, had a long day, often milking the cows or feeding the sheep before setting off to tramp to school and facing the same round of chores in the evening. One old-timer told me: 'It didna' leave a lot of time for skylarking.'

The name of philanthropist Andrew Carnegie is not perhaps as well known in Australia and New Zealand as it is in his adopted home of the United States, but the Dunfermline weaver's son who became a steel industry multi-millionaire also gave money for library construction in the Antipodes. One example was a gift of £2,000 which allowed a new library building to be opened in Mildura (VA) in 1908.

James Macandrew was an Aberdonian just filled to brimming with enthusiasm for the idea of a new life in New Zealand, so much so that he purchased a schooner and took his friends and his family Down Under. In Otago he became a leading member of the Constitutional Association which was seeking self-government for the colony and he began a trading company which rapidly expanded and soon was operating a fast mail service to the United Kingdom.

From various biographies and sketches it seems that Macandrew was a difficult man to keep pace with. He was soon the Provincial Superintendent and was considered a man of 'undoubted ability, patient sincerity, optimism and magnetic influence'. And yet there was a cloud building on the horizon. Macandrew was accused of pocketing some of the immigration funds and this forced his removal from the superintendency, although he denied the charges.

For Macandrew education was not just an adjunct to the religious life, it was almost a religion in its own right. He was closely involved in the founding of the University of Otago in 1870. His critics argue that while the man clearly had vision he was flawed as a businessman, being confident with broad issues but struggling with fine detail.

CHEMISTRY IN THE CUPBOARD

If William Littlejohn, the son of a Turiff watchmaker, did nothing in his academic career more than introduce Nobel prizewinner Ernest Rutherford to physics and chemistry he would have been entitled to a smile of satisfaction. However Littlejohn, a 'tall, burly, bearded fair young man with a strong Aberdeen burr', was a big bundle of energy who brightened and enriched the lives of a generation of New Zealand and Australian schoolboys. When his family moved to New Zealand in 1881 William completed his studies and joined them at Wellington. At Nelson College he obtained a post as third master and immediately began to be an influence in the school, as prominent on the football and cricket field after school hours as in the classroom.

This amazing man had studied the classics at Aberdeen but having contracted to take an elementary chemistry class at Nelson he did so by studying a lesson ahead of his class. On discovering that there was no laboratory, he persuaded the headmaster to convert a box-room. Once when the principal remarked on the Scotsman's heavy list of duties, Littlejohn responded saying that a man who was not brilliant had to do plenty to make up for it.

It was into this setting that young Ernest Rutherford, the son of a Scottish wheelwright who had immigrated in the 1840s, arrived and was later to be given special coaching by Littlejohn for a university scholarship. In 1903 Littlejohn, who by this time was principal at Nelson, applied and was appointed to Scotch College in Melbourne, the oldest secondary school in Victoria. Immediately he set out to broaden the interests of the school through sport, literary pursuits like the school magazine, drama and debating clubs and other measures. During World War I it was calculated that Scotch College had over 1,200 old boys at the front, of which over 200 were killed.

Littlejohn's biographers considered him a great organiser and schoolmaster, strict in discipline to the extent that he was known affectionately to his pupils as 'The Boss'.

When the slightly eccentric James Gordon Stuart Grant reached Dunedin he should have quickly become a disappointed and disillusioned Scot. Grant, born in the Glenlivet district of Banffshire in the 1830s, believed he had been appointed rector of the new Otago High School – yet to be completed. Grant opened his own academy, awaiting the launch of the high school, but soon lost his pupils when it eventually opened under the care of a man Grant always called 'the Second Rector'.

As an antidote to his disappointment Grant threw himself into a pro-education campaign and his battle against what he called 'darkness, ignorance and selfish mammonism'. His pet scheme was a library for Dunedin to fund which he made an amazing offer: he volunteered to lecture on any subject to any audience, indoors or outdoors, Unfortunately, as a speaker, he did not impress. In later years he became self-appointed champion of the working class, for instance in his demands for an eight-hour working day.

FROM PIT BOY TO PRIME MINISTER

Profiles of Scots who made an impact in the political arena in Australia and New Zealand from 1820 until World War II are so numerous that it would take a separate book to do justice to their contribution. When we look at the list of State Premiers, Prime Ministers and senior politicians in both countries it is an impressive contribution for a small feeder nation. For example three of New South Wales's first six governors were Scots (Hunter, Macquarie and Brisbane) and almost without exception their successors in high office seem to have been memorable characters. Sir William Macgregor of Queensland was once famously described as a 'great block of unhewn granite'. Being an Aberdonian, he would take that as a compliment.

However, by making the closer acquaintance of some individuals, two of whom made it to the top rung of the ladder in their respective nations and others who beavered away at the grass roots, a consensus of the Scots contribution may materialise.

Sir Robert Stout was born at Lerwick in the Shetland Isles and into money – his father was a merchant. Robert was a qualified surveyor when he came to New Zealand in 1864, tried teaching and then the law, giving himself the perfect springboard for a political career.

By all accounts Stout was a mighty serious individual, a strict Presbyterian with radical views on the rights of the poor and the underprivileged. Children's rights and votes for women figured high on his agenda first as Attorney-General, then as Minister of Land and Emigration and finally as Prime Minister. His term of office coincided with an economic depression but he concentrated on education and social welfare, doing much of the ground work in the 1880s for the reformers who were to follow. Stout died in 1930.

The year 1927 saw the biggest day for the Ayrshire village of Crosshouse that anyone could remember. In a storybook return Andrew Fisher, the young miner who had left forty-two years previously to seek his fortune in Queensland, and became three times Prime Minister of Australia, visited his home town.

What a contrasting start to life Fisher had in comparison with the Shetlander Stout. Andrew Fisher was brought up in a but and ben, with all the hard conditions found in 19th-century mining communities. Eventually he left Ayrshire after being victimised for his union activities. In Australia he worked again as a miner, read widely in economics and social sciences and became a union leader.

This tall, good-looking young Scot has been described as hardworking and courageous rather than brilliant. He was already active in Queensland politics when the first all-Australian elections after Federation at the start of the 20th century saw him elected to the House of Representatives and soon holding ministerial office. During his three terms as Prime Minister (1880–1915) over 100 Acts were passed connected with subjects as diverse as the transcontinental railway and maternity allowances.

Like his countryman Stout across the water, Andrew Fisher was a teetotaller but with a keen sense of the aspirations of the working man. He described himself as a Christian Socialist and his feeling for right and wrong is well illustrated by a story told in John Malkin's biography of how when Fisher found on returning home that an oil company who were seeking rights had gifted him a new oil lamp, he asked his wife: 'Would you ruin me, woman?' To dispel any lingering suggestion of graft Fisher took the lamp and left if burning in the street.

His return to Crosshouse to visit his old haunts was a gift to the headline writers of the day who celebrated Andrew Fisher – Pit Boy to Prime Minister.

At Christchurch on New Zealand's South Island stands an impressive and enduring memorial to another Ayrshire Scot who added to the record of his countrymen as civic leaders in Australian and New Zealand communities, large and small. Christchurch's beautiful tree-lined avenues, which still form much of the framework of the city, were the result of a planting plan formulated by Andrew Duncan, who was the third mayor of Christchurch in 1870. His father George took his family south in 1858, leaving from Renfrew on the *Zealandia* to found a New Zealand dynasty of nurserymen, landscape gardeners and horticulturalists. George Duncan's principal legacy in Scotland was the estate of Coodham, near Symington in Ayrshire.

After reaching Christchurch, George and his son Andrew operated a seed shop and plant nursery and introduced glasshouse culture to New Zealand. As a team they won many medals at exhibitions in New Zealand and Australia. Andrew also operated as an immigration agent in the United Kingdom for a year, encouraging many hard-working prospective settlers to take a chance in New Zealand. His treelined avenues are now familiar to visitors from all over the world.

THE EMPTIEST POOCH

It can often seem that young single Scotsmen arriving in New Zealand and

Bealey Avenue, Christchurch (CY). These beautiful avenues of beech trees resulted from a plan suggested by Ayrshire's Andrew Duncan during his term as mayor in 1870. (*Alistair Duncan, Taranaki*)

Australia were involved in some bizarre contest to see who could start their new life with the emptiest pooch.

George Dorward from Edzell in Angus left Scotland and worked at the gold diggings in New Zealand and South Africa. His success seems to have been limited because he stepped off the boat at Port Lincoln (SA) with nine pence in his pocket. However, he went on to successfully establish himself on the south coast as a farmer, road builder, auctioneer and active member of the local council. He was appointed a justice of the peace in 1901 but rarely sat on the bench. He was remembered as a kindly Scot and when he did take a case it usually meant good copy for the reporters. On one occasion he was dealing with a prisoner accused of drunkenness. Dorward fined him five shillings but the man declared himself penniless. Dorward's biographer reports the outcome:

> Noting that the prosecuting police officer had himself often kicked over the traces, Mr Dorward extracted two shillings and sixpence from him adding himself a similar amount to clear the fine.

The Angus man knew that every penny counted.

Chapter Six
Old Macdonald had a Sheep Station

A s your aircraft rolls out along the runway at Perth airport in Western Australia it's worth remembering that you are trundling across what was once Block 27, South Guildford, the 100-acre farm of settler John Scott from Lanark, who had the distinction of later becoming the first farmer at Bunbury (WA). The Scotts left a thriving and substantial farm in the Clyde Valley in 1831 to begin a new life as one of the earliest settler families in the vast region which was to become the state of Western Australia.

Descendants of the Scotts have puzzled over their departure (they arrived in Australia with four servants, including an Irish girl and two agricultural workers) but the feeling is that the great adventure may have been prompted by the possibility of almost boundless available land. They may also have been encouraged to go because the first Governor of Western Australia, Sir James Stirling, also came from Lanarkshire. It was Sir James who, on learning three years after the Scotts' arrival that they planned to pull up the tent pegs and move to Victoria, persuaded them to stay and gave land, rent free and from his own allocation, for a farm at Bunbury. The governor was clearly a shrewd man because John Scott had three sturdy sons and his wife was a nurse. They had all the credentials as Grade 1 settlers.

Sir James, considered by many to be the father-figure of Western Australia, saw that the pace of development in his colony was miserably slow, so was prompted to write to London asking that 'active and industrious settlers' like the Scotts be sent, rather than failures. The helpless and inefficient were dragging the colony under.

It's difficult to imagine the endless days of hard graft which lay ahead for the Scotts, building their new home from scratch – everything from the fence posts to the dwelling house and a complex of outbuildings. It soon grew

An early view of Bunbury, Western Australia, an important timber port and
target for early Scots settlers in the far southwest.
(*Battye Library, Perth, Western Australia: 6101P*)

into a little settlement in its own right with the Scotts quite literally living
off the land and, as the Governor had anticipated, Mrs Scott's nursing skills
proving a bonus in the developing area.

Watching from a tree for the arrival of the Governor's vessel *Champion*,
young Robert tore the backside out of his breeks – but his mother, quick
to improvise, slipped a section of bark into his trousers. His Excellency was
most amused, so much so that he presented Robert with a naval uniform.

Their biographer Theodora Sanders describes the family hunting kangaroo,
cultivating pear, mulberry and fig bushes around the house, beachcombing
for iron to fashion and repair ploughs. Their animals worked hard but were
well cared for. When too old to work they were killed for meat, their hides
tanned for leather and their bones ground into fertiliser. Their fat was
rendered for tallow and often the horns were polished as ornaments. No
part of these faithful beasts went to waste.

Idyllic? Not quite. Sir James Stirling left after his term of office was
complete but failed to pass on the deeds for the Scotts land at Bunbury, and
although public sympathy was on their side they lost a court case . . . and
the farm. The family had to start all over again. However, the numerous
descendants in present-day Western Australia are testimony to their resilience
and success at picking up the pieces.

Portrait of Lanarkshire's
Sir James Stirling, who
was first Governor of
Western Australia
(*c.* 1860). (*Battye Library,
Perth, Western Australia:*
668P)

It's clear on examining family records and local histories that the rural
settlers in the Antipodes, such as the Scotts of Bunbury, retained their
Scottish characteristics, outlook and behaviour far longer than their counter-
parts in the growing cities. The latter displayed assimilation at its best in the
urban melting pot.

Of course, there were those in the cities also who would cling to their Caledonian connection through clubs, bands and Scots-interest groups but many,
within a generation, were fully integrated. As Dr Tom Brooking of the University of Otago has said, they were left with the problem faced by all
immigrants: they wanted to be themselves but they also wanted to fit in with the
new and emerging nation. Each had their own way of dealing with this dilemma.

WHO'D BE A FARMER?

What is particularly interesting is the number who made up their minds to
swap a grimy city life in Scotland, or even a profession, for a stab at farming
and stock-raising. Some planned carefully, went to night school classes and
swotted up on every conceivable aspect of farming life, from irrigation to

sheep handling, from carpentry to basic veterinary medicine, and how these might apply in the very different conditions they were to find at their destination. Others scarcely knew one end of a sheep from another, but seemed undeterred by these mere technicalities. Little surprise then that many of the urban Scots who came to try their luck on the land managed to stick the hard physical labour and the long, long hours for just a few weeks or months before heading back to 'civilisation'. Of course, regular economic depressions also sent people to the cities, among them skilled farmers who were left with a simple choice, move or starve.

Those Scots who did make a go of farming life did not necessarily love the land in some misty-eyed Celtic manner as many would like to believe. Rather, according to Waterson, they believed in it, believed that despite all the hardships it had the capacity to secure their future, possibly even make them rich. What they all had was a completely new experience of life.

ROOTS SUNK DEEP

A compact and faded diary held by the Mitchell Library in Sydney, written by Glaswegian emigrant Robert Muir around 1839/40, provides intriguing detail of the life of the Scots settlers around Inverell in the New England district of New South Wales in those pioneering days.

Scotsman Alex Stuart used a combination of horse power and modern technology on his wheat farm in Manawatu between the World Wars.
(*Paul Melody, Manawatu*)

The Scots connection in Tasmania: Governor Sir William Allardyce leaves the
Gordon Highlander Hotel in Sorell after an official visit (c.1921) to the com-
munity where a number of Scots chose to settle.
(*Historical Society of the Municipality of Sorell*)

The earliest period of farming in New South Wales had been restricted
by poor soil and coastal forests but once the need for pastoral land developed
the Scots were out there in the vanguard of the push into the interior. Muir's
diary contains a vivid portrayal of life in the bush, of a man called Yorky,
murdered by the Aborigines and left 'much bruised and cut'; of natives
setting fire to the bush and almost causing the destruction of a newly-built
house. Regularly there seemed to have been trouble with the convict farm
workers refusing to work or crying off sick. One man, Flanagan by name,
was 'beset' with stomach pains which even a dose of Epsom salts failed to
cure and so he insisted on walking down country to the hospital in Newcastle.
He returned four days later, his ailment uncured.

On the culinary front mid-April proved to be a special period. Robert
Muir dined on kangaroo for the first time and found it 'very good'; and six
days later, having killed an emu, they dined on emu steaks. They were later
to discover that salting the emu's legs made wonderful hams.

A more typical settling experience would be that of the McGregors,
William and Nancy from Latheronwheel in Caithness, who sailed from
Liverpool on the *Carrier Dove*. Reaching Melbourne in 1857 they found
farm work until the Land Act of 1860 allowed them to 'select' 320 acres
thrown open for settlement in the Corop district. The terms were straightforward – the land was priced at one pound per acre payable in ten years

and the McGregors had to live on the block for at least ten months of the years and put £20 of improvement on it annually. Family records show that William brought with him a wagon, a dray, five draught horses, a light horse, seven cows, two single furrow ploughs, a harrow, a roller, a reaping machine and a carpenter. He camped alone for a month while the house was being built then sent for his wife and six children. From this start the McGregor holdings around Rochester grew to 3,000 acres and William is remembered for persuading local farmers to bind sheaves with twine rather than metal, which could find its way into beasts' stomachs. According to the family, William died in 1917 at the age of eighty-four never having returned to his native land, his roots having 'sunk deep in the soil of Australia'.

Women were often left with the care of pioneer farms in both countries, having lost their menfolk in accidents or through illness. The Scots lasses did not shirk a task which most men would baulk at today. Stuart Baillie from Arbroath worked for his widowed aunt in the Tumby Bay district of South Australia. She carted wheat in the bullock dray and loaded it on to the ship's cargo boat in the same manner as the men . . . ploughed the fields with a single furrow plough and sowed the seeds from a tin dish tied to her waist, broadcast by hand. The iron handles of the plough were too high for her but, full of initiative, she lit a fire and when the metal was sufficiently hot took a heavy post and bent them down until they were just the correct height for her to grasp. This formidable lady, who made the soles of her children's shoes from kangaroo hide, always had her muzzle loader at the ready – her first line of defence against whatever dangers life threw in her direction.

HUNGER FOR LAND

Settlement patterns begin to emerge on examination of the immigration diaries and family biographies. One very common scenario is that of the single Scotsman making his way to Australia and/or New Zealand, trying his luck on the goldfields with varying degrees of success, sending for his betrothed, then moving on to the land to farm despite, in some cases, having only basic farming techniques. Thomas Duncan was the son of the procurator fiscal at Perth and trained for the law before coming to Canterbury and taking up land, where he grafted for five tough years before realising that his strength was unequal to farming and so returned to the law – and politics.

But, of course, there were also success stories. The tale of Alexander Brydie from Anstruther in Fife has many familiar characteristics. Born in 1839, his father, a town bailie, used his influence to get Alex a place on a ship bound for Australia; effectively, the young man worked his passage to the new land. After spending a couple of years as a prospector in New South Wales, he took off for New Zealand in a vessel which the authorities considered unseaworthy but which slipped out into the Tasman Sea without a permit. Joining the 1862 'rush' in central Otago, he arranged for his bride-to-be Euphema Imrie to come out from Fife to join him. They were married by the renowned Dr Burns in First Church, Dunedin, and on a bullock dray they headed for Blue Spur at the head of the famous Gabriel's Gully, where Alex was a mining company manager. He also claimed to have created the first vegetable garden in the region. Children arrived in the Brydie family in due course and they moved again to a site where they built their stone house next to the McSkimming family – also from Fife! Alexander Brydie, the gold prospector, gained a new reputation in central Otago as a progressive farmer prepared to try new techniques to increase his yield.

WATCH OUT FOR THE AIRY GUFF

An amazing grapevine operated among the Scots as the new territories in New Zealand and Australia were opened up. When word got back of the good farming country in western Victoria, for example, the area was immediately targeted by thousands of Scots waiting to immigrate. Word was passed along the line by the few people travelling to Britain, in letters home from established settlers and in newspapers. Generally the down-to-earth Scots knew that, no matter how glowing the reports, only with hard work and their fair share of luck would sheep farming lead them to a comfortable life in the new lands. They were wary of what has been described as 'airy and irresponsible guff' produced to promote particular regions.

In South Australia, for example, Horton James who visited the colony when it opened to settlers went back to tell prospective immigrants that they could look to make an eighty per cent profit yearly. He gushed:

> It surpasses even grog selling, bullock driving or banking . . . the only
> thing it requires is ready money to begin with and the strictest attention
> to the sheep afterwards . . . there is a fortune to be made with sheep farm-
> ing in any part of South Australia.

Numerous Scots migrants made a comfortable living for themselves from the woollies, fewer made a fortune. But one pioneer summarised the sacrifice that had to be made in the early days:

> Sheep had to be watched from sunrise to sunset because of wild dogs and
> blacks . . . sleeping in a six foot by six foot watch box. No matter what
> the weather, storm or tempest, wet or dry, you must be with your sheep,
> no Sunday, no holiday, one continual always-at-it.

And the natural world took its toll on sheep and shepherd alike. Sombre monuments to a tough existence can be found. For instance, in the heart of the Mackenzie Country (CY) stands a stone memorial to John Brown, a shepherd from Skye who lost his life after being caught in a blizzard.

The scale of losses to the dingo or wild dog could be catastrophically high in Australia – up to ten per cent of the flock annually. Vast armies of rabbits which had bred from released pets and grazed on and undermined large areas of pasture were another enormous headache for the sheep farmers. The McKechnie brothers from Glasgow, who found a new home as sheep farmers on the Eyre Peninsula (SA) in the 1850s, get the doubtful credit for having introduced and liberated rabbits in the area. In the earliest days the McKech-nies considered them pets and the employees on the station were forbidden to kill them – soon, however, they were a pest of major proportions. Andrew Scott from Earlston in the Borders founded the vermin board in the Port Lincoln district (SA) and one of his lasting claims to fame was that he persuaded the government to give grants for 500 miles of anti-rabbit netting.

CUTTING A FURROW

The generally shy and retiring Scots did make one exception on the social front, attendance at the agricultural shows was compulsory. Not only did they enjoy showing off their animals, they just loved to display their prowess behind the plough and it's on record that pioneer James Cock was the outstanding ploughman in the Scots enclave of Mount Gambier (SA), winning the champion's prize at the region's very first ploughing competition. In the same area the Macarthur brothers, James and Donald, got a deserved reputation for their damned-near perfect ploughmanship.

Family histories often contain the declaration that Uncle Willie or Cousin George was the first to break ground with the plough in the new settlements. For example, John Kerr, a Perthshire agricultural labourer who might more reasonably have expected anonymity instead of immortality, found himself in the annals of New Zealand's Nelson district as the first to break the ground at Waimea West.

Skilled ploughmen many might have been but sometimes the Scots let the side down. Extensive land clearing took place and, particularly in Australia, not always for the benefit of the community at large but simply to create bigger and bigger holdings, allowing the new 'lairds' to become lords of vast (albeit often empty) domains.

Scots found their way into the forestry industry – timber was big business as the cities started to expand – but there was a hard price to be paid, for it was a dangerous calling at the best of times. Scots were killed in the rush to

The legendary square kauri tree on the Coromandel Peninsula of New Zealand's North Island. From the earliest days of settlement Scots were involved with the forests, whether gathering gum or in the important timber trade.
(*Isabel Mackenzie, Auckland*)

meet demand. Tragedy struck the McHardie family from Kirriemuir when Alexander, who had been working in the timber trade in the Hutt Valley north of Wellington after his arrival with the 1,840 pioneers, was killed by a falling tree. His immediate family decided to return to Scotland although his brother settled happily in North Island.

WATER, WATER EVERYWHERE

Fearsome droughts were something completely new for the Scots settlers. Those who arrived towards the end of the 19th century found themselves in the middle of a particularly severe four-year drought. Due to lack of pasture and extreme conditions which affected all of Australia, the population of sheep in Queensland, for example, dropped from twenty-one million to seven million.

The dry, barren interior of Australia blossoming like a garden – that was the vision of Glasgow man Hugh McColl (1819–1885) who spent most of his adult life as an advocate of a canal to bring water to the wilderness. He had worked for a time with the River Tyne conservancy committee in the north of England and this may have turned on his interest in irrigation.

After immigrating he worked as a commercial traveller and making his way through the countryside in the dry season convinced him that the watering of the parched lands could create a new garden of Australia. However, the rest of Australian society took some convincing. He became associated in a canal company and although a successful preliminary survey was carried out no financial backers could be found. Elected to the Victoria legislative assembly, he kept the water question to the forefront despite being a regular victim of the mockers. Eventually, through his insistence, a Royal Commission was appointed to look generally at the provision of water for the people's use. The chairman travelled the world gathering information. Sadly, McColl died before the commission reported but his persistence brought in many new water measures which helped the barren lands to bloom.

Drought – a distinctly un-Scottish phenomenon – was just one of the new experiences to which the settlers in the Waikato town of Te Awamutu had to become accustomed. Here children queue at the water cart.
(*Te Awamutu District Museum*)

The spectacular Cairns-Kuranda rail line in Queensland: Scots were involved in
every facet of the construction from navvying to surveying.
(*John Oxley Library, Brisbane, Queensland*)

Some immigrants found their ways into alien and un-Scottish aspects of
land use – for example, the sugar industry. Born in the north and educated
in Elgin, John Mann worked as a farm labourer and followed his brother to
far north Queensland, arriving at Cairns in 1889. As one of the legendary
swagmen, John threw his pack on his back and marched up and down the
Queensland coast – hundreds of miles – looking for work. Near Cairns he
had his first experience of working in a sugar mill. And John was not feart
o' hard work. He navvied both on the spectacular Cairns-Kuranda railway
and at the Mareeba goldfields.

He tried his hand at dairy farming but a combination of the 1893 Depression and a cattle tick plague forced him out of business with ninety per
cent of his animals lost. Reconnecting with the sugar trade, he helped build
a tramway from Port Douglas to carry the sugar cane. Finding his way back
to Cairns in 1897, he took up farming again and the homestead there is still
in the hands of the Mann family a century on. John also farmed in the
Burdekin River area for the production of sugar cane (another Scot, John
Drysdale, having opened up the district). In his later years John Mann was
a great advocate of the Queensland sugar industry, writing forceful letters
to newspapers and serving on the organising body of the State Sugar Cane
Growers. While serving in Parliament he met and married Janet King who

trenching equipment, and a technical school was built. Over the years Hugh McKay operated the largest agricultural implement factory in the southern hemisphere, units covering some twenty-eight acres.

There are other examples of Scots combining their traditional engineering and farming skills to good effect. When Alex Jones and his sons from Kirriemuir established themselves as blacksmiths and wheelwrights at Waipukurau (HB) they began to produce high quality farming equipment and every description of horse-drawn vehicle from traps, gigs and carriages to heavy farm drays. The skills of the Jones boys became well known beyond the confines of their home province of Hawkes Bay. An example of Alex Jones's talent is recorded by a Presbyterian minister who was called to the charge from the Dakotas in the United States in 1913. In a letter the Rev. Neil White tells how Alex repaired his wife's treadle sewing machine after the iron framework was smashed into twenty-three pieces on the voyage to New Zealand. The painstaking repair was so effective that the machine outlived the preacher's wife – who died fifty years later.

DAMN THOSE SHEEP!

In the areas of Australia most settled by the Scots – the Darling Downs, New England, the Hunter Valley, the western district of Victoria, Gippsland and Tasmania – there are farms which, though much reduced in extent, are still operated by descendants of those first Scots settlers. Wellington Vale in the Glen Innes district of New England is a case in point, having been first operated by Arthur Wellesley Robertson in 1849.

On the Darling Downs from 1840 onwards, as we've seen, the Scots were in the vanguard of settlement on these fertile plains west of Brisbane. The Scots station manager or owner lived in a homestead built of slab timber walls with a bark roof and stone fireplace and usually made do with crude, haun-knittet furniture. Perhaps some ten miles from the station smaller sheds were built, the six-by-sixes where the shepherds watched their flocks by day and night. They shared what has been described as a sordid existence of 'monotony and mutton fat'. A surprisingly high number of the squatters living in conditions of almost biblical simplicity were of good birth, education and social standing, sometimes the younger sons of the Scots aristocracy forced to make their own way in the world. Certainly the Darling Downs – although ideal sheep country – were no easy option. Ponder for a moment the difficulties faced on remote stations. Sheep scab, uncertain rainfall, little circulating money and a journey of 500 miles to Maitland on the Hunter River, the nearest market.

Patrick Leslie, the Scot who arrived with a party of Aberdonians, was

Bales of wool loaded and ready for shipment at the Gunn sheep farm at
Waranga Park, Victoria, c. 1920. (*Edith Christoe, Victoria*)

given the privilege of choosing the site for the first town on the Downs,
Warwick, which was gazetted in 1849. The Darling Downs remain a vital
part of Australia's economy. Sheep rearing played a central role in the spread
of settlement.

The Corriedale breed of sheep established in 1874, with a high yield of
mutton and wool, gave a tremendous boost to New Zealand agriculture.
Behind this success story is a noteworthy coincidence, the kind of spontan-
eous development in two or more centres usually reserved for scientific
research laboratories. The 'lab' on this occasion was the province of Otago.
William Davidson from Edinburgh is said to have registered his flock of
Merino-Lincoln crosses first – but James Little, a Scots shepherd who became
manager of the Corriedale run near Oamaru, had been conducting parallel
experiments. It is now generally accepted that neither man knew of the
other's work. Davidson went back to Scotland to manage the Australia and
New Zealand Land Company and Little, who hailed from Midlothian,
became a successful breeder of cattle, horses and, of course, sheep.

In Australia the influential figure of John Macarthur, offspring of an exiled
Jacobite family, played the central role in the establishment of the wool
industry. Starting in 1794, just six years after the First Fleet reached New
South Wales, he began experiments which resulted in a breed of Merino
sheep producing a fine fleece which today can give up to three-quarters of
the annual clip.

The life of the sheep farmer required determination and a capacity to deal
with isolation. While a few made their fortune, many – like Hawick's James

Anderson who ran a sheep farm in South Australia – in moments of frustration and fatigue might be heard to shout, 'Damn those sheep!'

DOG PADDLE FOR BEGINNERS

But what would a Scots shepherd be without his dogs, his faithful Border collies? The ten-strong McMaster family came to Australia from their home near Inverness on the *Brilliant*. In 1837 they were at Grafton on the Clarence River (NSW) en route to a job at the Wellingrove Station. Arriving at the estuary the ship met with heavy weather and the skipper, fearing for the safety of his vessel because of its heavy load, ordered all superfluous cargo and livestock to be thrown overboard. To the dismay and disbelief of the McMasters this order included their sheepdogs – but for the crew an order was an order. However, the McMaster boys were not about to see their canine companions of many a shearing consigned to a watery grave. When the crew cast the dogs overboard, to the amazement of passengers and crew, but probably not to their parents, the boys jumped into the choppy estuary and swam the dogs to shore. The father of the family, John McMaster, went on to work as station manager at a number of runs but sadly was drowned in 1851 crossing the flooded Severn River.

In Otago Trevor Ross of Palmerston remembers the Gaelic-speaking shepherds who came to work with their dogs at the Shag Valley station and recalls vividly to this day the difficulty some of the Highlanders experienced trying to get to grips with the English language. Trevor recalls a misty morning at the local sheepdog trials with a group of Scots shepherds who had been in New Zealand for a time and, although they had a good grasp of broad Scots, still struggled with their English.

Trevor remembers this particular incident even sixty years on because he got a clip around the ear for laughing at the antics. The dog had managed to head the sheep but as often happens the flock split. The judge, peering out into the gloom, waited a moment before shouting: 'Whaur are they, Wullie? I canna see them in the mist.'

'They're in that wee hollow,' came the response, 'and the dug's watchin' twa.'

'Whaur's the ither?' persisted the judge.

'The three o' them are there but there's one thegither and two by themselves.' Confusion reigned.

For the Lydiate family who sailed for New Zealand in the mid-1800s there was a deal of confusion over accents. Euphemia Lydiate, born in Roslin, Midlothian, had a broad Scots accent while her sailor husband from Lancashire had an equally strong northern brogue. The children were educated in

Otago and without any distinguishable accent of their own, and the confused neighbours often had great difficulty tuning into the family conversations. At the age of eighty-six Euphemia came back to visit her home village of Roslin as a minor celebrity, judging a fancy dress ball and kicking-off a football match.

REGULAR AS THE SUN

Finding new pasturage, as we've noted, was often the moving force which sent the Scots out into the uncharted territories. Moving north from Wellington in 1840 Andrew Duncan drove sheep one hundred miles along the beach to the Turakina River in Wanganui. The following year his countryman William Bell – having first walked the coastal route – drove a team of bullocks north along the same rough track to Wanganui.

With a big crowd to watch their departure, Bell and his two sons filed up the steep path from Kaiwarawara and disappeared among the woods on the crest of the hill. His wife, daughters and the farm equipment went by schooner. William Bell arrived safely although he reported some difficulty crossing the quicksands of the Turakina and Whangachu Rivers. According to an eye witness who had watched the departure of the Scots and their team, the pioneers set off 'slow, sure, and regular as the course of the sun'. Is there a more apt description of the dogged determination displayed by so many of these Scots settlers?

But it wasn't always the solitary settler family facing the wilderness. From time to time the process of settling could seem like a military operation. Peter Macintyre, born in Perthshire in 1783, was given the difficult task of selecting 20,000 acres in New South Wales on behalf of his employer, the British MP T. P. Macqueen, who had been rewarded for his investment of large sums of money in the colony with land grants. As Macqueen's Australian manager he landed at Sydney in April 1825 with a personal entourage of twenty-seven people as well as sheep and a valuable shorthorn bull.

He was set on making a fortune for himself as well as his employer. Macintyre had asked for and received 2,000 acres on the Upper Hunter River as a personal grant. In five years the sheltered river flats upstream from Aberdeen were transformed from bushland into a productive farm, the hard work on the land being done by 100 convicts allocated to the Macintyre operation. Through financial mismanagement and the constant menace of drought, flood, remoteness, and threat of Aborigine attack, the Macqueen enterprise collapsed. However, Macintyre struck out on his own in 1830, taking with him Alexander Campbell, one of his original party, as superintendent. As Macintyre prospered off the land, increasing the number of his worker-convicts and having a huge brick house built at Maitland on the Lower Hunter river, he still looked outward in search of fresh grazing. While the authorities turned a blind eye huge acreages were unofficially occupied.

It was through these districts that Alexander Campbell travelled into what became known as New England and opened vast new areas of pasture. Campbell settled finally in what was to be the Scottish triangle in the heart of New England (NSW), a district edged by the communities of Inverell, Glen Innes and Armidale. The location where Campbell settled couldn't have been more Scottish – it was named Blairmore, Scone. This was a land not discovered by death-or-glory explorers but by the very people who were to put down roots and commit themselves to its future.

The actual choice of locations made by the Scots to build their homes were always interesting. In Victoria, for example, the Scots farmers were to be found in the hillier sections where the pattern of farming was generally sheep and cattle grazing, whereas English and Irish settlers tended to gather on the flatter land and lower slopes. It was said that you could identify a Highlander's home in Victoria because it would always be built with a hill as a backdrop.

Many ambitious projects, or 'schemes' as they were known, were established over the years to assist immigrants to reach either Australia or New Zealand. One which was of particular importance to agricultural workers and deserves to be better known was the Flock House scheme, in Wanganui. Behind this particular programme was Edward Newman from Glasgow who came to New Zealand as a lad of seventeen in 1876, and over the next seventy-one years was a successful farmer, Member of Parliament for fourteen years and a local celebrity.

His most significant gift to New Zealand came near the end of World War I when he persuaded the nation's sheep farmers to donate their profits from a big sale in the UK to a fund for brave seafarers. Newman roamed up and down New Zealand seeking donations and more than 2,600 farmers agreed to contribute. Initially grants were made to the families of wartime seamen then the trust switched the emphasis and decided to bring the sons of seafaring families in the UK to New Zealand to train as farmers. In 1923 a huge homestead and 1,000-acre farm belonging to another Scots family, the McKelvies of Edinburgh, was purchased together with 7,000 acres of additional land. The McKelvie farm near the town of Bulls was known in the district as 'Flock House', thus the training plan acquired its name. In 1924 the first batch of twenty-five young men arrived and the following year girls were being trained at a separate establishment at Palmerston North, twenty-five miles away.

It was appropriate, bearing in mind Edward Newman's input, that this brilliant concept should attract among its draftees young Scots from

Aberdeen, Dundee, Banff, Glasgow, Stirling and Stornoway as well as a host of smaller communities. From 1924 until 1937, a total of 635 boys and 128 girls came to New Zealand under the Flock House mantle. Local historian Paul Melody says that as the youngsters learned their farm skills the Fund acted as parents, found jobs for the students and helped many acquire their own farms. Edward Newman died in 1946, aged eighty-eight.

Many different immigration programmes were attempted. In Western Australia in the early 1920s Premier Sir James Mitchell organised a project for British migrants to settle in the southwest of the State in loosely associated groups who would share the initial bush-clearing of a planned 6,000 holdings. This was the so-called Group Settlement Scheme which failed due to lack of technical know-how and the hostile environment. There were some 10,000 'Groupies'.

A FAMILY TORN APART

The story of the disintegration and regrouping of the Henry Muir family from Buchlyvie in Stirlingshire, who migrated to participate in Mitchell's ambitious but ill-fated scheme in 1923, is a real tear-jerker and illustrates how fate can so easily turn the best laid plans on their head. Within two years of stepping ashore their dreams of making a new home for themselves had fallen apart. They were allocated a block in the far south of the state and slowly began to build up the homestead. However, Florence Muir was preparing dinner one Sunday evening when she suffered severe burns, her dress having caught fire supposedly from the flames of the range. Despite their remote location a doctor was called and arranged for Florence to be taken to hospital in Bussleton where she died five days later from burns and shock.

A devastating blow in itself, it was only the start of the Muirs' troubles. Henry was left with five children to care for, the youngest only sixteen months. Two weeks after the accident the children were taken into the care of the Welfare Department, the Children's Court having decided in their wisdom that a man could not work and take care of five young children by himself. To lose his children so soon after his wife was a hammer blow. The wee ones were boarded out until they were placed in alternative homes, with Jeannie, the eldest, finding herself lodged in Perth Girls Orphanage.

Henry lost touch with his youngsters and their new families, having gone into the merchant navy as an engineer during World War II. However, eighteen years after their separation, a remarkable coincidence brought them together again, after the children had also gone their separate ways. Young Harry, one of the sons, had enlisted also but was injured and invalided back

Henry Muir from Buchlyvie in Stirlingshire whose children were taken away from him into care after their mother died in a tragic fire at their West Australian homestead. (*Helen Muir-Richardson, Western Australia*)

to the repatriation ward of a Perth (WA) hospital. Young Harry appeared on a forces radio programme and his sister Jeannie heard the interview. Harry senior was in Fremantle (WA) between ships and had actually begun the task of trying to trace his scattered family when he too heard his long-lost son's voice over the airwaves. A bedside reunion took place – 'I knew it was dad as soon as I saw him, standing at the foot of the bed smiling' – and then the lengthy task of contacting the rest of the family began. That year the Muirs had a very special family Christmas.

ONE HUMP OR TWO?

Regrettably, if Sir Thomas Elder from Kirkcaldy, Fife, is remembered at all outside Australia it is not as a pastoralist, businessman and benefactor, but

Ships of the desert, South Australian style, pictured here at Farina carrying bales of wool. Camels were introduced into the commercial life of Australia by Scot Sir Thomas Elder. (*Mortlock Library, Adelaide, South Australia: B24000*)

as the 'Camel Man'. In 1862 having already established himself in the sheep business in South Australia, Sir Thomas took the unusual step of importing camels from India complete with their Afghan handlers. It was felt that the camels could cope better with the arid conditions in what became known as 'Centralia', the northern reaches of South Australia, the hot core of the continent. His hunch paid off and the camels became a vital factor in the development of these vast wildernesses. The camels were marvellous pack animals and the Afghan handlers could set loads of up to 400 kg of piping, machinery, ore, gold, lead or asbestos, even poles for the Overland Telegraph. They carried wool to railheads and camel trains trekking across the interior were a familiar sight. Many animals were turned loose in the desert areas and their descendants roam the countryside to this day to the extent that they have been considered a pest.

Thomas Elder came to Adelaide in 1854 to join the family business but was soon branching out on his own. He bought the Paratoo and the famous Beltana Stations and eventually became the owner of vast tracts of countryside. It was said that at one time he held a pastoral area larger than Scotland. But it was difficult country with very low rainfall and Elder spent much of his time and energy and a great deal of his money sinking artesian wells.

As well as his camel coup Elder encouraged exploration, contributing to two important expeditions into the interior in the 1870s. He set his sights even further afield and tried, unsuccessfully, to raise support for an Antarctic expedition. Copper mines also proved another successful venture.

Despite the success of camels, horse power was still a vital feature of life before the widespread use of machinery; it was inevitable that the Scots would have a hand in the horse business. Robert Stuart made his home in New Zealand's South Island and in 1857 brought his first Clydesdale horse from Australia. Subsequently he was to breed many fine draught animals. Stuart later moved to Hawkes Bay and was the first mayor of the town of Napier.

In contrast with Stuart's huge draught horses, Robert Wilkin from Tinwald Downs and an FP of Dumfries Academy, a successful businessman both in Australia and New Zealand, began importing and breeding purebred race-horse stock after coming to live in Canterbury. A founder of the famous Middle Park Stud Company, he was responsible for importing the American sire Berlin whose progeny made a mark on the trotting history of New Zealand. Incidentally, he also gets the credit for introducing black swans and hedgehogs to that corner of New Zealand.

The first ship to carry frozen meat from Australia to the United Kingdom had strong Scottish connections in that the vessel was the *Strathleven* and she was owned by Andrew McIlwraith from Ayr and Malcolm McEachran

Kirkcaldy's Sir Thomas Elder, who was a renowned South Australia pastoralist, once held land with a bigger acreage than Scotland. Also the man who introduced camels to Australia. (*Mortlock Library, Adelaide, South Australia: B11292*)

from Islay. Established in 1875 the company operated eleven sailing ships, initially between London and Australia, carrying immigrants. When steam came on the scene the red, black-topped funnels of the company became a familiar sight around the Australian coast.

McIlwraith's great contribution to Australian history came when he learned that the French steamer *La Frigarifique* had brought the first-ever consignment of frozen meat to London from the River Plate in South America. The *Strathleven* reached London with the first cargo of frozen Australian meat in 1880 and at a luncheon to celebrate the success of the trip Queen Victoria was presented with a lamb carcass. Her reaction was not noted.

COBALT – THE X FACTOR

In the early years of the 20th century, as veterinary medicine made great strides, Donald McSporran McMillan from Campbeltown in Argyll and his wife Olive took over the running of the government farm at Mamaku (WO). Many long days were spent clearing tree stumps, some 400 acres of pasture being brought into use. The farm was the focus for much agricultural research and during droughts animals were sent to the station because they had developed a mysterious 'bush sickness' which caused them to lose weight and die. The animals were found to have a cobalt deficiency, an essential element lacking in the volcanic plateau region. An area in Western Australia experienced a similar problem and animals there went to lick a particular rock which held cobalt.

FORGET YOUR SPANISH ORANGES

George Stevenson was born at Berwick on 13 April 1799 and was a well-travelled young man by the time he voyaged to South Australia on the *Buffalo* as secretary to the new governor in 1836. It was Stevenson who read the proclamation creating the colony. He had intended founding a newspaper at Adelaide and on 3 June 1837 the *South Australian Gazette and Colonial Register* appeared for the first time in Australia. In four acres of ground which surrounded his house he planted every variety of fruit tree he could lay hands upon and when the settlers complained about the hardness of the soil he confidently predicted that the oranges of South Australia would match anything produced in the groves of Spain and Italy – and they did.

Pastoralist Peter Waite from Kirkcaldy is credited with having realised the value of fencing large runs and spent over £200,000 – a fortune in the second half of the 19th century – on fencing and irrigation projects.

Charlie Robertson from Torphins in Aberdeenshire could also claim an unusual contribution to the development of farming, this time in New Zealand. After he and his wife Isobel from Aberdeen's Marywell Street (they had immigrated independently in 1912 before meeting up and marrying) moved to the Bay of Plenty district, they discovered that large areas of the land had been covered by volcanic ash from the Mount Tarawera eruption of 1886. According to the local farmers this made around one-third of the land unusable and when Charlie questioned this they were adamant that the ash ground could never be made into pasture. Charlie, a typically indefatigable Scot, worked away on the supposedly sterile area, tending it, cultivating it, sowing it and to everyone's amazement turned it into profitable pasture. His Scottish tenacity was recognised by farming journals and he was pictured proudly displaying his rejuvenated acres.

Another Aberdonian, Alexander Rennie, a seedsman, was solely responsible for the introduction of the yellow turnip to New Zealand – he imported it from his home ground. Borderer James Runciman was a pioneer of New Zealand's dairy industry, a noted cheesemaker and the first to import dairy machinery from the United States.

When the late Eloise Sharp of Tincurrin in Western Australia recently compiled a fascinating list of drovers, stockmen, mailmen, teamsters, shepherds and boundary riders from the earliest days of settlement to the present day, she found a significant number of Scots among the ranks in the Wild West. There was Anthony Anderson, a good stockman who drowned in the Jeal Pool Bar; Alan Bain, stockman/drover who was an expert dingo trapper; Evan Bain, father of Alan, drover and camel-team driver; Alec Gray who did contract carting to the Murchison goldfields; John Macpherson who was a mail contractor who also carted wool; and Murray Paterson who helped his father drive sheep over long distances when he was still only six years old.

Chapter Seven
Damned Few Like Us . . .

EVERYWHERE is within walking distance if you just have the time, declared some wiseacre once upon a time. For the Scots in the Antipodes in the 19th century there was plenty of time and often no option. Walking was the business. The image of the swagman, pack on his back and cork-fringed hat at a jaunty angle, disappearing down an endless track in his quest for work, a square meal or the meaning of life is part of Australia's image the world over.

The Rangitikei district of New Zealand's North Island was the yomping ground for many successful Scots in the early days of the colony. From 1840 onwards they began to make their presence felt, taking administrative positions, pioneering new farms and setting up businesses. Names like McKelvie, McBeth, Glasgow, McDonald, Bruce, McDonnell, Wilson, McKenzie and Stuart were associated with this undeveloped district purchased from the Maoris.

Ferryman, storekeeper, publican, lighthouse keeper, harbour pilot and mailman were just some of the occupations of one of the most colourful of these early settlers, Thomas Scott from Largo in Fife. He lived in Rangitikei for half a century, arriving in 1841 to begin the job which made him a legend in his own lifetime – long-distance mailman on the Wanganui coast. His task was to carry letters between Wellington and New Plymouth in Taranaki, a distance of 216 miles along the beach. Roads had not yet been built at the time of Scott's twice-monthly postal pilgrimage and eleven rivers had to be crossed before the journey was half-over.

Incredibly, Tom Scott couldn't swim, nor could he ride a horse. So he walked along the beach beside his pack horse. Near the mouth of each major river he left a store of dried flax sticks from which he would fashion a makeshift raft and float across with his 100 lb pack of mail, some saleable goods and his clothing on his back, while his horse swam beside him. At night on these lonely journeys Scott slept among the dunes, first digging a hole then burying himself up to his neck in the dry sand to keep warm. A big strong Fifer, Tam kept up a rate of twenty-three miles daily and covered 7,000 miles a year, for which he got £1 weekly.

Dunedin's most famous postman in the pioneering years was surely Jock Graham who used to travel on horseback to Invercargill right at the southern tip of South Island. He not only carried the mail but brought news to the isolated settlements along the way. He wore a distinctive red coat which could be seen from miles away. Jock is remembered for one famous piece of Scottish enterprise when, on hearing that miners on the west coast were plagued by mice and rats, he bought up all the cats he could in Dunedin and took a shipload to the coast where he sold them all – at a useful profit.

Across in Western Australia Clarry Ross, a Dundee-born architect who designed many of the public buildings in the state in the first decades of this century, was another great walker who did not take kindly to the advent of the motor car. He felt sure, he told his family, that he would be knocked down and killed by an automobile. In a tragic irony he died in 1949, knocked down and killed . . . by a train.

WALKING IN THE WAY OF THE LORD

William Bannerman, a preacher at St Andrews in Edinburgh, was present when 470 ministers of the kirk renounced their allegiance to the Church of Scotland in 1843 and walked out to form the Free Church. It would have been no surprise at all if Bannerman had been first on his feet, ready to walk. He was the nearest thing to a professional pedestrian.

The First Church in Dunedin were looking for missionaries for central Otago. With the Rev. William Will, Bannerman took up the challenge and was allocated the vast and sparsely populated far south. Being unable to ride, he knew he was in for a power of walking. In fact, according to his biography he covered 3,600 miles in ten months, visiting small communities and offering pastoral care. When a horse was eventually allocated to him he became an accomplished rider and extended his visitations as far as Invercargill. He was often drenched, frequently lost but is said never to have missed a Sunday service.

Peter Dalrymple from Galloway was every inch the entrepreneurial Scot. Learning of an unsatisfied demand for accommodation in Victoria, he purchased sixty portable houses and shipped them to Melbourne where he made his money. After two years, he took off for New Zealand, walked for nineteen days to get from Dunedin to Bluff on the south coast and farmed there for the rest of his life.

Just in case we get the impression that only men were capable of these prodigious walks, let me introduce you to Janet McHardie Saunders, a carpenter's daughter from Kirriemuir who came to the Wellington area in 1841. She was a tough lady who worked on the farm 'like a man', even expecting her grandchildren to take the other end of her cross-cut saw. Janet was described as 'an indefatigable walker'. When living on the farm she thought nothing of walking to Foxton, a round trip of twenty-four miles, often with a baby in her arms. Two years before she died, aged seventy-four, she walked a distance of forty miles to Lillybank in one day. However, her most famous walk took place when she was still in her twenties, after she received a proposal of marriage and wrote back, declining. Having reconsidered and in order to arrive before the letter and announce her acceptance she set out on foot from the Hutt Valley in the evening over the Rimutaka Ranges to Featherston and accepted the proposal in person – before the letter was delivered.

The Highland Chief was the nickname of another Scottish pedestrian immigrant of note whose real name was Jock Mackenzie, also famed in Otago as one of the most efficient and speedy shearers ever seen around the sheds. Jack Lee reports that the Chief was of a 'race of men who worked hard, then drank hard' and when there was no work they slept in the open, 'great working class athletes' for whom the pub was the nearest thing they had to home. Mackenzie, for instance, would think nothing of drinking all evening then setting off, swag bag on his shoulder, to walk fifty miles overnight for the shearing roll call at first light on some distant farm. When Mackenzie boasted, as he often did, that he could outwork and outwalk any man in New Zealand no one doubted his word. The honesty of the man, however, is shown by the fact that he tramped five miles to return a borrowed medicine spoon to the lady of the house where he had been working.

Among the rough crew of drifters more than one could produce a certificate from a university. These were the 'remittance men', sent as far away from the family as possible because of their rakish behaviour.

MERCHANTS OF THE STINKING WATER

The drinking habits of the Chief bring us round neatly to another noteworthy Scottish contribution to the developing cultures of Australia and New Zealand – whisky. The story of the Scots and their fondness, or hatred, for drink is a saga every bit as exciting and relevant as more profound contributions to the Australasian cultures. The introduction of strong drink among the native peoples had occasionally catastrophic results. Although rum was soon being bartered by the sealers and whalers seeking supplies from the Maori tribes along the New Zealand coast, it was initially reported that the warriors detested strong drink, calling it *waiporo* or stinking water. Soon enough they were lapping it up.

But while the sealers and whalers, Scots among them, were introducing the native tribes to the 'delights' of strong drink, another Scot, Lachlan Macquarie from Mull, had taken over as Governor of New South Wales and in one of his first acts reduced the number of licensed premises in Sydney from seventy-five to twenty.

THE FAMOUS SKULL AND CROSSBONES

As Vincent Boyle of Winton (SD) told a genealogy conference in 1996, the story of the MacRaes and Hokonui Whisky is filled to the brim with impressive characters, suspense, romance, mystery and mystique – all the ingredients, in fact, worthy of a television series. It is fabulous folklore.

Clansfolk well accustomed to the skills of home distilling were the first settlers of the Hokonui Hills in New Zealand's Southland. Nine MacRae families were in that hilly region by the 1880s. The whisky they made in a totally illegal but widely supported industry found a ready sale, with the famous skull and crossbones motif on the label. Manufactured in carefully disguised stills hidden away in the bush, professional people, doctors, lawyers, surveyors were numbered among the MacRaes' best customers.

As confirmed by the New Zealand Dictionary, 'Hokonui' has become synonymous with illicitly distilled whisky. The original product, perhaps as a result of its romantic background, came to be considered as of a very high standard, although the worst of it, apparently, could be very bad. At the Invercargill conference Vince Boyle expressed the view that some of it was so bad that strong men gave up touching the stuff for good and some distillations produced a bouquet which was enough to turn off the most hardened toper. One can only imagine the damage it did if you succeeded in getting it over your neck. Southland writer Dan Davin is on record as saying that his mother could always tell when his father had been drinking the night before by the grim intensity with which he dug the garden; the grimmer and more silent the spade work, the rawer the Hokonui that had been drunk.

When police moved through the countryside in search of stills they were often confounded by the Gaelic speakers' apparent inability to understand English and the reluctance of non-Scottish farmers to shop them.

Widow Mary MacRae from Ross-shire arrived in Hokonui with her three daughters and four sons in 1872. During police raids it's recorded that Mary would sit on a small barrel, hiding it under her skirts. The MacRaes made the place their own. Her son, big, bearded Murdoch, was a legendary whisky maker. Even using planes to spot the tell-tale trailing smoke from the stills amid the hills failed to stop distilling in the 1930s. Legal distillation of whisky resumed in Dunedin in 1974.

SHOPPED BY THE IN-LAWS

In New Zealand's North Island John (Henech) Cameron was renowned for his illicit whisky distilled on his farm of 'Glenmore'. The Cameron family, John, his wife Janet and their nine children from Argyllshire, arrived on board the *Blenheim* on Christmas Day 1840, and after farming at Wellington they walked more than 100 miles along the beach to the Rangitikei land block. They were the first white settlers to reach the area and were quickly followed by shipmates from the *Blenheim*, Frasers, McKenzies, McFarlanes, Fergussons, McDonalds, McQuarries and McDonnells – and more Camerons.

Big John, whose great-grandfather fell at Prestonpans while fighting for Bonnie Prince Charlie, was a founder of the Turakina Caledonian Society. His distillery was a well-concealed sideline. However, an informer, thought to have been a disgruntled son-in-law, betrayed the whisky makers in 1869 and during a police raid the distilling apparatus was discovered. Two of Big John's sons – Charles and Dugald – were fined £50 each. Big John lived to be a hundred.

ANGUS WITH A SKINFUL

Across the Tasman Sea in New South Wales at around the same time as the Rangitikei Camerons were busy at their still, another member of the Cameron clan was occupied in a personal crusade against drink among the frontiersfolk. Religion played an important part in the lives of the early Scots settlers but, as Australian-Scots balladeer 'Banjo' Paterson pointed out, 'Men of religion were scanty'. One early arrival among the Scots settlers in the New England district (originally dubbed New Caledonia) was the Rev. Archie Cameron who was 'called' to a vast charge extending to many thousands of square miles. He was the first minister to penetrate so far into the outback and returned briefly to 'civilisation' at the Manning River to marry Christian McLeod who had come there with her parents from Skye.

The Camerons settled in the Glen Innes district and Archie made it clear he was out to defeat the demon drink. While teetotalism had a strong following in the area many of the old Scots, as local historian A. W. Cameron tells us, made 'good use of the Highland nectar'.

One of the Rev. Cameron's flock, a man called Angus, used to take a fill of drink more often than was good for him but, persuaded by the minister, jumped on the temperance wagon. However, a weak and drouthy soul, he fell by the wayside as Christmas approached and was locked up. When the minister went to bail him out Angus was resting on his cell bunk with his eyes closed. Archie gave him a shake and he opened one eye. Seeing who it was he sat bolt upright, concern written all over his face: 'Have they got thee too, parson?'

There is no doubt that when the Scots get together the national drink is never in short supply. At the pearling town of Broome in Western Australia in 1904, thirty Scotsmen gathered to honour the birthday of Robert Burns with 'song, toasting and verse'. According to local reports there was doubt in the cold light of day who had been most venerated – Burns or Johnnie Walker.

The Scotsman's first sip of whisky – childhood toddy apart – is an almost sacred moment. For Stuart Baillie from Arbroath, working in the bush in South Australia, it was a strangely unpatriotic affair. Stuart was sent down

Bush balladeer and Scots descendant Andrew 'Banjo' Paterson (1864–1941) who penned the lyrics of 'Waltzing Matilda'. (*Ravenscroft Album, National Library of Australia*)

to the shanty in Millicent by one of the Aborigine hands to a buy a bottle of whisky which they shared. Stuart remembered:

It nearly cooked me; I'd had more than enough and lay down and went to sleep.

When he woke he wandered about until he found a stranger to seek directions to his bivouac – and it turned out he was smack bang in the middle of his own encampment. Despite this salutary warning on the effects of strong drink Stuart admits enigmatically that although this was his first taste of whisky, it was not his last.

In the late 1860s when Alex Jones from Kirriemuir, the Hawkes Bay blacksmith, found his sons drunk he was completely horrified and vowed to remove all alcoholic temptation from his home. To prove his good faith he joined the Independent Order of Rechabites who advocated total abstinence. Fifty years later at a Hogmanay gathering in Dunedin old Jessie Jones, his wife, was persuaded to take a dram. 'Dinna tell faither,' she is said to have whispered. And no one did.

One famous temperance advocate was Robert Stout, the Shetland-born Prime Minister of New Zealand in the 1880s. He was a staunch advocate of total abolition and once declared:

I am absolutely against it. I would have no parley or truce with the sale of poison even if it be labelled alcohol.

Joan Fraser of Oak Park (VA) recalls a minor disaster at a Scottish Gaelic Society ceilidh in Melbourne in the middle years of the 20th century. The Society had been moved on from the Scots Church Hall in the city when, after a function attended by a particularly enthusiastic pipe band, a stash of empty whisky bottles was found beneath the speaker's podium.

The Society eventually found a new billet in the Wesleyan Church Hall where a strict no-drinks rule applied. On one occasion one of the personalities in the Scots community in Melbourne (who used to drive a Highland delivery van) turned up with a bottle in his bag. Told to leave it outside, he proceeded to trip over his bag, spilling the amber contents across the church hall floor. Under the watchful eye and twitching nose of the Wesleyan watchdog, one of the swiftest floor-mopping operations in history was organised. Wonder if they told that stern monitor that it was really just Irn Bru.

Two half-brothers from Orkney, James Harrold and Richard Craigie, saw opportunities for a ferry service across the Taeiri River soon after arriving in Otago in 1848. This in turn led them into the licensed trade. Almost as soon as they ventured into trading the population in the interior began to increase and the river mouth became a genuine little port with regular shiploads arriving and departing and an accommodation house being constructed. When the provincial council took over the ferry in 1857 and gave the location the name of Lower Taeiri Ferry, they were happy to give James and Richard the positions of ferryman and tavern keeper. James had assured the council that while keeping spirits for respectable travellers he was also determined not to turn the ferry inn into a common resort for drinking. It's known that among those who made use of its facilities were Bishop Harper on a parochial tour and the legendary Negro whaler Jimmy McKenzie (some Scots blood there, perhaps?) who asked the Orcadians to be witnesses at his third and fourth marriages.

There is no doubt, however, that alcohol did wreck lives among the Scottish communities. Alcoholism was not part of the Scottish face presented to the world but was very much an element in the day-to-day life of the expatriates, certainly in Australia, according to Malcolm Prentis who mentions ministers, teachers and even publicans among the victims.

While Willie Affleck of Gundaroo thought the death of his wife in 1870 was divine punishment for owning a hotel which dispensed liquor, John Smith from Kilmarnock arrived in Ballarat (VA) just before the gold rush. He built the first pub at Smythe's Creek and saw it filled nightly with a host of drouthy miners. Smith also put his good fortune down to divine intervention. He struck gold without having to raise a pick.

PIONEERS IN THE HOSPITALITY TRADE

It was said in Australia that in the late 1800s the Irish owned all the pubs and the Scots all the land – but the truth is the Scots also had their share of the hospitality trade. The first hotels in Sydney, Melbourne and Adelaide were all opened by Scots. Sydney's glorious number one, the Thistle Tavern, described as a 'rip-roarin' saloon' of a place opened its doors for business as early as February 1809. The proprietor was James Chisholm from Calder in Midlothian who had been a sergeant with the First Fleet and used his discharge money to build his hostelry.

George Guthrie gets the credit for opening Adelaide's first hotel in May 1837. Others were not slow on the uptake. Public records show that within a few years the number of licensed premises in the city had increased to 762. In Melbourne the two original hotels – Menzies and Scott being the pioneering proprietors – hosted many a wild Hogmanay celebration, opening the same year as Guthrie's establishment in Adelaide.

John Murray (1851–1916) was the son of Aberdeen parents who settled in Victoria, and rose to be Premier of the legislative assembly despite his liking for a wee dram. His biography tells us that his political career was endangered by his drinking and as often as not he turned up for debates with a good drink in him. Murray conquered his weakness and became a strong supporter of the temperance movement, lecturing on the evils of strong drink. He was apparently a 'big man, with a fund of humour and irony'.

Another Scot, Sir James Wilson (b. 1812) managed more successfully to mix the heady cocktail of drink and politics. Wilson, from Banff, was mayor of Hobart and Premier of Tasmania (novelist Anthony Trollope proposed him as a future Prime Minister of the joint colonies) as well as manager of the Cascade Brewery with which he was associated for fourteen years.

Black Sandy Cameron, who came to Australia in 1822 from Lochaber, had a drink problem in his later life. He was, according to local histories in South Australia, simply addicted to whisky. There was a fear that left alone he would drink himself to death. Friends and family arranged for an Aborigine to climb into a gumtree on the homestead with Black Sandy's keg and tie it there, high in the branches, while the old man was left alone on the station. He was told he would have to wait for a drink and was left in a black mood while the rest of the family went into town. Not to be beaten Sandy got his gun, placed a tin dish under the keg and shot a hole in the barrel, getting 'more than enough whisky to satisfy his wants'. On their return the drovers found Black Sandy dead on the ground, cuddling his tin dish.

THE UPSIDE-DOWN ORCHARD

A tragic tale, yet the drink could also make fools of the best of men. As the community at Penola (SA) began to grow, Inverness-shire's Alexander Cameron decided to mark the completion of his new house by importing the first fruit trees to the district. The group of Scots toasted the arrival of the rootlings late into the night before remembering that they had to be planted without delay.

The whole team rode out to the new farmstead and by moonlight and with due ceremony got the roots in the ground and went home to sleep off the booze. When, in the spring, the first sprigs failed to appear, a close inspection was made and, as local historian Peter Rymill remarks, this revealed that the paralytic pioneers had planted their orchard upside-down.

In the ranks of Scottish immigrants we have our share of people whose contribution is as off-beat as it is interesting. Among the forgotten Scottish geniuses of the Australian bush, for instance, we must number Robert Barr from the weaving village of Strathaven in Lanarkshire who took his ten children to South Australia in the second half of the 19th century. Farming was their destiny and after clearing land and battling the harsh conditions they decided to head west in search of greener grass. This, of course, meant a journey across the desert in a convoy of bullock carts for Robert and a long sea voyage for his family. After reaching Kalgoorlie (WA) and trying his hand at the gold mining Robert got down once again to the serious business of farming and looking after his huge brood.

According to his descendants he was an inventor of some repute, being the man responsible for the design of the stump-jump plough. You knew that, didn't you? The company who were commercialising his inventions went into liquidation, however, and all the rights were lost. However, his most famous 'unknown' invention, as the family put it, was a flying machine. In 1901, fully two years before the Wright brothers took to the air, Robert set off for London to unveil his plans to British scientists and was introduced to Lord Kelvin, generally considered to be one of the greatest intellects of his generation. Of course, Kelvin was a well-known balloon enthusiast and repeated to Bob his oft-quoted assertion that heavier-than-air flying machines were impossible. Robert Barr returned to Australia a broken man. It must be doubtful if it came as any consolation to Bob to learn that even the good and great can drop a clanger occasionally.

Banffshire-born James Horn was never going to feel homesick when he moved to New Zealand in 1875. In a long life as a storekeeper and trader, the man from Inverkeithney conducted his business in the land of the Maori in such exotically named places such as Bannockburn, Stirling and Clyde.

Bannockburn in Otago was the location of James Horn's far-famed grocery store where, as a sideline, he operated as the district dentist. Pictured in the 1890s. (*Mary Horn, Otago*)

Horn was a great believer in the future of central Otago, particularly if water could be brought to the arid land and he argued the cause of irrigation with the highest levels of government. He was also a great advocate of rail construction and again and again pressed for its extension into the outlying areas. He served in the national parliament for central Otago and his biggest but most successful gamble of his business career was investing in river-dredging for gold.

Horn's store at Bannockburn lives on in Otago folklore. A grocery, drapery, butcher's and baker's rolled into one, James Horn also provided a gold buying facility for the district. He was also the local dentist and swore by a good tot of whisky as the best anaesthetic. Many of the less well off in Bannockburn were given credit and when the family went through James's books on his death they found he had written off hundreds of pounds to help the poorest.

Miners were regular customers and up to all sorts of tricks. One digger used to buy tea by the chestload and on being questioned about his purchase admitted that he made the tea good and strong then soaked white pebbles until they were yellow. 'That's my gold,' he said proudly. Another old-timer had the habit of slipping eggs into the pockets of his coat until James, learning of the pilfering, came out into the shop and greeted the miner with a hearty 'Hello John, grand day', slapping him on both flanks and smashing the eggs in his coat pockets. No more egg thefts were reported. James Horn died in 1933.

Most folk imagine that Sir Edward Stafford, the first New Zealand Prime Minister to hold office for any length of time, was of Irish extraction. In fact, he was born in Edinburgh in 1819. Recognised as a moderate politician who was a great advocate of national education, he was as straight-laced as they come. But he had a secret. Having lived the life of a country gentleman in Ireland, often riding to the hounds, he had become an expert horseman and was once described as the best jockey in New Zealand.

Farmer's son Arthur Beverley from Alford, Aberdeenshire, was a watch-maker to trade but a man of wide-ranging talents with a natural flair for geology, botany and mathematics. He made important collections of plants and offered his services *gratis* to the Otago farmers in the construction of water races and power wheels. Strangely, if he is remembered at all it's as the individual who devised the formula for sag in the long steel tapes used in distance measuring. Beverley Tables were used the world over.

David Drummond from Fife made his name in the Nelson district running a timber mill but he also had a wee preoccupation with footwear. Arriving ready to face the rigours of forest life, he brought with him twenty-two pairs of patent leather boots. Within months, however, the heavy duty day-to-day work meant that the family were already having to make their own footwear. David, moreover, is remembered for having designed wooden block shoes for the front hooves of his bullock teams which were working in desperately muddy conditions in the forest.

INTRODUCING THE SCOTS

Attempts were made on and off during the 19th century to introduce grouse and heather to South Island, New Zealand. It is a significant testimonial to the hardihood of Scots heather that it flourished while the grouse soon disappeared. Pockets of heather are to be found in some of the most unlikely places in Australia and New Zealand – the legacy of Scots attempting to make themselves feel more at ease in their new home.

But it isn't only heather the Scots are credited with introducing. Melville Gray, a Canterbury farm manager born in Perthshire, is given the credit, or more accurately the blame, for having introduced both rabbits and gorse to the Mackenzie Country; Chinese pheasants found their way to New Zealand thanks to trader Thomas Henderson from Dundee who brought them to

The fiery kirk preacher John Dunmore Lang who was minister of the Scots church in Sydney for over fifty years and encouraged many Scots to try a new life in Australia, pictured here in 1873. (*Mitchell Library, State Library of New South Wales, Sydney*)

Auckland in his sailing ship the *Glencoe* in the 1850s; watercress was introduced to Christchurch at an early date by the Deans boys, the pioneering
Ayrshire brothers. Unfortunately the cress loved its new home in the tree-
shaded River Avon and soon choked the river.

But what of all those other little Scots peculiarities, idiosyncrasies so often
laid at our door?

Chauvinism

Almost inevitably this surfaces from time to time. Famously, the Rev. John
Dunmore Lang, possibly one of the most contentious Scottish exports ever,
told a young audience in 1863 that there's 'nae folk like oor ain folk'. This
extreme example of clinging together is said to have had an unsettling effect
on Presbyterian ministers of non-Scottish descent.

Emblems

Although it happened nearly seventy years ago, it's an incident the Scots of
Palmerston North (MW) don't like to talk about – the theft of the giant
Royal Standard from the showground after the annual Gathering of the Clans
in the 1930s. Gifted to the pipe band, the twelve-foot by six-foot flag was
a 'perfect example of the sailmaker's art' but had disappeared when the
clearing up began the following morning. It had changed hands many times
at Dutch auctions during World War I, when it helped to raise funds for
the war effort. The author of the *Manawatu Scottish Society Jubilee Review*
says that it was many years before the band members gave up checking every
Scottish standard which appeared above the district's rooftops. In a chilling
footnote the writer suggests that the flag carried with it a curse from every
Scot in the city – a heavy burden, indeed. The flag was never seen again.

Eccentricity

The antics of the Scots in their day-to-day lives could sometimes have the
other ethnic groups scratching their heads. Murdoch Finlayson was a West
Australian butcher, fiercely proud of his Scottish heritage. His neighbours
must have wondered about the Scots because people remember how, at the
age of ninety-six when most of us would be pinned to the rocking chair,
Murdoch would work with a sheep's carcass to provide the family's food
for a week. He used to remove the skin by punching it free from the carcass
with his fists, telling folk that the use of a knife damaged the flesh.

Meanness

Glasgow doctor James McKechnie who settled on the Eyre Peninsula (SA)
was described as 'quaint, formal, precise and old fashioned'. After a gent

called John Lewis had shown McKechnie how to shoe a horse, the auld Scot displayed a 'hard as nails' streak by refusing Lewis permission to yard some cattle for the night or drink at a more convenient well.

Reliability

George Miller from Gretna Green was an engine driver in Tasmania who was known to be the most meticulous timekeeper in the state. He was so reliable that the people of the Sandfly district set their watches by the whistle of Geordie's locomotive as it rumbled by.

Quick-Wittedness

Sir George Houston Reid, born in 1845 at Johnstone in Renfrewshire, was Premier of New South Wales around the turn of the century and a popular speaker at the rallies during the federation debate, as Australia finally came together. On one occasion he was struck by a bag of flour which 'covered his capacious waistcoat'. Quick as a flash, and dusting himself down, Sir George had his response ready:

> When I came to power the people had not enough flour to make bread for themselves and now they can afford to throw it about like this.

The Scots Mafia

One of the earliest examples of the Scots looking after their ain folk came in the allegations that Governor Lachlan Macquarie was using patronage to benefit his fellow Scots. The evidence suggests that there may be some truth in this but it is also worth remembering that he displayed a greater understanding of the difficulties faced by the Aborigines and the convict population than many of his contemporaries.

Honesty

Dunedin was no Utopia but the basic decency of the folk shines through in the story of the young Scot who, landing from an immigrant ship, heard of the goldrush so put his cabin trunk up against the wharf shed and headed for the goldfields. Three months later he returned to find it lying untouched.

AND ON THE SEVENTH DAY

Another characteristic which marked out the Scots was their insistence on making the Sabbath a day of rest. Annie Troup from Aberdeenshire, who had settled in Hawera (CY), knitted one ounce of wool daily into socks for soldiers during World War I but Sunday knitting was strictly taboo.

When the McLeod families arrived in New Zealand's North Island in the 1860s and started to build their sawmill at Helensville, the old Scottish tradition had to be put to one side as the vital construction work progressed. Janet McLeod was deeply religious and a powerful voice within the family, so as the McLeod men worked seven days a week to erect the sawmill and get it operating, she raised no objection to Sunday working. When the building was completed she asked her menfolk if they intended to run the mill on a Sunday and, not getting a satisfactory response, said that if it was their intention to do so she could promise them that there would be only one day of Sunday operating because she would burn it down before the next!

FROM ENTOMOLOGIST TO ESTATE AGENT

Not everyone's life was as exciting as Kelso's Robert Cunningham Bruce, who went to sea at the age of fourteen, was a fine boxer, loved botany, and worked the goldfields of California, Victoria and New Zealand, before settling on North Island in 1877 and becoming a farmer and politician.

The list of Scots who displayed this versatility, equipping them well for the pioneer's life, could fill volumes. Here are just a few from New Zealand: George Brodie, Edinburgh (gold miner, politician, journalist); Thomas Broun, Edinburgh (soldier, entomologist, farmer, teacher): William Fraser, Inverness (lawyer, soldier, miner, mayor); John Reid, Aberdeenshire (draughtsman, storekeeper, gold buyer, shipping agent, farmer, civil engineer, estate agent, tramway builder, public figure, churchman); George Clouston, Edinburgh (sea captain, coastal trader, meteorologist, jail warden).

The mildest-mannered man ever to run a strike was the strange accolade given to Orcadian William Spence who came with his family to Victoria in 1853. His mining experience started at a very early age and he is recorded working with a co-operative outfit of miners at the age of twelve. By 1878 he was a union organiser. When station owners tried to reduce payments to shearers in 1886 a Shearers Union was launched with Spence as treasurer – the struggle between the bosses and their shearers was to last for years. Although conciliation was Spence's watchword it was also said that once he got his teeth into something he never let go and eventually a deal was struck. The Orcadian was prominent again in the maritime strike and the Queensland shearers' strike of the early 1890s. He was elected to the federal House of Representatives in 1901 and held the seat for sixteen years. Ironically he was ejected from the Labour Party over the issue of conscription.

ECHOES OF HOME

It's a natural enough response to finding yourself in a strange land – naming everything around you, from a bend in the creek to a barren outcrop, after familiar sights and people from home. The Scots were, with one notable non-conformist, as guilty as any ethnic group of this self-indulgence. In some areas the effects are minimal. Most rivers in New Zealand, for example, retained their Maori names with one important exception being the Clutha River in southern Otago. Clutha is, of course, the old Scots name for the Clyde and indeed along its banks lived and farmed many Scottish immigrants. In Australia, by contrast, most rivers were renamed or named for the first time by Europeans and only a few of the Aborigine designations, impressive-sounding waterways like the Murrumbidgee, make the maps.

The naming of Perth (WA) by Scots Governor Sir James Stirling as a tribute to the town in Scotland for which his friend was a member of parliament caused an outcry among English officials angered by the Governor's Scottish preferences. But eight years earlier in 1821 there had been an altogether more spectacular naming expedition to Tasmania by Governor Lachlan Macquarie from Mull. Making his second and final tour of Van

Major-general Lachlan Macquarie from Mull, Governor of New South Wales (portrait, c. 1805). (*Mitchell Library, State Library of New South Wales, Sydney*)

An aerial view of the spectacular Southern Alps of New Zealand where Scottish
trailblazers can be traced. (*New Zealand Tourism*)

Diemen's Land, as it was then known, he brought along his wife Elizabeth
and son Lachlan. On a previous visit Macquarie had set the trend and this
time he was clearly determined to leave a permanent Scottish stamp on the
island. Another community called Perth was named by the Governor before
he made his way to the Argyle Plains which he had so dubbed on the previous
visit. Macquarie writes:

> Having determined on establishing a township on the north bank of the
> Elizabeth River [already named for his wife] I have named it Campbell-
> town in honour of Mrs Macquarie's maiden name.

This area was to become a world centre for wool production, with the highest
prices of the day paid. The district filled up with emigrant Scots.

Next on the agenda for the official party was the Ross station where
Macquarie was up early, notebook in hand, and attendant close by with paint
pot and signboards – 'Named last night's station Ross in honour of Mr
Buchanan, that being the name of his seat on Loch Lomond' (Ross Priory).
The Rev. W. H. Macfarlane says that Macquarie had an almost insatiable
appetite for place names and few spots had been left without a Scottish title
after the hooves of his horse had marked the track. This infuriated Englishmen like Edward Currie who wanted the original settlers' names like Gallows
Hill and Hell's Corners retained. Later he was to comment:

The mountains of central Tasmania where Governor Lachlan Macquarie went on his spectacular naming spree. (*Australian Tourist Commission*)

We cannot bring ourselves to be Highlanders and Shetlanders in a moment notwithstanding our late Governor-in-Chief would appear to desire it.

And on that 1821 expedition the naming frenzy continued . . . Mount Stewart, Gordon Valley, Strathallan Creek, Roseneath. To be fair to Macquarie, he also made use of non-Scottish names, although they might be equally inappropriate – Brighton (because the king was living there), Price and Harcourt, Curzon and Meredith (for friends of Mrs Macquarie). Wylde Hill was named for the judge-advocate who was riding with them. He changed the Thames River to the Lachlan and named Lachlan Island in honour of his young son. As the sailing ship *Caroline* pulled out of Hobart, Macquarie looked back on Tasmania for the last time . . . an island now filled with Scottish connections.

In New Zealand's South Island, with a sparser population than the North, mountains, ranges and lakes were named by Scots settlers – Ben Lomond, Ben More, Ben Nevis and the Lammermuirs among them; and the Scottish influence is easily traced in hundreds of town and community names throughout the Antipodes, ranging from the aforementioned modern city of Perth (WA) to out-of-the-way places such as Strathmore (QD), Melrose (WA), Struan (SA), Roxburgh (OO), Balmoral (CY) and medium-sized towns like Hamilton (WO) and Ayr (QD).

Non-Scots have always had trouble with 'Lock' Lomond so it is no real surprise to find a community in western Tasmania which, according to local tradition, had originally been called Strachan. Try as they might the non-Scots just couldn't get their tongue around Strachan and today the town, founded by storekeeper Frederick Henry from Edinburgh, is Strahan.

The presence of Scots can also lead to a deal of confusion in the naming process. Huntershill in Sydney, you might reasonably expect, would be named after Governor John Hunter. Not a bit of it. It was named after transported political reformer Thomas Muir's family estate in Glasgow.

Even down to street names the Scots just wouldn't leave it alone. Palmerston (OO) is filled with echoes of Orkney in the street names . . . Sanday, Stromness, Brough, Auskerry, all given by Orcadian immigrants in the 1800s in tribute to their island home beyond the Pentland Firth. Across the provincial boundary in Canterbury the township of Fairlie had Ayr, Alloway and Doon streets named by a pioneer called Rapsey Struthers after his home ground. It's said that the town itself was named by an Ayrshire couple, Margaret and David Hamilton, after the town on the Clyde coast where they spent their honeymoon.

John Alston Wallace, born in 1824 in the Royal Burgh of Rutherglen, arrived in Melbourne in 1852 as one of the thousands of Scots drawn to the goldfields. He joined his brother at the diggings but again spotted the opportunity to make a killing in the service industries and opened several

For tourists on the threshold of the 21st century the Barrier Reef off the Queensland coast is a wonderful playground; for Scots immigrant ships it could be a death trap. (*Australian Tourist Commission*)

stores and the chain of Star hotels. In 1860 Wallace named a new town in northeast Victoria after his home burgh, but to receive the privilege he had to agree to close his hotel bar. Wallace later went into mine management, selling out the hotel and stores business. He also represented Eastern Province in the Victoria legislative council.

Among the more remote locations in Australia which harken back to Scotland is a group of islands on the Barrier Reef named after a Berwickshire military man, Lieutenant-Colonel James Molle from Chirnside. Across the Tasman Sea the famous name of Robert Bruce, on this occasion an immigrant from East Lothian, is recalled in the town of Hunterville (MW) by a street, a forest and the road to a skiing resort.

James Henry came to New Zealand in the 1860s and after trying his hand in the Thames goldfields he settled at a small town south of Auckland where, among various community roles, he took on the job of postmaster. The place had a longish Maori name – Rahuipukeko – which none of the Europeans could manage so it fell to James to suggest an alternative. Patriotic Scot that he was, he chose the town nearest to his birthplace, Huntly – and Huntly it is to this day.

Maybe more than most races the Scots found themselves described in Australia and New Zealand by a whole host of generic nicknames, among the most popular being Jock, Scotty and Mac. I've also found them dubbed 'the folk from the land o' cakes', and more traditionally 'Haggis Bashers'.

In the Thames district Alex Brodie is remembered as the source of all worthwhile knowledge about draining mines and for his uncanny ability to get money out of central government while serving as county chairman. Alex arrived in New Zealand as a military engineer during the Maori Wars beginning in 1863 and was responsible for erecting telegraph lines to the seat of the fighting in Waikato. In his later years his nickname in the corridors of political power was the deliberately ambiguous 'Big Pump', an epithet which recognised his ability to draw the last drop out of the Treasury as well as his skills in water control.

JUMPING ON THE BANDWAGON

If there was ever any doubt about the popularity, indeed the necessity, of having a Scottish handle in certain areas of the Antipodes then you would only have had to ask sheep station boss Hop Lee McNab. New shearers arriving to give his 12,000 woollies a trim at his Otago station were amazed to find that this particular clansman was Chinese. Hop Lee would patiently explain that he adopted the name when he first came to New Zealand because McNab seemed a good solid, local name. A memorial stone records the

New, hybrid Scots names popped up all over the settled areas of Australia and New Zealand. This is the Glenorkney homestead at Bunnaloo, Victoria, pictured in 1919. It belonged to a Norquoy family. (*Ann Berryman, Victoria*)

passing of this self-appointed Scot. This was by no means a unique occurrence. A leading light in the Caledonian Society of Sydney was city restaurateur, Quong Tart.

Often the Scots would find themselves outflanked in the naming game. Not only did Caledonia Australis become Gippsland, New Caledonia in northern New South Wales (a description which the Scots continued to use in their correspondence) was not to Anglo-Saxon tastes and weight of numbers saw it altered to New England, which it remains to this day.

The process of naming communities reached a simple perfection when, instead of being called after Scottish locations and great Scottish achievers, names paid tribute to an ordinary Scot who had lived and worked in the area. Such a distinction went to Dumfries-born James Linton who came to Manawatu-Wanganui by way of the Victoria and Otago goldfields. In 1871 he moved to the town of Palmerston North where as mayor he argued powerfully for the rail link with Wellington. The community which takes his name is situated only a few miles from Palmerston North.

Legend has it that Bernisdale (VA), now with a population of 11,000, proved such an excellent place for producing offspring that within a few years of being named by two Macleod brothers after the crofting township on Skye, it had become Bairnsdale which it remains to this day. On the other hand experience suggests that somewhere along the line a clerical error would be the explanation, much in the way that the Forbes clan became Farrabas when they were transported to America.

The entire naming process could, however, get out of hand – and not just when Lachlan Macquarie was around. Sir Thomas Brisbane, the Ayrshire Governor of New South Wales, named his first two children Thomas Australius and Eleanor Australia. In Dunedin, the Antipodean Edinburgh, so many street and district names have a derivation from Scotland's capital that it's difficult to keep track. Dunedin has a Princes Street, a George Street, Hanover Street, Castle Street, Frederick Street and suburbs such as Corstorphine, Portobello and Musselburgh, even a Water of Leith.

The Stirlingshire-born Surveyor-General of New South Wales in the early 1800s, Sir Thomas Livingstone Mitchell, generally bucked the trend of naming everything that passed across the line of view after a Scots hillock or hamlet. Ironically, although he was insistent on the retention of the Aboriginal names he is himself commemorated in roads, rivers, mountains and townships. But from time to time even the fair-minded Mitchell weakened, for instance on the occasion when he climbed a mountain near the site of Maryborough (VA) and named his conquest Mount Greenock.

Also widely found are original names constructed from Scottish elements, such as Glenorkney (VA) or Glengyle (QD), and odd hybrids of Scots/ Aborigine or Scots/Maori words, such as Ben Ohau.

Inevitably the most popular Scottish names are repeated. It is an interesting but confusing fact that the Antipodes boasts *three* Ben Lomonds: Australia, rather greedily, has two – in New South Wales and Tasmania – while the Kiwi Ben Lomond is in South Island.

Chapter Eight
Killed, Cooked and Eaten

ONE OF THE GREAT IRONIES of the Scottish immigration to Australia and New Zealand is that many of the Caledonians were victims of the Clearances (roughly 1746–1880), having left directly for the Antipodes from the crofts or from the cities in the Lowlands where they had been forced to settle, leaving willingly or virtually in chains. They then arrived in their new homelands and proceeded to displace the native populations much as they themselves had been pushed off the land to make way for sheep and 'improvements'. This is something over which many Scots descendants still feel guilt. Yet although the Scots were in the front line in asserting settler superiority they were also occasionally active in defence of the rights of the native peoples; the Highlanders, with their clan heritage, may often have had a more profound understanding of the needs of the Maoris and Aborigines than other immigrant groups.

An interesting case study: although adopted, Australian Douglas Grant was proud of his Scottish family background and while serving with the Australian Infantry Force in World War I took the chance while on leave to visit the auld country. Professor Malcolm Prentis tells of Grant's sensational appearance at his foster-father's native village where in speaking to a shop girl in his best Scots accent he confused the lass behind the counter. 'There's a Scotty here from Australia who's been burnt black by the sun!' she is said to have declared. Of course, you're way ahead of me, Douglas was a full-blooded Aborigine, raised by an expatriate Scots family in Sydney and fiercely proud of his adopted homeland and its culture. His story is not unique.

On the other hand, Berwickshire's Henry Clark (b. 1821) was on the *Blundell* when it arrived in Otago in 1848 and his claim to fame is that in the first provincial elections he actively canvassed against giving the Maoris the vote. In both Australia and New Zealand governments are now trying to make good some of the perceived sins of their forefathers against the native peoples. From the start of organised settlement there was a feeling that the native peoples were a downright inconvenience. Scots seaman James Herd, in charge of the New Zealand Company's first expedition from Leith in 1825, reported a hostile reception – from the missionaries! It seems they feared that colonisation would impair their influence over the Maoris. Mind you, Herd in turn was accused of dishonest dealing with the natives when in 1822 he commanded the *Providence* in a trading expedition to New Zealand.

History has indeed shown that the Maoris were exploited in land deals, happy to accept nick-nacks and token gifts in exchange for vast areas of virgin bush which, because of the complex concept of land-ownership among the Maoris, was never theirs to trade away. If they were proving reluctant to deal, they were often plied with drink and once befuddled would agree to almost anything.

Gordon Gray, a Scots descendant from Roxburgh in central Otago, pin-pointed this strange arrangement and wonders why so many Scots apparently unwittingly entered with enthusiasm into these flawed contracts. His ante-cedent Henry Gray from Orkney had arrived in Dunedin on board the *Oamaru* on New Year's Eve 1878:

> His application to the administration of the Queen's Grant Scheme was successful which meant that five acres of densely covered bush in South-land belonged to him. That this land did not belong to Queen Victoria to give, and that Henry, a Scot of strict Calvinist beliefs should accept stolen property seems difficult to understand.

However, neither Henry nor Her Majesty, nor for that matter the thousands of others who took up land grants seemed to be bothered by such niceties.

In fact, anyone trying to walk or steer a middle course at the expense of the European advantage could find themselves under attack. James Campbell of Skerrington in Ayrshire was appointed to arbitrate with the Maori tribes in the 1850s. A battle-hardened soldier having fought in the Peninsular War, he had been elected a member of the Society of Canterbury Colonists. After his arrival he was appointed Commissioner of Crown Lands and government agent in Canterbury. In this job he was required to investigate all lands claims and adjudicate on them but he soon angered the settlers with his efforts to be equitable and was the subject of a series of complaints to Governor Sir George Grey.

AN EMPTY LAND – SURELY NOT?

In Australia the historical idea of Terra Nullus – that the great island continent was effectively an empty land before the arrival of the First Fleet – has been overturned and recognition given to the traditional land rights of the Aborigines. By 1993 the Aborigines could claim native title to land if they could prove uninterrupted traditional use. This condition obviously prevented claims against urban Australia and the vast pastureland. In Darwin (NT), however, the nation's newest capital, the local Aborigine council were looking at a claim over the undeveloped land in the city prefacing bids for compensation when building takes place. Difficulties have also arisen when oil, gas, uranium or diamonds are found in remote spots and claims are made that they are located on 'traditional' and sacred aboriginal sites. At least, as one cynical Australian-Scots correspondent suggested to me, all this litigation keeps constitutional lawyers in new Mercedes cars.

In New Zealand settlement claims by Maori tribes are also being dealt with. Compensation was conceded in 1996, for example, by the Wellington government relating to a land grab or wrongful seizure by the settler population in 1865 of ancestral lands belonging to the Whakatohea tribe.

Some of the more conservative elements among the Scots descendants see these recent legal restorations and compensations as 'money grabs' just as deplorable in their own way as the 'land grabs' by the whites in the 1800s. However, the Scottish connections with the Maori and Aborigine populations are in place and can take many fascinating forms. As we've seen, other ethnic groups are desperate, it seems, to claim some Scottish link, any Scottish link. A Maori speaker at a recent genealogy conference in Southland confused his audience by claiming Scottish ancestry 'through absorption'. He went on to explain that he could make this assertion because his great-grandfather had eaten a Presbyterian missionary!

New Zealand's police force has always had its share of Scots descendants including, in the 1990s, a tall, fuzzy-haired Fijian with the grand name of Hector Seaforth Mackenzie.

The proliferation of Maori Macdonalds in the Nelson area of South Island is down in legend to the Highlander who chased a Maori lass round a flax bush – the fact he eventually caught her is in no doubt, given the crowds of dusky Macdonald descendants in the region. The close relationship which developed between the Scots and the Maoris, particularly in Otago, is further illustrated by the astonishment of Scots from North Island who, arriving in Otago for the sheep shearing, heard the Maoris speak with a strong Scottish brogue.

The men whose task it was to survey the vast interior of Australia could never be quite sure of the reception from the local tribes. Ayrshire geologist

Many early links were forged between the Maoris and the Scots; similarities
between the clan and the tribal social systems are often cited as the reason for
this coming together. Here we see traditional Maori Poi dancers.
(*New Zealand Tourism*)

Robert Jack was speared through the shoulder by hostile Aborigines while on an expedition to seek gold deposits in northern Queensland.

WRECK OF THE STIRLING CASTLE

Of the many stories of endurance and hardship experienced by travellers to Australia the saga of Eliza Fraser, a captain's wife from Dundas Street in Stromness, Orkney, and her ordeal among the Queensland Aborigines takes some beating.

After the wreck of the *Stirling Castle* on the Barrier Reef in 1836 and a nightmarish journey in an open boat, Mrs Fraser faced six weeks as a prisoner of a particularly cruel group of native Australians before eventual rescue. Her experiences fascinated people around the world who had been fed stories of the atrocities carried out by Aborigine tribes and they were astonished to learn of her return to civilisation, an escape from what must have seemed an inevitable and terrible end.

As the *Stirling Castle* left the Thames on the outward leg, with a cargo of 900 barrels of ale, she collided with another brig and departure was delayed – among the superstitious seamen this was seen as an ominous portent. With eighteen people on board, mostly inexperienced sailors, the ship left Sydney on the return journey and seven days later was grounded on a reef to the northeast of Rockhampton, the skerry known thereafter as Eliza's Reef. When the vessel began to break up the two ship's boats were launched into the surf, the longboat having eleven people on board including the Frasers. The pinnace had to be used to tow the waterlogged longboat and for weeks the two tiny craft floundered about off the coast trying to reach Moreton Bay penal settlement (later Brisbane). Five days after the wreck, waist deep in water, Mrs Fraser gave birth to a child which drowned after a few breaths. The party lived on small quantities of shellfish and fresh water gathered along the chain of small islands which they passed. Eventually they landed on a vast sandy stretch of territory which was to become known as Fraser's Island, the largest sand island in the world, some eighty miles in length.

At first the Kabi Kabi Aborigines gave no trouble but became progressively more hostile as the party's possessions, which they had bartered for kangaroo meat, began to dwindle. As they decided to head overland to Moreton Bay the party was overrun by the tribesmen who stripped them and left Mrs Fraser with only one garment; the survivors of the *Stirling Castle* were enslaved and split up. It seemed that when they became too weak to work they were tortured.

Captain Fraser was murdered, his chief officer was burned alive and Mrs

Eliza Fraser from
Stromness in Orkney
who survived the wreck
of the *Stirling Castle* on
the Barrier Reef only to
be taken prisoner by a
band of Aborigines.
(*John Oxley Library,
State Library of
Queensland, Brisbane*)

Fraser selected as a slave to the tribeswomen. She was made to climb high trees in search of honeycombs, forced to stain her skin and was soon, like the Aborigines, infested with vermin. The ship's cook, a Negro who had been treated more leniently, escaped and alerted the military at Moreton Bay who sent out a search party. A convict called Graham, attached to the rescue mission, is said to have snatched Mrs Fraser away from Aborigines during a native celebration, an act for which he gained his freedom and a reward. However, the story has a distressing conclusion. After being received as a heroine in Moreton Bay and Sydney, with a thanksgiving service and a collection taken, Eliza secretly married the skipper of the vessel which took her back to the United Kingdom. Although her circumstances had much improved, she still applied for the relief fund money which had been gathered on her behalf. There was public indignation when news emerged of her marriage and last word of Eliza sadly found her as a sideshow curiosity behind a placard which read:

Stirling Castle. Wrecked off the coast of New Holland. All Killed and
Eaten by Savages. Only survivor a woman; To be seen – Admission 6d.

Contrast the loss of the *Stirling Castle* and the sufferings of the voyagers
with the wreck of the Dundee barque *Peruvian* which also fell victim to the
Barrier Reef, a little further north in the same period. Records show that
when the longboat from the *Peruvian* reached shore near the present-day
town of Bowen, only four of the twenty-two crew and passengers were still
alive forty-two days after the grounding. Survivors were Captain George
Pitkethly from Newburgh in Fife, his wife, a seaman named Morrill and an
apprentice called Wilson. The Aborigines who discovered the stricken party
on this occasion were friendly to a fault, and seemed to deem it of particular
importance that they should take care of Mrs Pitkethly. After a few years
they had all died with the exception of Morrill who was found by white
prospectors, having 'gone native'. Within a few years of his return to 'civilisation' he too had died.

DOING THE DEAL

The purchase of Maori lands which has caused so much controversy right
down to the present day was carried out by the government, district by
district. The Rangitikei area of North Island, for example, covered 435 square
kilometres. This was one of numerous negotiations conducted by Donald
McLean (later Sir Donald), a six-foot-two-inch Highlander of whom one
historian recorded his dancing feat: 'In Highland company he jumped on
the table where he had no rival in the sword dance, Scottish reel or Highland
Fling.' Then aged twenty-nine, McLean, from Tiree, Argyllshire, faced a
Maori legend in the Rangitikei negotiations. This was Te Rauparaha, a brutal,
warlike leader; however, McLean is said to have kept a confident, agreeable
and reasonable face during the fortnight's parleying. Probably a wise move
when you consider that the chief had gathered 4,000 Maori warriors and
camp-followers at the land sale. But Donald's tactful approach paid off and
he talked the chief round to selling.

Plain James McDonnell from Inverness-shire was the first farmer to settle
in the newly-bought Rangitikei. In fact, James was said to be the heir to the
noble title of Lord Glengarry but in the new egalitarian environment decided
against making use of it. Soon after arriving in late 1849 he married Anne
Cameron, also from Inverness, one of the band of Scots who reached
Wellington on the *Blenheim* in 1840. This was a real Scottish voyage. Of
the 177 migrants on board more than half were Scots – fifty-nine Camerons,
twelve Frasers, ten McQuarries, eight Mackenzies and nine Sinclairs.

Just before New Year 1850 James and Anne rode 100 miles along the sandy beach from Wellington, fording the deep Rangitikei River on horseback to reach their property which they named Inverhoe after a spot near Glengarry which James had known as a child. Big Mac, as he was not surprisingly known, had been in business as a stock buyer before settling down. His job involved travelling back and forward to Sydney, 1,000 miles away, to accompany consignments of sheep, cattle and horses. Eventually he stayed in New Zealand to handle the import side of the business. Anne and James had ten children.

BLAME IT ON THE DINGOS

Robert Fairbairn, whose father came from Berwickshire, may well have received his first lessons in Euclidean maths and arithmetic while sitting on a tree stump. In the early 1840s the only school in the vast expanse of Western Australia was at Perth.

Fairbairn, who became a magistrate and government representative in the developing colony, is remembered for his controversial report on race strife on the Gascoyne River. The settlers felt that one police officer to cover 600 miles of wild country without a horse was next to useless; and reports of trouble between the whites and the Aborigines were reaching the authorities on an almost daily basis. In 1882 two white shepherds had been murdered on a property called Swandagee. Almost as an afterthought, it's mentioned in the official records that eight natives were killed and a number wounded in the same mêlée. There were reports of a missing chubby Chinaman and most of the settlers had convinced themselves that he had been eaten.

Into this fraught situation Fairbairn, the governor's appointee, arrived armed with a series of questions designed, perhaps surprisingly, to find if the immigrants had brought the troubles on themselves by their harsh treatment of the Aborigines. When details of his remit filtered out to the tough pioneers, they were furious. Fairbairn visited the settlers in their homes and they were informed that they did not have to respond to the questions. They poured scorn on many of the ideas suggested for making the lives of the Aborigines more civilised and tolerable. Iron huts were suggested as accommodation. Robert Fairbairn had a next to impossible task and his final report was considered exaggerated and unfair, the general feeling being that he had been 'stuffed' with improbable and stupid stories and, however well intentioned he was, he could never give a true portrait of the state of play along the Gascoyne River.

Fairbairn even expressed the belief that sheep theft was down in large part

Encounter with Aborigines at Attack Creek in central Australia during John
McDouall Stuart's groundbreaking expeditions in the 1860s which culminated in
the crossing of the continent from south to north.
(*Mortlock Library, Adelaide, South Australia: B1355*)

to dingos rather than the Aborigines. In their turn the settlers, with heavy
sarcasm, wrote to the Press pointing out that dingos did not usually skin
and roast an animal, bury the bones under the fire and cover everything up
with ashes . . . Fairbairn's good intentions had done nothing to further the
cause of conciliation.

The quest for cheap labour also brought the Scots into contact with the
Pacific Islanders at an early date. Benjamin Boyd from Wigtown shipped in
natives to his whaling settlement at Twofold Bay (NSW) hoping to create
an unlimited supply of cheap labour but his project failed principally because
of public objections.

THE VAST TRIBE OF NEWTON

Amid stories of strife and recrimination between the races the saga of Kirkcaldy whaler George Newton (b. 1803) restores faith in the successful
outcome of early mixed marriages. As noted elsewhere, whaling and sealing
brought many Scots to New Zealand in the early 1800s when white settlement
had not yet begun. These hardy seamen traded their catches to Port Jackson
(Sydney) for transhipment to the United Kingdom. It is certain that as a
result of the great number of shipwrecks in which the flimsy craft simply

vanished, many a whaler's family back in Scotland would never have known exactly where and how their kin died. But some survived to put down roots.

Wharetutu Anne Newton was baptised in 1844 and at the same time she married George Newton. This was no fleeting, whirlwind romance, however – the couple already had ten children. As a young woman Wharetutu had gone to live with George at Codfish Island off the coast of Rakiura (the original Maori name for Stewart Island). George's brother John came to New Zealand to join him and also married a Maori lass.

With sealing in decline the Newtons and four other mixed couples founded a settlement on Stewart Island itself, creating a timber milling business which supplied wood for ship and house building. George and Wharetutu had a total of thirteen children and visitors to the little community were impressed by the industriousness of the place. The marriage of their children also produced large families and the Newtons were to be the founders of a vast network of mixed families throughout southern New Zealand. According to her biographer, Atholl Anderson, Wharetutu's descendants numbered 5,000 by 1986, by far the largest mixed group traced to that date.

Some of the extended Scots families generally can be enormous. The Taylor family came to Winton (SD) in 1863 with thirteen children who in turn had a fruitful average of eleven children each. In 1996 family biographer George A. Smith reckoned a grand total of 8,081 descendants, probably more than half of them still living in Southland.

TRY A LITTLE TENDERNESS

Robert Christison, the son of a minister from Foulden in Berwickshire, was long remembered among the Aborigine peoples of northern Queensland for one final act before he retired to the United Kingdom in 1903. His first concern during the sale negotiations of his property was to ensure the right of the native peoples to remain on the station as their home. His success in living in friendship and harmony with the Aborigines is one of the remarkable stories of early Queensland settlement.

Arriving in Victoria in 1852 with his brother Tom and with neither friends, contacts or money, they worked for a time at Werribee for the affluent Chirnside family who also had their roots in Berwickshire. Robert quickly achieved success as a horseman and as a boxer. His reputation as a steeplechase jockey also grew. Setbacks appear to have been meat and drink to young Robert: he tried gold mining and failed; he tried to join the ill-fated Burke and Wills expedition but his letter went unanswered. Around this

Berwickshire's Robert Christison, a Queensland pioneer who is remembered for his enlightened, compassionate approach to relationships with the Aborigine tribes. (*John Oxley Library, State Library of Queensland, Brisbane*)

time he realised that before traipsing off into the bush he should learn navigation and went off to classes in Melbourne.

By 1863 we find him in northern Queensland where, to learn the conditions of the country, he took a job as a shepherd for three months. He then returned to Bowen on the coast, bought stores and with an Aborigine boy and several horses struck out west. By chance he met another Scot, explorer/surveyor William Landsborough, who steered him out towards the western watershed. Settlement was spreading rapidly even into this far-flung area so Christison rode back to Bowen and obtained an occupation licence for a district he called Lammermoor. In partnership he bought a small flock of sheep and spent most of the time trying to protect them from rampaging dingos. His early encounters with the Aborigines are intriguing. A settler had shot some natives deciding they had stolen his sheep, the Aborigines retaliated by killing a settler and his family and a dangerous tit-for-tat was developing. Christison, much against the received wisdom, decided to try a little kindness. He captured a young Aborigine, treated him so well that the young man was glad to work for the Scotsman and then sent him back to his tribe as an ambassador. It worked a treat.

Hardship was a daily companion. In his explorations further west Robert almost died of thirst. More than once, now assisted by his brothers Tom and William, they had to survive on mutton when flour ran out. In 1870 he drove 7,000 sheep all the way to Adelaide (SA) to get a decent price. The canny Scot got five times the price per animal he had been offered in the north.

The man Robert Christison met in the bush, Landsborough, was a fascinating individual in his own right, a man who also provided much early information on the Aborigines of the interior. Brought up in Ayrshire, he came to Australia as a young man. After trying farming and gold mining he pushed forward in 1853 into the rich agricultural land at the head of Queensland's Thomson River. In 1861 he was put in charge of an expedition setting off from the Gulf of Carpentaria in search of the Burke and Wills party. He worked his way into the heart of Australia, eventually finding his way to Melbourne, a hero's welcome and the presentation of a plate worth £500 – just the ticket for an explorer of the outback. However, Landsborough had discovered the first practicable north-south route across Australia.

Dumfries artist Thomas Watling, who had been transported to New South Wales for forgery, wrote home in 1792 telling his aunt of the strange customs he had found among the native peoples. Apart from fixing bones in their noses and smearing their bodies with red and white earth, they were required to donate part of their body to a tribal leader at an early age – men, one of their front teeth, and the women, the first joint of the little finger of the left hand. Explorer Allan Cunningham found Aborigines who wore kangaroo teeth in their ears and cockatoo feathers in their hair. The young men had their beards formed in three pleated tails.

Setting out from the Hunter River (NSW) in 1840 with a party of eight men, Hugh Gordon from Rhynie in Aberdeenshire passed through runs which had been occupied by settlers until they came to the area north of where the town of Glen Innes stands today – free land, the domain of the Aborigine, which they called Strathbogie Station. In Gordon's party was Frederick Lamatte who kept a detailed log of the expedition. He made many notes on the trek:

> I think this is a favourite spot of the blacks as we came across several of their fires, and some of them very recent; the trees all about are notched with their tomahawks.

There always seemed to be anxiety about the unpredictability of the local

Aborigines. At the station site their only shelter initially was a tarpaulin stretched over a ridge pole. Lamatte said his seat was a tobacco keg, Gordon's a bale of hops. What do you think of our situation, he asks:

> By Heaven, I believe it to be one of the hardest and roughest of lots . . . if Gordon leaves my only companions are three or four discontented convicts. Beyond the reach of social intercourse we live, in a wilderness with no possibility of assistance should the blacks prove troublesome.

And such problems were common. In South Australia, George Dorward, a migrant from Lamlash on the Isle of Arran who had taken up sheep farming, regularly found Aborigines haunting his homestead and sheep encampments. On one occasion one of his children was carried away but Dorward followed the kidnappers, gun in hand, to recover his child unharmed.

THE GILFILLAN MASSACRE

Even more serious incidents were recorded. When white settlers started to buy land from the Maori tribes in an organised manner, offering blankets, fish hooks, tomahawks, even umbrellas and Jew's-harps, there was little understanding among the Europeans of the complex, unwritten laws which governed the ownership of land. This failing was to lead to animosity and eventually to war, just as it had done with the Indian nations of North America.

Into such tension in the province of Wanganui in 1842 arrived the Gilfillan family from Edinburgh. John Gilfillan, doctor and painter (encouraged by Sir Henry Raeburn he had painted 'Bonny Jean' Armour, wife of Robert Burns), was an organised man and had studied carpentry, engineering and farming in London to equip himself for the life of a settler. But as Miriam Macgregor tells us the Gilfillan family found Wanganui seething with unrest due to haphazard purchase negotiation between the New Zealand Company and the Maoris. The insensitivity shown by the settlers to the native population is indicated by the fact that the name of the district had been changed to honour a director of the New Zealand Company. Ironically, John Gilfillan was prominent in a successful campaign to have it revert to the original Maori name.

Like most incoming families the Gilfillans were granted a town section and a block of 110 country acres, theirs in the Matawara Valley. It seems for the first three years things were almost idyllic, hard work spiced with family picnics upriver and fireside music-making. Earthquakes were a frequent hazard, the earth opening up in front of John once as he stopped for a rest while pushing a wheelbarrow.

Survivors of a Maori massacre on New Zealand's North Island – Glasgow artist John Gilfillan and his daughters Mary (*centre*) and Sarah. (*Whanganui Regional Museum*)

Their home in the Matawara Valley was completed in the spring of 1845. Two years later an incident involving a young Royal Navy midshipman who accidentally injured a Maori with a pistol was to tear the Gilfillan family apart. Seeking vengeance, or *utu*, a group of headstrong warriors attacked the Gilfillan house, seemingly at random, striking down John Gilfillan at his front door. Although he managed to stagger inside and the door was barred the Maoris hung about outside. Tragically, the Gilfillans decided that the Maoris would not harm women and children and under cover of dusk John crawled off for help. Shortly after Mary and her seven children and grandchild found the house under attack with windows being smashed and wooden staves being driven through the clay walls. As they made their escape through a window they were slashed and battered by the natives waiting in the garden. Fleeing in different directions Mary and three of her children died under a hail of blows. Four Maoris were apprehended upriver and hanged within forty-eight hours. Within months two more of the children had died, their passing directly attributed to this tragic incident. John Gilfillan, with the sad remnants of his family, began a new life in South Australia and continued to paint.

DINNA MESS WI' 'RED' McGREGOR

The fear of suffering at the hands of the natives – whether Maori or Aborigine – was a very real one in Scotland in the middle years of the 19th century. When Anna Allen from Slamannan in Stirlingshire sailed from Liverpool for South Australia it was with the words of her neighbours ringing in her ears. If she went to that wild, outlandish place they feared she would surely 'get eaten'. Others were less easily daunted.

Alex 'Red' McGregor was a Dornoch stonemason and builder who brought his family to Wanganui and only a few years after the Gilfillan massacre bought the property next door to what had been the scene of the tragedy. Calling the farm Auchmore, they found that since the incident the area had been avoided by settlers but the McGregors were hardy souls – Alex apparently stood six-foot-four-inches with flaming red hair. Once finding a group of Maoris gathering menacingly around the house he put on his kilt and fastened on his long sword (taken by his father from the Pyramids, so it was said) and marched out to meet the warriors. Instead of trying out his primitive Maori vocabulary Big Eck recited the Lord's prayer in Gaelic at the top of his voice – there seems to have been no further trouble with the locals.

Glaswegian John Bryce arrived at Wellington as a child in 1840 and grew up to be what is best described as a hard-liner in relation to the Maori 'problem'. It was his firm belief that as long as the Maoris considered themselves a match for the troops there would never be peace and his views were those of a 'fighting frontiersman who had seen neighbours shot down on their own doorsteps'. In the Maori Wars Bryce helped found volunteer units but in 1869 was accused of a My Lai-style massacre at a location called Handley's Wood (MW) in which Maori women and children were said to have been cut down. He sued for damages after publication of these allegations and was awarded £5,000.

As a firm and forthright Native Minister appointed in 1879, he personally led a force into the Maori settlement to arrest a pair of troublemaking prophets. To his credit Bryce, as well as helping to draft legislation to pacify the Maoris, also helped address their many grievances, particularly over land purchases. Bryce's biographer assessed him as a man of resolute will, uncompromising though fair, unsubtle, plain-spoken – in the patois of his native Glasgow he would have been classified as a tough nut.

OLD HABITS DYING HARD?

Hero or villain? Of the relationships between the Scots settlers and the Aborigine peoples one of the most enigmatic was that of Skye's Angus McMillan, discoverer of Gippsland and a giant figure in the early history of Victoria. This pioneer immigrated in 1837 and with the aid of an Aboriginal guide, Jimmy Gibber, pushed through to the Bass Strait, opening up the area for settlement. His role in the swift Europeanisation of the district is a source of controversy to this day.

Recently the Koorie (Aboriginal) community in East Gippsland published a brochure for the Bataluk Cultural Trail which assists visitors to explore the Aboriginal heritage of the area. It includes a controversial section on what they choose to call the 'Gippsland Massacres' which took place as the Aborigines resisted European invasion of their land but lost out to the technical superiority of the settlers' weapons. In a list of alleged atrocities levelled against the newcomers the name of Angus McMillan (1810–1865) figures prominently. For example:

1840, Oct.– Dec. – Unknown number killed by Angus McMillan's men.

1841 – 30–35 shot by McMillan's men.

1843, June – Between 60 and 180 shot by Angus McMillan and his men.

Some, perhaps many, of the hundreds of alleged killings may, it was suggested to me, have been the result of inter-tribal fighting rather than direct European aggression by the so-called Highland Brigade. However, even this strife was probably occasioned by one group of families being pushed from their traditional hunting grounds by white settlers, forcing a clash with their neighbours.

Another book published on the topic of the behaviour of the early settlers has an unequivocal and pointed title – *Our Murdering Founding Fathers*. It is a highly contentious topic to this day and some people living around the Bushy Park area where McMillan's homestead stands in sad dereliction stoutly defend the man to all-comers. Woe betide anyone who enters this vicinity with a preconceived notion of McMillan's guilt. One interesting theory put to me by McMillan's apologists was that the Scots were simply dealing with local difficulties in the traditional Highland way, a kind of evolutionary process which justified the survival of the most determined and best-equipped: clan warfare transmitted to the bush.

NOT HUMAN AT ALL

Kerr Johnston in his book *The Scots Factor* says that at the Hunter River penal colony north of Sydney, home to the no-hopers among the transported prisoners, army personnel in the early days treated convicts as sub-human and the Aborigines as not human at all.

It's worth nothing that the Scots themselves, and in particular the Highlanders, could find themselves victims of ethnic prejudice because of their Celtic roots and because they were members of a culture alien to the Anglo-Saxon powerbrokers. Sir Charles Nicolson pompously declared that the sluggish and listless habits of the Highlanders would suit well with the life of a shepherd. Gaelic-only speakers inevitably ran into difficulties, especially in the earliest days of settlement.

Violent incidents were common in the early pastoral days and not just in Victoria. In South Australia Glasgow doctor James McKechnie took a lease of land, forty-three square miles on the Eyre Peninsula. Two years later one of his shepherds was 'fatally speared' by four Aborigines. They were tried and sentenced to death at Adelaide and ordered to be taken back to Franklin Harbor where 'in front of as many blacks as could be mustered' they were to be hanged, punishment apparently designed to discourage further Aborigine misbehaviour.

Aborigine prisoners in the custody of police officers in the Northern Territory in the early 1900s. (*Miller Collection, Northern Territory Library, Darwin*)

According to one report of this horrific affair, the executioner who travelled with his victims on the schooner *Yatala* was a 'terrible looking scamp', an ancient New South Wales lag who had been liberated from Adelaide jail specifically for this gruesome task. Police inspector Holroyd described the bizarre scene at the gallows as the four men, apparently quite indifferent to the fate that awaited them, ate and talked casually as if being launched into eternity was an everyday occurrence. They had been chained together by their military escort, the prisoners wearing only striped shirts, no trousers and white night caps. The execution was watched by about forty hurriedly gathered natives, Dr McKechnie and his two brothers. Holroyd says

> The prisoners were placed on the scaffold, the nightcaps over their faces . . . the doctor looked on fixedly as if to see that full justice was done to the murderers of his inoffensive shepherd.

All this time the natives crouched on the sand betraying no emotion, even when the bodies were swinging at the end of their ropes and the old executioner was hanging on to their legs to speed their departure. As the party prepared to leave they agreed to let the Aborigines, who had been clamouring for the men's clothes, take them on condition that they buried the bodies. McKechnie's biographer suggests that, no matter how indecent this whole business might have been, it did have a salutary effect on the future conduct of natives in the district.

Ironically, at almost the same time as this sad episode, along the coast at the new community of Mount Gambier (SA), another Scot, Christina Smith (b. 1814), who had worked with the Aborigines since arriving in South Australia in 1845 opened a school and was already planning a home to accommodate orphaned and distressed native children. She also wrote a book on the Booandik tribe.

Skyemen do seem to figure prominently in these unsettled times. When the sons of Major Donald McLeod of Talisker on Skye crossed from Van Diemen's Land (Tasmania) with other Scots to begin the settlement and opening up of the Port Phillip district (Melbourne), they quickly moved inland with their stock. Apparently they felt in control only after what has been described as a 'sickening series of confrontations' with the local Aborigines.

Some Scots, including Gideon Lang (1819–1880), stressed the responsibility of the settlers to the Aborigines; but generally the welfare of the indigenous peoples seems to have taken a low priority in the scramble for land, simply because land equalled wealth and power. A few enlightened individuals warned very early on about the likely effects on the tribes of this land mania. Stirlingshire explorer and surveyor Sir Thomas Livingstone Mitchell remarked in 1850:

> The only kindness we could do for them, would be to let them and their wide range of territory alone; to act otherwise and profess good-will is but hypocrisy.

Occupation of the land, he said, carried as a natural consequence enormous change. He suggested that the native peoples of Australia would be happier left in ignorance of the need to wear a fig leaf or use a plough. Mitchell was also one of the more alert Scots who realised that there was much to be learned from the Aborigines – and not just in terms of bushcraft. He even read a paper to the Philosophical Society of New South Wales describing his proposal for a ship's propeller which operated on the principle of the boomerang.

A BIT OF LOCAL KNOWLEDGE

And there is evidence that the arrogant approach adopted by some of the settlers to the native people could occasionally backfire. As early as March 1799 the Aborigines on the Hawkesbury River north of Sydney warned the settlers of an impending flood but 'not liking to be taught by untutored savages' the settlers treated the warnings with contempt. Very soon an extensive area of farmland was under water and the country resembled the open sea. Much precious stock was lost and a valuable lesson learned.

A founder of Brisbane (QD), Sir Evan Mackenzie, was accused of being a land speculator and of guilt in the poisoning of Aborigines on his station at Kilcoy. His biographer John Mackenzie-Smith says he was innocent of both charges, adding that his apparently uncaring attitude towards the blacks was little different from most of his white colleagues in 1840s Queensland. He was only in Australia for a few years but single-mindedly worked to develop northern autonomy from Sydney – a task in which he was able to claim success although he did fail in his declared target of establishing a direct trading link between Brisbane and London.

Certainly the general attitude of the pastoralists filters through in the obituary columns and local histories of the times, column after column paying tribute to the Scots pioneers. You'll find descriptions of this 'black-infested country' or perhaps 'the murdering natives' or a passing observation that the sore-pressed settlers 'suffered much from the depredations of the blacks'.

Explorer David Lindsay of Dundee was a tall, broad-shouldered Scot whose principle claim to fame is that he mapped some 80,000 square miles, the extent of Queensland's arterial water system. While in charge of a government expedition into the Northern Territory in 1883 his party was attacked by hostile Aborigines who were chased off only after the use of firearms. Some of the horses had been stampeded during the skirmish and the party had a hard time making it home.

As ever there are two sides to this coin. Premier of Victoria, John 'Jack' Murray (1851–1916), the son of Aberdonian parents, was a consistent defender of the Aborigine people. He fought a government attempt to disperse native populations from a reserve and very tellingly is said to have been the first chairman of the Board for the Protection of the Aborigines to take his duties seriously, often intervening in disputes.

From the composing room at the *Scotsman* to the battlefields of North Island, New Zealand, where he was a war correspondent during the Hauhau Uprising – that was the dramatic career charge for William Berry who came to New Zealand to join the Southern Cross. He learned Maori and wrote powerful despatches exposing the treatment of the Hauhau women and children.

Samuel Martin from Kilmuir in Skye edited the first newspaper in Auckland and was often at loggerheads with the authorities; after leaving New Zealand he petitioned the House of Commons protesting about the ill treatment of the Maoris by settlers.

A LITTLE DARK IN THE SKIN

Hector and Agnes McDonald met and married in New Zealand in 1854, embarking on as fascinating and colourful a life as any pioneer couple in the middle years of the century. Hector, who hailed from the Western Highlands, was a genuine character from the day he arrived in Tasmania at the age of six to settle in a McDonald enclave on the Derwent River.

The excitement of whaling appealed more to Hector than the relative security of farming and in 1832 he landed at Kapiti Island (WN) where he was met by the ferocious and infamous warrior chieftain Te Rauparaha. Historians now agree that Hector, who lived as a chief among the Maori, was the first settler along that coast and was respected by the native peoples for his characteristic Scottish traits of firmness of character and stout honesty. He even married a Maori princess although, sadly, she died in childbirth.

When Wellington became established in 1840 Hector opened his trading empire buying pigs and potatoes to supply the new community. After marrying Agnes, originally from Castle Douglas, the couple settled at Otaki in a primitive shack. Later, after the birth of their children, the couple went into the hospitality trade, opening a rooming house and selling liquor, their main customers for the latter being Maoris.

Hector and Agnes McDonald – this adventurous Highland couple lived and
worked among the Maoris on the Kapiti Coast of New Zealand's North Island.
(*Mary Dorset, Manakau*)

Agnes, having seen her brood of children on their way in life, became
concerned with the high mortality rate among the Maoris who often seemed
to die from the simplest of ailments, and she persuaded the authorities to
give her a medicine chest. She nursed in a very forceful way and because of
Maori reluctance to report in for treatment she would trek out to their
encampments. During these bush expeditions Agnes discovered that iodine
could cure scrofula.

In later years at Horowhenua the McDonalds were the only white people
living among hundreds of Maoris but Agnes is said to have worked to make
sure her children retained their white identity. Histories suggest that the
Maoris still felt an innate need for tribal warfare and once a battle was fought
around the McDonald house with bullets zipping past the building. In the
midst of all this uncertainty the McDonald boys went about their daily tasks,
checking sheep and milking the cows.

Another youngster, schoolboy Andrew Miller from Falkland in Fife, found
Dunedin strange, wonderful and just a wee bit confusing. Writing to his
cousin back home in 1862 he declared that he liked 'first rate' to live in
New Zealand but admitted he found it very strange that cattle ('we call
them bullocks') hauled the carts instead of horses. Of the Maoris he had this
to say:

MARY NEICH McEWEN 1819-1876   DAVID McEWEN 1818-1905

Fifers Mary and David McEwen who sailed with the *Bengal Merchant* in 1839 and pioneered the Hutt Valley and Manawatu districts of New Zealand's North Island. (*Christina Powell, Wellington*)

I do not know any of the languages the natives of this place speak. They are a little dark in the skin and a great many of them are sort of painted on the face.

Another Fifer, David McEwen, with his Tam o' Shanter at a jaunty angle, was a familiar sight along the tracks and among the farmsteads of the community that is today known as Palmerston North (MW). As often happened it was the enthusiasm of one individual – David in this case – for immigration which eventually persuaded a whole family to New Zealand.

It was in 1839 that David, a flax dresser who had been working in Dundee when he read the immigration literature and heard the agency talks, decided to try the Antipodean adventure. His wife Mary was soon convinced of the plan and his parents expressed a willingness to travel also – his mother, having heard that the place was peopled by savages, suggested that they might as well go along and be killed, cooked and eaten too. Shortly after David's sister Ann and her husband decided to join the expedition. The party sailed on the *Bengal Merchant* from Greenock, the first of the new-generation New Zealand Company's ships to sail from Scotland, and old Mrs McEwen's fears about native unrest were not without foundation. After landing at Petone (near Wellington) they settled in the Hutt Valley. The McEwen family was growing but so was the unrest, the troubles of 1846 culminating in the famous Maori attack on Boulcott's Farm, an outpost held by only twenty-five regular troops. At this action thirteen-year-old bugler Allen lost his life trying to sound the alarm. Three children were born to Mary during these troubled times.

New land was being opened up to the north and thus the McEwens became Palmerston pioneers, welcoming travellers who had come to see the new district and providing the areas's first postal service. Again in 1868 Maori unrest threatened their new life but a catastrophic attack by Taranaki warriors was avoided by the intervention of local Maoris, records biographer of the McEwens, Miriam Macgregor.

Also in Taranaki we have evidence in the 1880s of a growing self-confidence among the Maori people in the settled period after the war. They seemed in no way cowed by the white presence. Groups of Maoris collected mushrooms for export and one afternoon a party were making their way home when they were met by a cheeky group of Scots settler schoolboys. One of the Maoris was a large, jovial gent known to everyone as 'Smiler' because of his pleasant nature. Boys will be boys, of course, and one of the bold lads yelled 'Yah, big fat Maori' and sprinted off down the road. Smiler soon proved that his weight was no handicap and, sprinting, caught up with the boy, grabbed him by the scruff of the neck and, pulling up a good stout fern stick from the roadside, he dusted the seat of his pants. 'Little boys best mind,' was his message.

INTO THE ENEMY CAMP

The Mackay family from Sutherland chartered the *Slains Castle* to take them as settlers to the Nelson District of New Zealand in 1844, bringing with them sheep, cattle, dogs, farm implements, furniture and timber, ready cut for the construction of their new home.

The Mackay children all became notable pioneer colonists but the story of James Mackay (1831–1912) is particularly informative. A tough lad who soon learned the basics of farming, he was on very friendly terms with the Maoris, fluent in their language and anxious to understand their culture. Having begun a series of journeys along the West Coast with his native guides, he was given the responsibility by the government in 1859 of completing the purchase of seven and a half million acres of land from the South Island Maoris.

His adventures during the Maori troubles of the 1860s and 70s have become the stuff of legend. In 1873 a settler had been killed and his head and heart passed through the district as trophies. A war loomed and Mackay, already a celebrity for his explorations and his role as a warden in the goldfields, was selected by Sir Donald Maclean of Tiree, the Native Minister, as an ideal local administrator, government agent in the troubled Waikato province.

Mackay prepared defences around the settlements but was determined to find out how forcibly the Maori leaders felt about entering another war and so one morning saddled his horse and rode alone into the heart of Maori country. Resolute and apparently fearless, Mackay entered the Maori encampment to an uproar. He sought out the old chieftain Rewi Maniapoto and introduced himself, demanding that the settler's murderers be handed over. Brave or foolhardy – both probably!

The Maoris gathered to consider his request at a night-time conference which was a strange mixture of religious service and council meeting. After lengthy debate with much chanting and noisy exchanges of opinion, everyone retired for the night. However, a priestess had stirred up her warriors to such an extent that one volunteered to assassinate the white man known to them as 'Hemi Maki'. Mackay was on his guard in this hostile environment. When he woke to hear someone at the tent flaps he was ready for the attack and, although suffering a wound to the face, grappled with his assailant. They rolled out of the tent and on to a grassy square and the tribes were wakened by the commotion. There were those who would have joined in slaying Mackay on the spot but the old chief led him to his quarters, shouting as he went 'Ko Maki taku ingoa', meaning 'My name is Mackay'. By this declaration he threw his personal protection around the Scotsman.

Mackay's adventure achieved little though he was hailed as a hero along the frontier that winter. He tended to play down the affair himself, saying in later years:

> As for tight corners that wasn't the first. I once had the pleasure of sitting for ten minutes while a group of Maoris debated whether they would shoot me or not.

There seems no doubt that the native peoples of Australia and New Zealand held a fascination for the settlers and in particular the youngsters. Edinburgh's Thomas Petrie was a builder, explorer, and discoverer, believe it or not, of the bunya-bunya tree, a native of coastal Queensland. But it was his son by the same name who established a close relationship with the Aborigine tribespeople. As a child Thomas ran away from home and was found in an Aborigine encampment. Thereafter he never lost his interest in the native peoples, becoming a recognised authority on their language and customs. Unusually he often accompanied Aborigine treks into the bush and the trust displayed in him saw Petrie involved in the organisation of the first Aboriginal reserve on Bribie Island near Brisbane.

Born in Edinburgh and brought up in Glasgow, Alexander Reid (1821–91) became a New Zealand missionary after joining the Methodist Church and got as close as anyone to the Maori peoples during the middle years of the 19th century. First of all he took charge of a training institution for native teachers where he mastered the language and was impressed by the idealism of the Waikato tribes. Taking over the mission station at Te Kopua he introduced sheep farming on a practical scale, persuaded the Maoris to send their wool to market in Auckland and was fully in sympathy with Maori demands for self-determination. As war threatened, the Maoris advised him that they could no longer guarantee Reid's safety and he withdrew. During the conflict he ministered to the British soldiers. He preached and taught widely and served on the committee that oversaw the translation of the Scriptures into Maori.

Chapter Nine
Pride, Pianos and Presbyterians

THE STUBBORN SCOT, displaying a gritty determination in the face of seemingly insurmountable problems surfaces regularly in the annals of Australian and New Zealand settlement. Of all the Caledonian characteristics noted by social historians this steely single-mindedness must have been the most significant attribute. On occasions it must have made us seem a serious bunch indeed but this ability to apply ourselves to the task in hand to the exclusion of everything else made ordinary people capable of almost super-human feats.

Take for instance the story of James Adam who single-handedly persuaded thousands of Scots to immigrate to the Otago settlement in New Zealand. If he had passed along the other side of Belmont Street in Aberdeen one rainy afternoon he might never have left the northeast, and the Antipodean experience would have been denied to many. On the street corner flyers were being handed out for a meeting in the Free Church that evening to discuss the Otago scheme so James, his attention captured, went along, listened to the speakers and had an interview, apparently making some useful suggestions. This prompted a letter from the Otago Association offering him free passage if he was prepared to stay on in Otago to assist with the development of the Free Church colony. He sailed with his wife on the *Philip Laing* on 20 November 1847.

Having settled to his new life, James was elected to the first provincial council. He immediately complained about the slow rate of immigration, warning that if it continued it would take 4,000 years to adequately settle Otago. This raised a few eyebrows and as a result the council set aside the sum of £25,000 specifically to encourage immigration, sending James Adam back to the United Kingdom as their immigration agent. Often criticised for his rough and ready working man's manner, James Adam was nevertheless a winner and after his arrival in Edinburgh in June 1857 the first boatload of Otago recruits was ready to sail by August. Adam remained in Scotland until the *Jura* sailed a year later.

It's interesting to consider the *Jura* voyage from the standpoint of one of the immigrant families, the Mathiesons from Mid Calder near Edinburgh. John Mathieson and his wife Catherine were among the last families to be persuaded to try the New Zealand adventure by James Adam. They had probably attended one or more of the meetings during his hectic tour of Scotland as he attempted to sell Otago. In his journal John Mathieson noted that there were 400 people on board the *Jura* including none other than the illustrious immigration agent himself. Of the steerage passengers 220 were assisted immigrants. The Mathiesons had paid their own way.

One of the most intriguing planks of Adam's immigration sales pitch had been that 'every immigrant should supply himself with a really useful woman for his wife for those who settle in Otago with such a partner in trade are sure to succeed'. Evidence suggests this was a very shrewd assessment.

On his return to Otago Adam took up sheep farming in South Tokomairiro but when gold was discovered his men disappeared to the diggings and Adam was destined to spend long solitary hours in the saddle looking after his flock. When gold was discovered on his own land 700 miners agreed to pay a weekly royalty of 2/6d to dig there but payments were irregular and difficult to collect and the business troublesome; he was glad to accept a government offer of land elsewhere. Adam, never forgetting his roots in the northeast, called his Otago homestead Bon Accord.

Those wily Scots of Otago never missed a trick when it came to attracting colonists – even from within New Zealand. Hearing of unemployment in Auckland in 1859 a recruiting party went north and carried off 100 settlers from 'mild, temperate and faithful Auckland to the frigid, bleak and snowy south' which, according to the *Auckland Weekly Register* was inhabited only by the squatters of Otago – 'lords of wastes and princes of deserts'. The Scots knew better.

CALTON HILL TO CLUTHA

And when the Scots met up in these distant lands, when auld acquaintance-ships were renewed, it was always a cause for rejoicing. Arriving in Otago from Edinburgh in 1858 Andrew Smaill and John Darling set out for the Clutha River to seek advice about land, leaving their families in Dunedin. As they trekked along the river finding the best sections already taken up, darkness fell and they sat down for a bite to eat, noticing at the same time a house light in the distance across the river. Reaching the riverbank they shouted to attract attention and the woman of the house, Mrs Mitchell, who was alone that night, persuaded some Maoris fishing a little way along the river to bring the two strangers across. As the two men came up the bank into the light from the doorway Mrs Mitchell stood back and gasped – 'Mr Smaill, where have you come from?'

Andrew Smaill looked at the woman and in turn said, 'Katie Lindsay, how are you here?'

Katie Lindsay, now Mrs Mitchell, had recently immigrated from Scotland and had last seen Andrew Smaill behind the counter of his Edinburgh grocer's shop. The next day, on his return, Willie Mitchell told them of a couple of hundred acres of good 'if peaty' land close by and there they settled.

THE LANG ROAD TO SUCCESS

When John Dunmore Lang, minister to the first Scots congregation in Australia, moaned about the batch of Church of Scotland ministers sent to Australia in 1837 he did not mince his words. They were 'four Judas Iscariots and eight full-grown specimens of contempible [sic] shufflers and drivellers'. Outspoken, he was.

Lang (1799–1878) was born in Greenock and went south to start the first Presbyterian church in Australia which opened its doors in Sydney in 1826. Of the legion of Scots who made for the Antipodes over two centuries Lang can be regarded as one of the most controversial, a man who found himself head-to-head with two governors and an establishment which didn't seem quite ready for his innovative social ideas. As one writer rather softly put it, 'Lang was a fiery gadfly'. Having visited America and admired their democratic system Lang spoke and wrote openly mooting the possibility of an Australian republic. He also travelled thousands of miles between Australia and the United Kingdom during the years 1823–74, recruiting immigrants, Presbyterians and radicals, many of them from Scotland. Lang's one-man recruiting drive was perhaps the most spectacular solo effort during the busiest period of immigration to Australia. Lang believed that only by the introduction of hardworking, sober, skilled and – most importantly – Protestant Scots could Australia be transformed from what he saw as a nest of vipers, thieves and adulterers, and at the same time keep the Roman Catholics at bay. No colonial controversy was complete without Lang having his ten-pennies-worth. Gaol often beckoned for debt and libel.

His pet project was the building of a Presbyterian College in Sydney and after receiving a loan from the Colonial Office he returned to Australia in 1831 with 140 migrants, chiefly 'Scotch mechanics', whose passage was paid from their earnings in constructing the college. The institution was eventually opened in 1832 under the name of the Australian College.

In every spare moment Lang wrote – books, treatises, speeches, pamphlets – a grand total of 300 publications from a man who was certainly the most energetic individual in the Scottish exodus and who easily qualifies for the label of the Scot who had an opinion on everything and didn't mind who knew it.

Many little communities dotted around Australia have cause to remember Dunmore Lang but Albany (WA) more than most. Constantly politicising, Lang was on one of his journeys to the UK when his ship stopped off at Albany in 1837. Lang never missed an opportunity and immediately fired off a pastoral letter explaining how if the townsfolk could get 100 signatures pledging allegiance to the Presbyterian Church all sorts of government aid to build a church and manse would be forthcoming. It was nevertheless a further fifty years before those signatures could be gathered, the Scots in Albany attending the Anglican church in the intervening period 'with reservation'.

THE PIANO LEGACY

That haunting film *The Piano*, which won three Academy Awards and tells of the mute Scotswoman arriving with her daughter to an arranged marriage in New Zealand complete with her piano has strange echoes in the story of Jane MacLean from Cromarty on the Black Isle. In 1905 at the age of sixteen, Jane, a sea captain's daughter, was sent to New Zealand as housekeeper for an uncle who lived in Hastings (HB). Her descendant Lyndsay Brock of Auckland says that the parting from the family was a painful and unwilling wrench but the MacLeans believed there would be more opportunities for Jane in a classless society and a fast-developing nation. In addition, the uncle had promised that Jane could return home if she failed to adapt or was unhappy.

Jane brought many accomplishments with her to New Zealand. She was well schooled, intelligent, a talented pianist and the owner of a beautiful soprano voice. Her uncle, alas, turned out not to be the kind and sympathetic individual for which they had hoped and Hastings not so cosmopolitan and filled with opportunities as Jane had expected; but she applied herself, got on with the job and took solace in her connection with the church. However, after four years Jane had had enough and asked her uncle if he would keep his promise, release her and provide a ticket home. He refused. Jane was devastated. Her payments had been in board and keep and small cash sums. She had no opportunity to save and certainly no money for her passage home. She couldn't bear to write and tell her parents of the dreadful situation

Jane MacLean from Cromarty whose new life in New Zealand turned into a nightmare at the hands of her despotic uncle. Left: as a child in Scotland.
(*Lyndsay Brock, Auckland*)

and her constant pleading with her uncle failed to break down his icy exterior. Within months of each other in 1912 both of Jane's parents died but by the time she got news they were, of course, long buried. Her life by this stage must have been miserable.

Then the uncle took ill and died, taking his obstinacy with him to the grave. After his funds and property had been distributed among his immediate family, it emerged that Jane had been left the piano. For a return trip to Scotland much more cash was needed than the sale of the piano could provide so Jane was stranded – and to add to her heartaches, she was now without a home or a job. It was a desperate time and if it hadn't been for the charity of the local minister and his wife the Cromarty lass would surely have been sleeping in the street. Finally an offer came. A local accountant needed a housekeeper and when Jane agreed to take on the post a second offer soon followed, this time of marriage. Jane and Clarence Masters had five children and Jane's life was transformed as financial security arrived through Mr Masters' judicious investments.

Lyndsay Brock feels that her grandmother's soft ways masked a remarkable tenacity, adaptability and a willingness to accept adversity without bitterness. In many ways Jane personifies the resilience of the Scots womenfolk who ventured to the Antipodes. For most of her years, she longed for

The Dick family – father, sons and employees – outside their engineering works at Newcastle (NSW) in the early 20th century. . . another Scottish success story in Australia. (*Snowball Collection, Newcastle Region Public Library*)

her homeland but realised that her commitment was now in New Zealand. After her death in 1971 her ashes were sent back to Cromarty, to the little cemetery on the arc of the bay. She was home at last.

OPEN 25 HOURS A DAY

This unflinching resolution is seen in the development of a thousand small Scots-run businesses across Australia and New Zealand. The Dick family's engineering works in Hamilton, a suburb of Newcastle (NSW), repaired and produced a variety of heavy equipment including steam, gas and oil engines as well as pumps and boilers. The founder of the family concern had arrived from Glasgow in the 1880s.

As you might expect enterprise was the family watchword. A 1927 Dodge car was jacked up and used to drive a sausage-making machine which son James patented in 1924. In a local newspaper feature on the company in 1912 the Scots made sure everyone knew they were geared up and ready for business. The last sentence read: 'The firm's telephone number is 25, Hamilton – night and day.'

The Rev. Simon Fraser Mackenzie, an Aberdeen minister who migrated to Australia in 1857, found himself in great demand seven days a week because he was able to preach in Gaelic and English. Eventually it was left to the Presbytery of Sydney to find him the most suitable charge.

Pride and a difficulty in accepting charity have always been Scots traits and the story of Catherine and Ralph Douglas in the Waipukurau district (HB) in 1872 shows this phenomenon clearly at work. Ralph was already an experienced shepherd when he sailed for New Zealand, having helped previously to ship sheep to South America. However, even with his background in the sheep business he, like so many others, found the early days Down Under tough going.

Catherine was the daughter of an Orkney shoemaker and her brothers, like so many other Orcadians had flown the nest for a new life in America. They had prospered beyond their wildest imaginings and, anxious about their sister and her family on the Antipodean frontier, wrote offering financial support. The money certainly would have eased the Douglas's domestic situation as Ralph and Catherine struggled to establish themselves but she wrote back tartly telling them that she and her husband were prospering and certainly didn't need any money, thank you very much. Catherine is remembered as a formidable cook, a very hospitable person but with a rather sharp manner.

Pride and misplaced honour could have dire consequences. Malcolm Prentis relates the following story of the destitute family back in Scotland. A young son – with the co-operation of his mother – brought home a sheep from the hills to feed the hungry mouths but when the father found out about this 'crime' he ordered them to hand themselves over to justice – and they were transported to Australia.

Benjamin Boyd was overflowing with ideas about how to develop Australia but history's verdict is that his schemes were just too ambitious for the Australia of the mid-1800s. Coming from a well-off Wigtownshire family he sent off a vessel to trade in Australian waters in 1830 at his own expense and, while still working in Britain as a stockbroker, floated the Royal Bank of Australia. Boyd himself then headed off to Australia as the bank's representative and later claimed that within a couple of years he was one of the largest squatters in the country with eighteen stations and over 381,000 acres of land in the south. Around the same time Boyd & Company had three steamers and three sailing ships in operation.

His most ambitious project was the founding of Boyd Town in Twofold Bay (NSW) where he soon had nine whalers working from the port.

Insurance claims for a wrecked ship saw his business damaged and he took off for California and the gold rush. Boyd was killed by natives in the manner of the perennial adventurer while out shooting game in the Solomon Islands. To add to his charisma a story circulated to the effect that he had staged his own death to foil his creditors. Whatever the explanation, Boyd was never seen again.

TAKING THE KNOCKS

Steerage passengers who arrived at Lyttleton Harbour over the hill from Christchurch (CY) were promised spots in the centre of the new town where they could squat until finding more permanent accommodation.

The first task therefore for these Canterbury colonists was to climb the Bridle Path across the Port Hills and stake out their claims. Within hours of the *Randolph*, one of the First Four Ships as they are known, anchoring in Lyttleton harbour in December 1850, John Williams, a Dunfermline baker and confectioner, joined his fellow passengers on the trek over the hill. However, three months without exercise, the harsh terrain and the boiling sun were too much for John, whose wife Isabella and their seven children waited for his return. As he reached the crest of the hill and, like Moses, gazed upon his promised land, John collapsed and died from a stroke. Fitter souls who had already staked their claim and were on their way back found his lifeless body beside the track.

On the threshold of a new beginning, this was the cruellest of blows but the histories of Canterbury tell us that Isabella kept a cool head, sold yeast to fellow immigrants in order to raise some capital and allowed the Anglican clergyman in Christchurch to open a subscription on her behalf.

On 15 January the Williams family, whose plight had been the talk of town, took refuge with the Deans brothers at Riccarton and Isabella wrote home asking for tweeds, knitting worsted, linseys and socks to be sent out in order that she might open a drapery. Glasgow House, as the 'little shop' was called, opened in 1852 and was a success. One of Isabella's daughters, Elizabeth, married William 'Cabbage' Wilson, the 'richest man in town', a nurseryman who had turned to politics. In 1868 the couple were the first mayor and mayoress of Christchurch.

FOURTEEN TONS AGAINST THE TASMAN

It was an ambitious scheme, thought the more generous among the business community in Sydney and in the newly opened settlement area of Wanganui on New Zealand's North Island; others thought it was just plain daft. But

Elizabeth Yates from
Caithness who as civic
leader in Onehunga,
Auckland, was the
first female mayor in
the British Empire
(1894). (*Alexander
Turnbull Library,
Wellington*)

William Watt from Dundee and his young partner T. B. Taylor were not to
be swayed. They saw a great future in a regular shipping service between
Australia and Wanganui and having served all over the world together as
apprentices with the White Star Line they felt they were up to the task.

It was 1841 and in that part of the world, in those exciting, pioneering
days, anything was possible. Together the Scots bought the tiny 14-ton
schooner *Katherine Johnstone* with which, in the face of scepticism and the
might of the Tasman Sea, they launched their service. Watt took over the
land-based business in North Island while Taylor remained as skipper and
to general delight they brought down their first cargo from Sydney in 1842.
Later they acquired a fleet of little vessels, the *Edward Stanley*, *Governor
Grey*, *Rosebud*, *Seagull* and *Tyne*, with which they developed their service,
always keeping one vessel operating to and from Wellington. Their enterprise
and business acumen is well illustrated by the purchase of their largest vessel,
the brig *Lady Dennison*, bought as a wreck for salvage but which became a
vital part of their fleet. At a crucial time in the development of the region
Watt and Taylor provided a vital lifeline to the outside world. It's no surprise

A panorama of the waterfront at Sydney in 1885, the first view of the new
land for many Scots arrivals. (*St Andrews University Photographic Collection*)

to learn that after his contribution Willie Watt was elected Wanganui's first
mayor in 1872 and in all held the post on five occasions.

Persistence and hard work were also the keynotes in the success story of
Sir James Burns who came from a well-known Edinburgh family to found
a trading empire in Australia. With an elder brother he was in Queensland
by the early 1860s and immediately sought to broaden his experience by
working in the back country. He then began opening stores on the goldfields.
Going into partnership with Robert Philp, Burns made Sydney his new base
and established a shipping line which traded up and down the east coast.
Soon enough this was the Queensland Steam Shipping Company operating
steamer links into the Pacific and the East Indies.

Burns realised the potential of sheep in the development of the Australian
economy and the company also took up pastoral interests. Here was a man
of shrewdness and vision, who although he became a classic Australian
entrepreneur, never forgot his Scottish roots. He was president of the local
Caledonian Society for twenty years and had the Burnside Home for Scottish
Orphans built at Parramatta, near Sydney. Two of his sons were killed in
the Great War but his third son James took over the business.

DON'T MESS WI' BIG AGGIE

Bald Hills, Gippsland, was a rip-roaring Australian frontier town, a wild and violent place at the best of times in the 1860s, so when a spluttering and swaying drunk started to harass and insult a local girl on the sidewalk, most folk just looked the other way. However, on to the scene, across the muddy cart tracks, on this occasion strode a large, powerfully-built bullock driver, whip in hand. According to one correspondent the driver laid into the drunk with the bullwhip without mercy and nearly 'thrashed him sober'. 'You may be as hard as you like but even here in the bush a man should be civil,' the whimpering miner was lectured by the bullock driver. Here we have a classic example of Scotland's very own 'Calamity Jane' in action. One of Australia's few women 'bullockies', Agnes Buntine from Glasgow was also known as the White Mother of the Gippsland district of Victoria where so many Scots settled.

Agnes, although born in Govan, had been living in Mauchline in Ayrshire before immigrating with her parents from Greenock in 1840. Still a teenager she married Kilwinning man Hugh Buntine only a few months after arriving

Glasgow-born Agnes Buntine, bullock-cart driver and pioneer of Victoria, a larger than life character who was also known as the White Mother of Gippsland.
(*Davidson Family*)

in Australia. His first wife and child had died following a typhus outbreak on the *William Rodgers* on the way south. Soon Agnes was showing the qualities needed for a pioneer's spouse: toughness, self-reliance, and a willingness to tackle all the jobs her husband might encounter.

In 1851 the Victoria gold rush prompted Agnes and Hugh to open a haulage business with bullocks, the only pulling power available in the difficult terrain. Her first adventure saw Agnes drive the team to the Bendigo goldfields carrying a ton of cheese and half a ton of butter for the hungry diggers. It was the start of regular journeys between Melbourne and the goldfields. Her husband ran a store at Forrest Creek and, according to her descendants, Agnes operated what was splendidly described as the 'bullock motivated carrying enterprise'. It may be that Hugh – eighteen years her senior – was in poor health and this forced Agnes to take on the bullock driving while he minded the shop. Whatever the reason, she proved a natural. In an age when women generally wore crinolines, bonnets and shawls, Agnes must have cut an impressive figure in the main streets of central Victoria. She wore a cabbage-tree hat, a long kilt over breeches which were tucked into her boots, and a heavy overcoat. As gold fever spread, the Buntines followed in its wake opening stores and the legends of Agnes, or Mother Buntine as the tough miners knew her, began to grow. Most, but not all, correspondents were impressed by this formidable lady, Howitt in *Land, Labour and Gold* related how Agnes rode around the countryside with a pair of pistols in her 'capacious' belt:

> Nothing could exceed her dignity and bulk except it were a Turkish dome or a steam boiler on horseback.

Bushfires were an ever-present danger in summer and one February day in 1863 Agnes was caught in a terrible inferno which later became known as Black Monday. The *Gippsland Times* described how she sought out a clear patch of ground to ride out the fire and when the flames passed the bullocks were singed but alive: Agnes was badly burned, saved only from certain death by her thick clothing and heavy boots. After Hugh's death Agnes continued on the trail until, in her early fifties, she retired and remarried, living out her days at Flynn's Creek where she died in February 1896.

Like thousands of others George Miller of Gretna Green was convinced that by migrating to Australia with his wife and two daughters he would make his fortune, or at very least, a comfortable living. By 1901 the family had settled in Tasmania but the times were hard and George took off for the Kalgoorlie goldfields. Months passed and the family heard nothing from George so, with their daughters in tow, his wife set off on the long and arduous trip to Western Australia. She found Kalgoorlie was a large, bustling boom town. No one seemed to have heard of George and there seemed only the remotest chance of tracking him down. Finally, almost in despair, she was walking the length of the single men's quarters when on a clothes line outside one hut she recognised a flannel handkerchief she has sewn for George before his departure. Inside the hut the family were reunited and eventually returned to Tasmania where George worked in the West Coast mines.

Australia was indeed the land of opportunity, even for the very young. Stuart Baillie, aged only eleven, from Arbroath, was offered a job within minutes of stepping ashore at Port Adelaide. Much discussion followed between the boy's father and the farmer and off north to a new life went Stuart. His father had been reluctant but Stuart had persisted. He recalled:

> I went away in what I stood; my Scotch bonnet perched on my head, my worldly wealth was nil; nonetheless, it was a start.

Wages were four shillings a week and he slept in a slab hut. At first, remembering the tales of fierce natives, there were no doubt some restless nights.

THE TOUGHEST OF CALLINGS

Railway construction work was one of the toughest jobs for the Scots pioneers and since many of them already had experience of the work in the old country they were in great demand. But it was a hazardous calling.

Andrew Scott from Peebles and Jane Laurie, born in Ratho, Midlothian, came to Australia in the 1860s and by 1875 were working on the laying of the rail line between Rockhampton on the Queensland coast and the town of Barcaldine (named by Scots after a castle in the Western Highlands). Flooding hit the region as work continued and the *Capricornia*, the Rockhampton newspaper, reported destitution among the settlers and chaos in the rail work camps. Some people had been without food and fresh water for four days. The newspapers reported:

> There are 45 bullock teams underwater and 20 are loaded with wool. Overflow from the river extends ten miles from side to side.

Jane had been with her husband throughout the flooding but took ill and died the same day the *Capricornia* was reporting the deluge. It is easy to imagine the desperate conditions of the work camp at the best of times but after the downpour it must have been dreadful without fresh water. A few months later, amid all the celebrations of the July 1877 opening of the line, there was ironically a new problem facing the people of central Queensland – drought. Scott family tradition has it that Jane was buried at the work camp site, a lonely spot beside the tracks.

THE CAPTAIN AND MISS C

Maori legend abounds with stories of larger than life characters but the Scots writer and traveller, Miss C. G. Gordon Cumming, holds a special place in the traditions, known to the tribes as the 'man-woman' and noted for her boxing ability. In 1877 she visited the volcanic wonderland around Rotorua and Tarawere in North Island. At the request of her cousin, the Governor of New Zealand Sir Arthur Hamilton Gordon, Captain Gilbert Mair who was the son of the Peterhead-born pioneer of the Bay of Islands was asked to guide this lady through the thermal districts of hot springs and weird lava formations.

In his diaries Gilbert Mair records how at his first meeting with Miss

Bay of Islands on New Zealand's North Island where settlers got their first foothold in the new land in the early 1800s. (*New Zealand Tourism*)

Lava terraces at Rotorua on New Zealand's North Island. Scots were among the
first to see the tourist potential of these spectacular volcanic locations.
(*New Zealand Tourism*)

Gordon Cumming he had been stunned to a find a tall, even massive person,
clad in a large shepherd's coat, vest and short skirt, stout grey hose and a
huge Kilmarnock bunnet adorned with an entire grouse wing. Apparently
the traveller was inclined to speak her mind and was highly critical of the
sulphurous smells and the native inhabitants.

Together the Captain and Miss C. visited the marvellous pink and white
terraces near Te Awairoa (destroyed in a subsequent eruption) and Miss
Gordon Cumming set out to sketch the rock formations unaware that the
Maoris, not being slow in catching on to the benefits of tourism, had a fixed
charge of £5 for photographing or sketching the rock formations, officially
a measure to discourage land grabbers. Mair was called to the lakeside because
of a commotion and found fifty villagers gathered at the foot of a rock
pinnacle where the Scotswoman was seated and the Maori ranger Tamihana
Rangiheuea was climbing upwards towards her. Tam was shouting at her
'No money, no pikitia' but the lady's response, according to Mair was: 'You'll
no' get a bawbee out of me'. The Maori made a grab for her ankle and as
he clambered over the edge she rolled up her sleeve and fetched him a right
uppercut. The ranger staggered and rolled backwards down the slope. From
her rock perch above the fiery Scot shouted:

Come on . . . if there's any more o' your kidney down there, come on up,
I'm just in the mood to take on the lot o' you.

When told that his assailant was merely a Scotswoman, the Maori ranger had responded with a Maori phrase which indicated that she may have been a Scotswomen but she had a punch like a Scotsman.

WEDDED TO SOUTHLAND

A stubborn, independent streak certainly lay close to the surface with some Scots. Witness the leading role of James Alexander Robertson Menzies (b. 1821) from Rannoch in Perthshire in the quest for provincial status for New Zealand's Southland.

After qualifying as a doctor James was in Otago by 1854 and walked to Bluff on the south coast through an area called by the Maoris, Murihiku. He was among the first settlers in the Wyndham district and despite being a retiring individual was persuaded to take up a seat on the Otago legislative council. In this forum he was soon championing the cause of Southland and accusing the town voters in distant Dunedin of leading the southerners by the nose. From merely being a critic Menzies soon emerged as a front man for a separation movement for Murihiku and its creation as a new province. With an act of 1861 this was achieved and Menzies moved into the principal town, Invercargill, where he personally guaranteed the sum needed to allow the new province to proceed with the election of its first council. Without opposition he was chosen as superintendent. The authority, unfortunately, in trying to justify its new-found independence launched into a costly programme of harbour and rail improvements, ventures far beyond its meagre resources. To add to their misfortune gold was discovered at Gabriel's Gully – but just on the Otago side of the new boundary.

Southland stumbled along from one financial crisis to another, council meetings dissolved into slanging matches and it became obvious by the late 1860s that a return to the Otago fold was the only option. Southland as a province ceased to exist in 1870, but the independent streak in the people persists. Biographers have suggested that Menzies would have had a wider impact if he had not been wedded, single-mindedly, to the future of Southland.

It's said that when a moment of crisis is reached an individual often materialises to resolve the situation. For the colony of Victoria in the mid-1850s, for just a fleeting moment, that man was Alexander Thomson. The son of an Aberdeen shipowner, he sailed to Tasmania in 1825 as a surgeon on a convict ship, made several voyages then decided to settle there. Operating two small coastal steamers he became interested in the colonisation of Port Phillip (Melbourne) across the Bass Strait and in 1835 sent across the first cattle. The following year he crossed with his wife and daughter to serve as settlement medical officer. He had land on the site of present-day Geelong and exploring the locality he expanded his land holding until in 1846 he had around 150,000 acres. He is said to have driven the first bullock cart to Melbourne despite hostility from the local Aborigines.

His contribution in getting Victoria off the ground included his willingness to make cash advances on wool. By 1849, with a population of 8,000, Geelong had its first mayor – Alexander Thomson. He was also prominent in the movement for the separation of Victoria from New South Wales, refusing to attend meetings in Sydney even when elected to the legislative council. By 1851 Victoria was a colony in its own right but always on its guard in case its rights were eroded. Seeking information about the Australian Colonies Bills, Thomson went to London. When he got there he discovered that there had been a change of minister and Lord John Russell, who had been put in charge of the Colonial Office, had gone to Vienna for a conference. Undaunted, Thomson followed him to Austria, persuaded his officials to allow him an interview and was able to return to Australia with the assurance that there would be a separate consititution bill for the colony of Victoria. In his later years Alex and his old horse Creamy were a familiar sight around Geelong. Because of financial problems he had to accept the post of medical officer at a boys' home to make ends meet. He died at Geelong in 1866.

William Westgarth (b. Edinburgh, 1815) also played an important part in the separation movement in Victoria. In 1840 when he arrived in Melbourne the town had only some 3,000 inhabitants and Aborigine tribes held *corrobees*

The vineyards of the Hunter Valley, one of the early areas of New South Wales settlement to the north of Sydney. (*Australia Tourist Commission*)

Sunrise, 29 April 1864, and General Duncan Cameron is pictured (leaning with
his back on the cannon wheel) with officers and men from the Royal Artillery
as they prepare for the attack at Gate Pa during the Maori Wars.
(*Turnbull Library, Wellington*)

or get-togethers attended by many hundreds of tribespeople in the middle of
what is now the city's business district. Among Westgarth's contributions
to the separation debate was the interesting suggestion that the best way of
drawing the New South Wales/Victoria border was to read the hooftracks
of the bullocks – where the herds moved generally south, this land should
be included in Victoria; where they moved north, this land should be retained
by New South Wales.

Perthshire's Ann Robertson (b. 1825) came to the Bay of Plenty district
of New Zealand with her husband who, as a police officer, was involved in
the Maori Wars. In fact Ann gave birth to her fourth child Helen at the
redoubt during the Battle of Gate Pa. However, she is best remembered as
a pioneer of the tourist trade at Tauranga where she and her son Ted ran
Robertson's Boarding House from the early 1870s.

They moved on to Rotorua and again led the way in the hospitality trade.
Ann was involved in a long-running legal battle over the disputed ownership
of a hotel which saw her forcibly evicted by a group of Maori women and
her bakery attacked by a mob. This prompted Ann to walk hundreds of
miles to Wellington to protest about an Act which threatened to take away
all her rights. Eventually her claims were recognised and she received compensation.

John Tinline from Jedburgh was one of the *Bengal Merchant* pioneers of

1839 who set up business in Wellington but was almost ruined by a disastrous fire. He then began to concentrate his interests across the Cook Strait at the town of Nelson. An adventurous type, Tinline rode his own horse at early race meetings and was never happier than when exploring the interior; a river in the Richmond Range was named after him. Although he pushed for extensions of the rail network and telegraph lines into the area, he was also responsible for planting willow cuttings from St Helena in north Canterbury.

SCOTSWOMEN SHOW THE WAY

The achievements of immigrant Scotswomen in the Antipodes have been just as great as that of their menfolk when you consider that for a century or more they were seen as mere camp-followers to the dominant male. Reading the national (and family) histories it is quite clear that the women provided the steel which saw significant numbers of Scots families through the toughest times. And when women began to assert their rights politically and socially the Scotswomen in Australia and New Zealand were in the vanguard.

Louisa Dalrymple arrived from Scotland in 1853 and had an important and early role in setting up the Girls High School in Otago, a model for others throughout the country. Louisa almost single-handedly persuaded the authorities that when the University of New Zealand opened it should be available, without any restriction, to women as well as men. Her success in this campaign was confirmed when the first degree to a woman in the British Empire was awarded – by the University of New Zealand.

Prohibition and rights for women were familiar battle cries around the world in the second half of the 19th century. In New Zealand the Women's Christian Temperance Society – with its roots in the United States – had a group of Scotswomen among its pioneers.

Kate Sheppard was born on Islay in 1848 and is considered the foremost advocate of women's suffrage in New Zealand history. A feminist long before it became a trendy stance, Kate was responsible for much of the crusading journalism in the women's cause and having achieved the vote in 1893, she turned her attention to running women's groups throughout the country. Though Kate died in 1934 only months after the election of the first woman to the New Zealand parliament, she is still remembered on the country's ten-dollar bill.

Teacher and poet Jessie Mackay was the daughter of a Highlander who had migrated to Canterbury. As a close friend of Kate Sheppard, she worked for social justice and reform throughout her life.

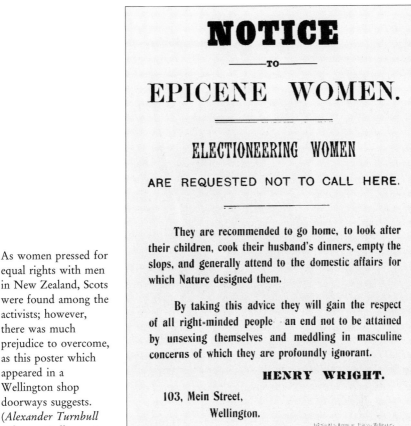

NOTICE

——TO——

EPICENE WOMEN.

ELECTIONEERING WOMEN

ARE REQUESTED NOT TO CALL HERE.

They are recommended to go home, to look after their children, cook their husband's dinners, empty the slops, and generally attend to the domestic affairs for which Nature designed them.

By taking this advice they will gain the respect of all right-minded people — an end not to be attained by unsexing themselves and meddling in masculine concerns of which they are profoundly ignorant.

HENRY WRIGHT.

103, Mein Street,
    Wellington.

As women pressed for equal rights with men in New Zealand, Scots were found among the activists; however, there was much prejudice to overcome, as this poster which appeared in a Wellington shop doorways suggests. (*Alexander Turnbull Library, Wellington*)

NO ESCAPING SUCCESS

Many motives are encountered for taking the immigration trail but one of the more unusual concerns William Gunn from Halkirk in Caithness. The dramatic escape of two prisoners from his custody was the spark which sent PC Gunn to the goldfields of Victoria in 1853. In search of a fresh start he left behind his wife Cecilia and three children to seek his fortune.

After panning for gold at Rushworth, Gunn gained experience in sheep farming and took the lease of a large grazing property near the town of Murchison. With the help of thirteen Chinese shepherds he developed his farm and by 1857 his wife was able to join him driving, as so many did, from the coast to their new home in a bullock dray. She brought William Jnr, leaving her two daughters behind to complete their education. William's clouded departure from Caithness was forgotten as he established himself as a pastoralist at his farm known as Waranga Park. Rehabilitation was complete when he was appointed a justice of the peace for the district, and

William Gunn (1804–1888) from Halkirk in Caithness who immigrated in 1853 and became a successful pastoralist at Waranga Park near Rushworth (VA) where he employed thirteen Chinese shepherds. (*Edith Christoe, Victoria*)

in time-honoured colonial tradition he had a local landmark named after him although on this occasion it is one of the least glamorous which we've encountered – near the homestead a piece of marshy ground (now a reservoir) was nicknamed Gunn's Swamp.

The power of advertising was a concept which Duncan Waterson took with him to New Zealand in 1909 when he left Glasgow in a quest for Waterson relatives Down Under. Home furnishing and funeral undertaking was his business but his search for a place to settle was interrupted by World War I in which he served with the Auckland Infantry Regiment.

For a time Duncan was employed by Governor-General Lord Jellicoe at Government House as a cabinetmaker before moving to Matamata (WO) to found his furniture and cabinetmaking business. Duncan or 'Don' as he was known in the town bought the community's first motor cars in 1923 and maintained his interest in Scots affairs, being the first chieftain of the Caledonian Society and a great devotee of rugby and football. His firm belief in the medium of advertising is shown by the stories of how he was often seen in the outlying districts of Matamata, stopping his car at a strategic corner and producing hammer, nails and spade from the boot of the car, swiftly erecting a brightly painted hoarding advertising his business and making a swift exit. Planning permission – what exactly is that?

Alexander Duthie immigrated from Shetland to New Zealand in 1927, selling his fishing boat to help fund the great journey. In his adopted country, as well as continuing fishing, he served as skipper of the marine research vessel *Ikatere* between the World Wars and conducted the first organised scientific research into the breeding of fish, particularly the famous 'snapper' or bream. Alec's was a well-kent face along the Auckland waterfront.

THE LONG AND WINDING TRAIL

When the MacDonald family left Cromarty for New South Wales in the 1830s they surely did not expect to write themselves into the history books as the organisers of the longest-ever overland cattle drive. This took them from one end of Australia to another and lasted an incredible *three years*!

Arriving at Goulburn (NSW) in 1838 they built up their property and though the sons roamed far and near, droving, shearing and prospecting, they remained a close family. When Donald MacDonald learned of the vast open spaces of northwest Australia he approached his McKenzie relations and put to them the quite stunning proposal that they should secure leases of vast blocks in the Kimberleys and together they should overland the cattle right to the new territories. They calculated this might take two years. Planning got under way.

The great expedition began in March 1883 with 670 head of cattle, forty-six bullocks, sixty horses and two bullock wagons filled with equipment and provisions, everything from dried fruit to nuts and bolts. Swollen rivers had to be forded, and yet as they moved into southwest Queensland they found the place in the grip of a drought. Local property owners did not want the itinerant herd on their land and native attacks were happening regularly. Other difficulties included having to pay an unexpected tax on every beast at the Queensland border. Water, or the lack of it, was the main problem and they even chased thunderstorms in the hope of catching a downpour. Descendant Charles MacDonald, writing of this stage in the drive, paints a vivid picture of conditions:

Often no water was found . . . Tongues swollen, eyes red and squinted against dust and glare, leaving dying cattle behind for the ever present eager natives, the shimmering mirage tormenting them in this nightmare simulation of hell.

Imagine then the elation when the rains came. They had been static for three months. Other 'mobs' of cattle were heading for the Kimberleys and there were fresh problems on the so-called 'Gulf Road' with pleurisy caused by an abundance of young spring grass.

The rivers to ford now had the added hazard of crocodiles, and the natives were more aggressive. But they were making progress, slow progress. Throughout the epic trek crew had come and gone but it was Willie Mac-Donald who was left to finish the drive and he records in a matter-of-fact way: 'I arrived here June 1886 and called it Fossil.' With him were 370 head of cattle and thirteen horses. The station was managed by Charles and William MacDonald until their deaths in 1903 and 1910 respectively. This expedition ranks alongside any of the great treks of the American West.

It is an indication of the hardiness of the Scots who made the passage south that even after reaching Australia and New Zealand they were prepared to set off on such epic hikes, journeys which people today would find tough beyond endurance, simply to find a new home.

James Stirling from Lamlash on the Isle of Arran travelled out to Australia on the same immigrant ship (the barque *Indus* which sailed from Dundee) as the great explorer John McDouall Stuart – first man to cross Australia south to north, you'll remember. Some of Stuart's sense of adventure must surely have rubbed off and the men remained friends all their lives.

For a few years Stirling remained with his family near the town of Nairne but decided that the Port Lincoln district on the Eyre Peninsula would offer greater opportunities. With scarcely a second thought he set off around the head of Spencer Gulf with his wife, three children and 1,800 sheep on a journey that was the equivalent of a trek between London and Aberdeen. On route they passed through almost unknown country with hostile Aborigines and uncertain water supplies. They were also joined by other westward travellers for a time but they parted again because James Stirling, the cautious Scot, insisted on hugging the coastline. The party which headed for the interior was never seen again, apparently a common occurrence on the Eyre Peninsula in the 1840s and 50s. Also in the group by this time were two convicts who threw in their lot with the trekking party and whenever a camp was formed and the Aborigines came near the sheep the convicts went out with muzzle-loading guns and chased them off. Eventually the Stirlings settled near Port Lincoln at the homestead which they called Green-patch.

TAMING THE BUSH

Group settlement was a feature of life in the vast, undeveloped areas of Western Australia in the 1920s. This was the experience of Maggie and Alex Clark from Forres in Morayshire. In May 1925 Alex Clark arrived in Fremantle. His wife and child, all on assisted passage, were to follow in six months after he had shared in the backbreaking and dangerous work of forest clearance. Along with Bill Read and Herby Shilling, Alex was allocated Block 85 at Cowamarup, right down on the southwestern tip of Australia. In his diary Alex notes that he was met by an Aberdonian, which must have been some consolation in such an unfamiliar setting.

Their journey to the settlement was not an inspiring one, the horses having to drag the cart through feet-deep bogs on the roughest of rough tracks. At the encampment were over forty settlers living in 'humpys' or improvised huts who were paid three dollars weekly sustenance with every second Saturday off. Clearing the timber was a day-by-day task and Alex's first memory is of boring and blasting the timber with gelignite, lighting the fuses in twenty-five charged trees with a glowing nine-inch Banksia fir cone which lasted through a full day's work. The trees were dragged away by steam traction engines.

Then the big day came for the balloting of blocks. People moved on to

A riverbank humpy which was often the first home for Scots settlers in the Australian bush. (*Ron Michael, Greater Shepparton City Council, Victoria*)

their sites and Alex secured a ploughing job with a four-horse team 'simply because at that time I was the only one who knew which end kicked'. Many of the settlers had been city dwellers. To get nearer the creek in order to guarantee water supply Alex moved his humpy. When a letter reached Forres explaining this move Maggie became extremely anxious about the mobile house, wondering just what she had let herself in for.

Christmas 1925 saw the arrival of the families at Perth (WA) and for ten years the Clarks developed their little dairy farm until the Depression forced them off the land and into the city, like so many others. Edna Carruthers, the eldest of their children, remembers the hard times in settling on the land and accepting the inevitable return to city life. Of her parents she says:

> You would never hear them complain, no matter the difficulties. They simply accepted it as part of their lot.

Chapter Ten
Whores and Hard Cases

WHISPER IT – but among the sober, industrious and upright legions of the Scots diaspora (Australia/New Zealand Division), there were some rank badjins; rogues and villains we would rather consign to the scrapheap of history but who hold our interest, nonetheless.

Most accurate estimates suggest that around 9,000 Scots were transported to Australia during the years 1787 to 1868 when the great continent served as a penal colony in the aftermath of the loss of the American colonies. In fact, during the first twelve years of Botany Bay only seventy Scots had been received and it was the mid-1820s before that total approached 1,000.

Historians tell us that there was another reason for the establishment of the penal colony and that was to get a foothold in the Antipodes and counteract increasing French activity in the area. However, the prisoners who made that often horrendous voyage to the other end of the earth were little concerned about the politics of it all – their first target was simply to survive to see Botany Bay.

Proportionately there were far fewer Scots than English and Irish among the transportees simply because Scotland's distinctive legal system less often imposed the death penalty and transportation. It is therefore likely that most Scots who found themselves in the convict ships would have a string of previous convictions, the women were often prostitutes, the men generally hardened criminals.

HEADING SOUTH IN CHAINS

A list of some of the earliest transportees, the bulk of whom came from the densely populated Central Lowlands, gives an idea of the sort of calibre of

Scot we lost to the Australian penal colony. They include George Black, burglar (banished 1811 from Glasgow); Hugh Allan, vagrant (banished for seven years in 1793); Margaret Brown with her many aliases, vagrant and fortune teller (banished, 1793); Charles Cameron, butcher/sheep stealer (transported for fourteen years from Inverness); Janet Catenach, a Braemar thief (seven years); Janet Hislop, for assisting an escapee (seven years); and Margaret Scott, prostitute and thief (transported 1833 from Perth).

There were two important groups of Scots 'political' prisoners, untarnished by previous criminal record but sent from Scotland because of their subversive beliefs or revolutionary politics. First were the so-called Scottish Martyrs, arriving in 1794, the best-known of whom was the advocate Thomas Muir; and secondly there were the Scottish Radicals of 1820, who had taken part in a weavers' revolt which saw three of their number hanged. The

Woodcut on a linen handkercheif from 1793 decorated with portraits of the
Scottish Martyrs and a view of Botany Bay.
(*Mitchell Library, State Library of New South Wales, Sydney*)

nineteen transported Radicals were by and large skilled tradesmen, well educated and active Christians. In this case Scotland's loss was very much Australia's gain because these men brought much to the development of the nation that became their home.

Scots were often in charge of the convict outposts such as Norfolk Island, Hunter River (later Newcastle) and Moreton Bay (Brisbane). Norfolk Island is an isolated dot in the Pacific Ocean most noted for having been settled by the descendants of the *Bounty* crew. It was discovered by James Cook and served as a penal settlement during the first half of the 19th century. During its final years as a prison island it witnessed some of the worst brutalities of the convict system.

Two Scots have a prominent connection with this forbidding place. John Piper from Maybole in Ayrshire had a sixteen-year link with Norfolk Island, firstly as an officer and latterly as acting commandant. He was credited with being a fairly benevolent overseer, certainly in comparison with the later commanders. Alexander Maconochie from Edinburgh arrived in Tasmania in 1837 as secretary to Sir John Franklin and wrote vigorously against the prevailing convict system. He gained many enemies who must have smiled when he was posted to Norfolk Island in 1840 as commander. For four years he put his radical theories on the rehabilitation of prisoners into practice, 'with some success' according to contemporary commentators. As a prison reformer Maconochie was years ahead of his time.

Settlement at the mouth of the Hunter River north of Sydney began as early as 1804 with the economy of the community – eventually to become the town of Newcastle – based on cedar, coal and convicts. It served as the repository for the worst no-hopers among the transported convicts and in command was a Scot, Lieutenant Charles Menzies. With the closure of the penal colony the river valley began to fill up with free settlers and freed convicts. Although there were many Scots along the river it was not as distinctively Caledonian as say the Western District of Victoria, or the southeast of South Australia, or New England (NSW) were to become.

John McIntyre, who settled on the Upper Hunter River, suffered badly from marauding by escaped convicts and the hostility of local Aborigine tribes, which was more than occasionally prompted by precipitate action from the settlers themselves. John was by any definition a hard man, known to be swift in retribution and generally described as mean and tyrannical. In one instance after an Aborigine had taken some corn from the plantation he was caught and strung up from a tree with a corn cob jammed in his mouth.

According to Dr A. K. Johnston, hanging was regarded with stark horror by some Aborigines who, unlike the whites, had not become hardened to the idea of lynch law. The native people of the district schemed their revenge and had a fire ready upon which to toss John McIntyre after waylaying him. As it happens McIntyre was warned and escaped. His violent end was only delayed, however, as he was murdered in the bush in 1830, probably not by Aborigines but by escaped convicts.

WORKING ON THE CHAIN GANG

Overland routes between Sydney and the Hunter River were opened up mostly by fleeing convicts and in this way the first viable road was built over the Mangrove Mountain to Wollombi. It's said that convicts on the work gangs suffered terribly in the conditions during construction.

There was one particularly brutal Scots overseer on this job, a man by the name of John McDougall, himself a freed convict. His cruelty to the men had a sadistic streak and many a prisoner silently swore vengeance. He was later trapped in a hotel by a gang of escaped convicts led by a daring character called 'Jewboy' Davis. In an act of cruel though perhaps understandable revenge, McDougall was tied to a post outside the hotel and the men attacked him in turn with a lash. By the time they had finished, it's said he had no shirt and very little flesh left on his back and for the remainder of his days had difficulty walking.

Still on roads duty, Alex Stuart was the son of a Banffshire crofter who arrived in New Zealand with just half a crown in his pocket then progressed

Tasmania's Port Arthur prison, landfall for many convicts transported Down Under during the 19th century. (*Australian Tourist Commission*)

to owning a 650-acre farm and becoming a Member of Parliament. He was described as a 'rugged individualist', and a man who knew how to use a shovel. In Wanganui he went into partnership with his brother as a road contractor which in the early 1900s was solid, unrelenting toil, even without a cruel overseer. Stuart's workers each had to be able to shovel thirty yards of broken stone for bottoming daily. Alex delighted in competing against his men and was always the fastest shoveller.

Other convict settlements were set up in Tasmania and in Western Australia but South Australia decided against taking convicts and instead used assisted emigration to attract farmers, business folk and tradesmen.

For years it was a kind of stigma to have a convict ancestor, it was not spoken of. However, today, with the burgeoning interest in genealogy, having a transported antecedent, particularly one who travelled with the First Fleet, carries with it a certain kudos, indeed it is almost trendy.

THE YETHOLM THIEF MAKES GOOD

Despite their relatively small numbers the Scots convicts present a few interesting case studies. Arguably the most celebrated and possibly most successful of all freed convict settlers was Andrew Thompson. This Borderer from Yetholm arrived in the *Pitt* in 1792 having been sentenced to fourteen years' transportation for theft at Jedburgh. In 1797 he was pardoned and two years later had put up a granary, bought ships for coastal and international trading and built a salt works and a bridge across the Hawkesbury River. By 1806 he had become the biggest grain grower in the district. He was virtually the right-hand man of Governor Bligh of *Bounty* fame, and when Thompson died in 1810 he was reckoned the wealthiest man in the colony.

Margaret McKinnon from Skye was transported with the First Fleet for torching her neighbour's croft in a fit of jealousy. A Gaelic speaker, Margaret's claim to fame is that she married a German who has come to be regarded as the first free immigrant to Australia.

Among the many other stories of convict settlers who knuckled down, secured their freedom and got on with notable success in building new lives for themselves, the tale of David Gibson who went from convict to capitalist is one of the most remarkable – and that of Bonaw postmaster John Cameron deserves to be better known too.

Gibson, from Perthshire, is said by tradition to have been banished from Scotland for shooting a bull which was eating his barley, but his actual crime was the theft of jewellery in Hull in 1802, for which he was sentenced to death but then reprieved and transported. Within a couple of months of

Transported Scots convict David Gibson who escaped the executioner twice to become one of Tasmania's leading runholders. (*Evandale Historical Society, Tasmania*)

arriving at Port Phillip (Melbourne) he had made a break for freedom (earliest convicts believed China lay just beyond the Blue Mountains behind Sydney) only to return emaciated from his ordeal in the bush but having discovered the Yarra River, which runs through the heart of Melbourne.

When the settlement moved to Tasmania Gibson proved just as troublesome, receiving 300 lashes for absenting himself from public labour in 1806. Two years later, on a much more serious charge of piracy, with seven others Gibson again found himself sentenced to death before once more being reprieved. By 1813 he had been pardoned.

He immediately launched himself into frontier society, acting initially as government storekeeper in Tasmania and state overseer. By this time he also had a 'bidey-in' in the shape of Elizabeth Nichols. Trouble with bushrangers and escaped convicts plagued Gibson's early attempts to build up a flock and a reputation as a solid citizen. Nevertheless, by 1818 he had constructed a large house at Launceston on the north coast. The building was demolished in 1915 but was an elegant home by the standards of the time and place. By 1820 he was married to Elizabeth and on his farms were thousands of sheep and hundreds of cattle. He entertained Governor Lachlan Macquarie during his 1821 visit to Tasmania. As the years went by he acquired many more properties and fathered numerous children, pioneered many agricultural techniques and won the respectability for which he had worked so hard. His status as a farmer and land owner is perhaps best indicated by the fact that he sent wheat to the Paris Exhibition of 1855. David died three years later.

Argyllshire postmaster John Cameron was transported for fourteen years for fraud at the High Court in Inveraray in 1847 and by 1850 he was at Hobart, Tasmania, assigned as a servant. The story of how John met and married another Scots transportee Jane Park has been researched by Jeff Parkes of the Inveraray Jail heritage attraction.

John had been assigned as a clerk to the owner of the *Hobart Guardian* newspaper and Jane, accused of theft from her employer in Musselburgh, eventually was placed in Hobart also. They met, Jane became pregnant and

Pleasant Banks, David Gibson's home in Tasmania where he cast off the 'convict' tag to become a society figure. (*Evandale Historical Society, Tasmania*)

was banished to the community of Bothwell, forty miles north of Hobart, and told to keep away from John. However, the Argyll man was freed just before the baby arrived and they were married. The family grew and the Scots tried to put their convict life behind them, moving to Maitland in New South Wales. Now the descendants of the couple, with the help of Jeff Parkes, are trying to unravel further strands in the story. One possibility is that the Camerons moved to New Zealand where many of the clan, as we've already discovered, had settled.

Non-conformist is probably the best description of Alexander Gammack, a Scot in the English stronghold of Canterbury who seemed to have been sympathetic to the Methodists but when asked his religion on a census form noted that he was a 'Gammackite' and was fined for his cheek.

The early years of the New South Wales colony were unstable and occasionally downright dangerous, with the officer class and leading settlers (usually former military men) like John Macarthur vying for power. When Governor John Hunter from Leith took over in New South Wales he found the military very much in control, the officers making an enormous profit from traffic in spirits.

ANNANDALE'S HARD MAN

On to this dramatic stage as an officer with the First Fleet had come George Johnston from Annandale in Dumfries-shire. He negotiated the tangled politics of the colony to end up governor and is remembered for two historic incidents – the way in which he crushed the Castle Hill convict rising, and for stunning Governor William Bligh by staging a mutiny and throwing him in jail.

Johnston was one of the first officers to receive a land grant (1793) which he called Annandale after his birthplace. On 4 March 1804 hundreds of Irish convicts led by his namesake William Johnston, who had been transported for his part in the Irish rebellion, armed themselves with pikes and rifles and began a march on Sydney swearing vengeance on their Protestant overlords. After covering only a few miles, however, they were confronted at Vinegar Hill by a force under Major Johnston. When the rebel leaders came forward under a flag of truce they were seized and Johnston ordered a charge in which over a dozen convicts were killed; three were later hanged, many flogged and others sent to Coal River (Newcastle), the outstation of the penal colony reserved for the hardest cases.

It was in 1808 that Bligh's opponents, most notably Macarthur, asked Johnston to arrest Bligh because of what they claimed was his overbearing and autocratic style of governorship. Johnston obliged, assumed the title of Lieutenant-Governor and operated for six months as Macarthur's puppet until he was, on Bligh's exoneration, court-martialled and cashiered.

THE SCOUNDREL MACARTHUR

John Macarthur's father had fought for Bonnie Prince Charlie – and John, generally regarded as the founder of Australia's wool industry, was a scrapper in the same mould. He arrived as a young officer in Sydney in 1790 and in the years to follow managed to break three governors, whom history generally rates as honest men trying to do their duty conscientiously.

The ship which brought Macarthur to Australia wasn't even out of Plymouth Harbour before he had challenged the captain to a duel. Eventually Macarthur (1767–1834) became the richest man in New South Wales but his behaviour generally was that of a bully and a power-hungry troublemaker. He was a man who believed he could do no wrong and was merciless in pursuing others who did not fall in line with his way of thinking. Macarthur fought hard to maintain the officers' monopoly in the rum trade and when he wasn't firing off angry and viciously-worded letters complaining about the way the colony was being governed, he was fighting duels and swapping

This stamp pays tribute to John Macarthur, a controversial character and Jacobite descendant, who introduced the Merino breed of sheep to Australia. (*National Philatelic Collection: Australia Post*)

insults. According to one biographer, he could at the same time be charming and viperish.

RUSTLING UP A STORM

Out of gold rush Victoria, Ross-shire's James 'Jock' McKenzie arrived in New Zealand's South Island about 1852, an anti-social sort of buddie who still spoke Gaelic as his first language. He is now something of a legend in south Canterbury, his story familiar to every tour bus driver who enters the district. Jock remains an enigma, however. It is not even certain that the Mackenzie Country where his exploits took place actually bears his name or that of some other clan member. Many McKenzies settled thereabouts.

The official line is that Jock, obliged to stock his block of land within a specific period, went down to the lowlands on a series of sheep stealing missions accompanied by his 'barkless' collie and a bullock. In 1885 when he raided the Levels Station and drove away up to 1,000 sheep he found himself in trouble. John Sidebottom, the station manager, and two Maori guides pursued him into the high country, caught him, trussed him up after sharing a pot of stew then, as the mist rolled in, they settled down for the night. In the dawn's light Jock was found to have scarpered. He went into hiding in a boarding house in the port of Lyttleton near Christchurch, waiting for an outward bound sailing. However, the local constabulary in the shape of Sergeant Seager arrived and Jock was nicked. A few weeks later he began a five-year term with hard labour. However, Jock clearly felt he had been wronged and made several unsuccessful escape attempts, being shot at in the process, and on the final occasion was recaptured by Maori bounty hunters who carried him into Lyttleton trussed and hanging from a pole like a prize hog.

All along McKenzie insisted he had been paid by a man called Mossman to steal the sheep (right enough, £20 had been found in his pocket) and eventually he was pardoned on condition that he left on the first ship out of Lyttleton. His later years are a complete mystery. Daring and dangerous he might have been, bold and honourable, perhaps. One fact is certain. The Ross-shire adventurer has done wonders for the south Canterbury tourist trade.

The founder of the amazing religious community of Zion City near Chicago was John Alexander Dowie from Edinburgh but the Australian connections of this strange and enigmatic man are less well known. In 1860 he was brought to Adelaide by his parents and grew up with an interest in all matters religious. After working in the established churches in Sydney and Melbourne he decided in 1870 to go 'freelance' and as an independent evangelist he was soon holding services in a theatre and claiming healing powers. Coming to Melbourne in the early 1880s, he had attracted sufficient followers and enough financial backing to have his own tabernacle constructed. After a successful tour of New Zealand he looked to the United States and landed at San Francisco, eventually drawing more than 5,000 adherents to his model community, Zion City. The empire crumbled eventually, with Dowie having shown megalomaniacal tendencies.

THE TERRIBLE TWOSOME

Mudie and Larnach were a Scots double-act who operated a regime of tyranny on the Hunter River (NSW) and who were despised by the convict population. Lieutenant James Mudie from Angus (b. 1799) was granted thousands of acres of land in 1822. There he was joined by his farm manager, John Larnach from Caithness, the following year. They were strict disciplinarians and the talk was that Mudie was unbalanced. Their behaviour even prompted a convict uprising.

Serving soldiers, hardened campaigners who opted to stay in Australia after completing their military service and made use of land grants, soon found that the hostile environment and the vagaries of world economics were as formidable as any enemy they had encountered.

Such was the tale of Archibald Innes from the coastal village of Thrumster in Caithness, for whom the barometer seemed set fair. He had joined the British Army in 1813 and was a captain by the time he arrived in Sydney in 1822. He distinguished himself by recapturing convicts in Tasmania. By 1826 he was commandant at Port Macquarie and two years later resigned his commission to become magistrate and police chief at Parramatta. When he became police magistrate at Port Macquarie he was granted 2,500 acres at a place called Lake Innes where he built a homestead. His contract was to supply food for the convicts. He bought up a number of properties including the Furracabad Station in northern New South Wales and changed the property name to Glen Innes, now a town in the heart of a Scottish enclave paradoxically known as New England. Archibald Innes was ruined by the rural depression of the 1840s when wool became valueless and sheep were being boiled down for tallow. The collapse ruined his health and wiped out practically all his assets.

Scots soldier Sir Duncan Cameron, a veteran of the Crimean War, was sent to New Zealand in 1860 to take charge of British forces when the distinctive aroma of war was in the air. His first demand was for more troops and he personally led his soldiers into the Waikato Campaign where he relentlessly carved out military successes at such exotically named locations as Koheroa and Rangriri, Rangiaowhia and Hairini. He continued to lead his troops for the next two years but increasingly found himself embroiled in a debate with the governor over tactics. These disagreements eventually led to Cameron's resignation in 1865.

The influence of the Scots in the services was always a considerable one. Several distinctively Scots volunteer units were formed in New Zealand during the second half of the 19th century and they took part in the Maori Wars. In Australia, the Royal Australian Navy was founded in 1911 by Sir William Cresswell and Major General William Bridges, first commander of the Australian Infantry Force in World War I, who was born in Greenock in 1861. He served in the South African War and headed the Australian military college before being fatally wounded at Gallipoli.

Many Australian-Scots served in the Royal Air Force and its predecessor, the Royal Flying Corps. Robert Logan from Berwickshire, as a colonel, commanded the expeditionary force which captured German Samoa where he was to become territorial administrator. Today Scottish pipe band music remains a prerequisite for Anzac Day parades.

In New Zealand Murry Urquhart from Glasgow, who arrived in Taranaki in the 1890s, had a remarkable record of military service which saw him take part in the Boer War around the turn of the century and both World Wars before retiring as a Lieutenant-Colonel in the New Zealand Army. The Premier of Victoria J. G. B. McDonald, an immigrant to Shepparton with his widowed mother, falsified his age and volunteered with many settlers to join the Australian forces in the Great War.

THE MISSING YEARS

There are many wartime stories of simple heroism and loss bravely borne but the two-year disappearance of Jim Bennie from Western Australia remains a riddle to this day. The Bennie family came from Dunfermline to Western Australia initially to try their luck on the land. Jim Bennie was born in Bunbury in 1893 and was in at the start of Australian involvement in World War I, seeing action on the Gallipoli peninsula before transferring to France with the 51st Battalion. On 16 August they had moved into a German trench taken shortly before by the Black Watch. In heavy shelling which killed two of his mates, Jim was badly injured and buried. Dug out and taken along the trench he was buried again by a second shell which exploded close by. This time he dug himself out. A traumatic experience, for sure.

Sent to England to recuperate he had a visit from his younger brother who was a cook in another unit of the Australian army and at this point both his diary entries and his army records ceased. He had vanished. Two

Jim Bennie, from a Scots immigrant family to Western Australia. He went missing for two years, possibly in Scotland, after being wounded in the trenches during World War I. (*Bill Bennie, Western Australia*)

years and three months later he was found wandering around London, still in his uniform. He had no explanation for the missing years and was assumed to be shell-shocked. His son, Bill Bennie of Kalamunda (WA), has spent years puzzling over the mystery. The most substantial clue was the fact that in his diary was a list of addresses for single young ladies in the Glasgow area.

Bill Bennie wonders if his dad had had a gutful of this foreign war that had no connection with his own folks at home; did brother Bob encourage him to take a train ride north; did he meet and fall in love with one of the girls on the list; did he perhaps even marry; was he indeed shell-shocked, suffering complete memory loss? Back in Australia he waited until he was forty to marry. A guilty conscience? Bill Bennie believes the tantalising mystery of those missing months may yet be solved eighty years on.

Expatriates and Scots descendants, from field general to foot soldiers, fought with great valour in the two World Wars under the Anzac standard but the story of Duncan McCormack from Troon in Ayrshire, who came to Auckland in 1913 as a confirmed socialist, tells of a very special stamp of bravery. On the outbreak of the Great War Duncan espoused the philosophy of socialist pacificism – he had decided he had no quarrel with the ordinary people of Germany. He would not go to war. To go 10,000 miles to fight an enemy could never be construed as simply defending hearth and home.

Although Duncan was a Sunday school teacher and subscribed to the Christian tenet of 'loving thy neighbour', he and the other conscientious objectors were abandoned by the Church. Compulsory conscription was introduced in 1916 and Duncan, having been given a few minutes to gather together his gear, was marched off to jail through the streets of Auckland. He remembered a group of building workers cheering him as he went.

After close questioning Duncan was lodged up and down the country both in military prisons and prison camps, including the grim Terrace Jail in Wellington. It was there that he met another Scot and future Prime Minister Peter Fraser, who had spoken out against conscription. Years later they met again and Fraser's embarrassment over their shared experience had been quite apparent to Duncan.

After serving two years he was released from military barracks (the objectors were still technically soldiers) with the sum total of a half-penny per day prison pay. Outside Duncan found no animosity because of his stand, in fact one man expressed the view that he'd wished he'd had the courage to refuse to fight. Between the Wars Duncan came to realise, he later told his family, that there were different kinds of wars, some of which – the struggles for freedom such as Scotland underwent – were perhaps more easily justified. However, he died in 1988 at the age of ninety-five convinced that the millions killed in the Great War had been lost in a conflict fought to redistribute the spoils of colonialism.

Pocket anecdotes which help illustrate tough Scots are plentiful. Fifer David Drummond, who settled on the edge of the forests of Nelson in 1842, is reported to have sliced his nose down the middle with a bill hook while trimming a vine. Hardy Davie bound it with his lunch cloth and, bloodied but unbowed, went pig shooting that same afternoon.

The first pistol duel in Australia took place between Scottish surgeons Colin White from Musselburgh and William Balmain of Balhepburn, Perthshire (who has a district of Sydney named after him). They had arrived in Sydney with the First Fleet and after a series of quarrels agreed, as officers and gentlemen, to give each other satisfaction on the field of honour. In the duel which took place on 3 August 1788 both men were slightly injured.

A Scot also figured, according to reports, in perhaps the last duel fought in Australia, in 1851. It involved Stirlingshire's famous surveyor Sir Thomas Mitchell. He was actually rather too near pension age to be taking part in duels – Mitchell was fifty-nine – but he survived to retirement.

In the Inverell district of New South Wales legend has it that two Scots, Viviers and Campbell, arrived simultaneously at one of the best unoccupied runs in the area. Neither was prepared to move on, so a square-go was arranged from which Campbell emerged the victor, taking the territory. Viviers moved on to King's Plains where he successfully settled.

Some Scots migrants seemed destined to fail no matter how tough they proved. Andrew Hamilton Hume was employed as superintendent of convicts at Woolwich in London and had impressed the colonial authorities with his knowledge of farming. He applied for the post of one of the nine superintendents at Sydney Cove and by 1790 found himself in Australia. First of all his ship had been wrecked off the Cape of Good Hope and as soon as he reached New South Wales he was sent to oversee flax processing at the austere Norfolk Island prison settlement. Returning to Sydney he was accused of embezzlement and rape but acquitted. It was left to his son, Hamilton, to bring some pride and honour back to the family name. In the heyday of Australian exploration he walked from Sydney Cove to Port Phillip (Melbourne) and back.

Of all the 'firsts' which Scots claimed in the exploration and development of Australia and New Zealand one of the most unlikely was made by George Dorward from Edzell in Angus (b. 1842), one of fifteen children who came to South Australia via South Africa. George claimed the 'distinction' of having organised the first strike in South Australia over shearing rates of pay. He was working as a farm-hand near Koppio, refusing to commence shearing at the rate offered. He was followed out in sympathy by three more shearers. After going on strike he undertook road and fencing work and rented a small farm, earning a living later as an auctioneer. Despite his militant background, George ended up a respected figure in the community, a JP and a member of Port Lincoln district council, although his life was forever changed by the death of his wife and three children in a diphtheria outbreak.

NAE LUCK FOR THE WILD SCOTCHMAN

Bushrangers were Australian highwaymen, originally escaped convicts, who plagued the countryside for half a century. The Irish camp can certainly claim the most notorious member of this bandit clan in tinman Ned Kelly, but Scotland has its very own romantic villain among the ranks.

Scots-born James Alpin McPherson, alias John Bruce, alias Mar, alias Kerr, alias Scotia or Scotchie and generally known as the Wild Scotchman, arrived in Queensland in 1849 as a child. It would be fair also to dub him the unluckiest bushranger in Australian history. During a three-year career he went to New South Wales to join the notorious Hall gang only to find it had been wiped out; discovered that £1,600 he had stolen was in non-negotiable cheques; stole Black Eagle, Queensland's finest racehorse only for it to run away from him in a storm; and evaded police and military in two states only to be finally captured by a group of civilians.

A good student, he ran away from home and began his bushranging career by threatening a sheep foreman, who had underpaid him, with a rifle and then holding up an hotel. Moving to New South Wales he had an odd obsession, a determination to fight a duel with Sir Frederick Pottinger, head of the colony's police force. He did exchange shots with Sir Frederick's party but returned to Queensland and to a routine of robbing the mails and waylaying travellers. McPherson loved fast horses and was, as a result, usually one step ahead of his pursuers. Sympathisers were agreed that he was a fine horseman, a good shot, and a Robin Hood character who lived on Hospital Mountain and dropped into the Star Hotel, Naningo, for a drink with the boys.

After a citizens' arrest by a group of farm-hands he was sent to Sydney to face charges of attacking Sir Frederick; these were dropped when the police chief was killed in an accident on his way to give evidence. Returning to Queensland to face further charges, he slipped his handcuffs at Mackay and escaped only to be quickly recaptured.

The only act of alleged violence held against McPherson had taken place in northern Queensland early in his career while he was operating with a couple of rogues and a hotel owner was shot in the jaw. Acquitted of this charge McPherson was, however, jailed for twenty-five years for armed

A Queensland homestead as portrayed by Stenhousemuir-born artist Harry McVey. (*Betty Markwell, Queensland*)

robbery. Intriguingly, he was freed in 1874 after serving only eight years. It has been suggested that this dramatic cut in his sentence may have been connected with the fact that as a young man he had protected the Attorney-General at a public meeting. On his release he became a stockman and respected member of the community, husband and father of six children. In a life filled with adventure it was somehow fitting that he met his death when a horse fell and rolled on him.

However, it was not only in Queensland that the bushrangers made their presence felt. In fact, apart from the Wild Scotchman, Queensland got off relatively lightly compared with the more densely populated areas such as New South Wales, Victoria and Tasmania. In the latter, for example, one of the most notorious bushrangers was a Scotsman known popularly as 'Captain Melville'.

THIS FAR AND NO FURTHER

There is a telling report of one Scots family's encounter with the bushrangers of Tasmania in the records of the Clyde Company formed in Glasgow in 1836. The Reids – husband, wife and two children – eventually achieved a comfortable life in what was then Van Dieman's Land; but arriving in 1822 on the *Castle Forbes*, comfort and security must have seemed a long way off. They built their hut on the Clyde near the settlement of Bothwell (yes, there were lots of Scots in the vicinity) but in already planning for a more sumptuous lifestyle had even sent to Hobart for a piano, silver plate and furniture.

One night Mrs Reid was giving her children some tuition in the Shorter Catechism, when a gang of bushrangers burst into the hut and started filling bedsheets with the family's possessions. The husband's response on returning next day was to vow that he would not stay in the God-forsaken country one day longer, but Mrs Reid was made of sterner stuff and declared her intention to carve a new life, saying: 'I have come this far and I can go no further.' Mr Reid stayed and put his faith in the Lord, a couple of loaded pistols and a drawn sword which he kept on the bedside chest in case of a return visit by the bushrangers.

A FORTUNE UP A GUM TREE

By the time Gilbert Mair of Peterhead reached New Zealand he was already a seasoned voyager, having worked on his father's trading sloops. To the community of Russell, then known as Kororareka, he came for the first time in 1821, settling there three years later. He was an early trader in kauri gum and shipped a load to the United States where the value of the gum as a base for varnish had quickly become apparent.

Both his sons, Gilbert and William, were born in New Zealand and at an early age had acquired a deep knowledge of the Maori language and people on expeditions with their father to collect gum. Young Gilbert became a surveyor and joined up with the outbreak of the Maori Wars in 1863, taking part in a number of daring escapades including swimming a river at midnight to attack a Maori position, having his horse shot from under him, and leading an attack on the Maori rifle pits. Forced marches and dangerous pursuits through dense bush all confirmed that Mair was a natural-born scrapper. We have, of course, already encountered him as an escort to that formidable traveller and pugilist Miss Gordon Cumming.

It's somehow pleasant to be able to record that, after the hostilities as well being a government agent among the Maori people Gilbert was also native interpreter to the House of Representatives. He had been on such friendly terms with the Arawas during his gum-gathering trips that he was admitted to full membership of the tribe . . . a rare honour for a European. An Arawa native contingent had joined him in the government ranks in the Maori War.

William fought also, was injured in the Wars and like his father and brother was a tough adventurer, having tried the Victoria goldfields before the outbreak of fighting in New Zealand's North Island. He was called to parley with the Maoris because of his understanding of their ways.

It was unlike the Scots to miss an opportunity – war or no war. Baker

William Black from Muiravonside in Stirlingshire had opened his own business in New Plymouth (TI) when war broke out with the Maori tribes. An imaginative Scot, he was able to successfully combine a role of captain in the militia while undertaking contracts to supply the hungry troops with bread.

To the casual observer John Bathgate, a pupil of the High School of Edinburgh, banker and newspaper mogul, was a rational, level-headed member of the Otago business community in the 1860s and 70s. He served in the Scottish company of volunteers as a captain, on various public bodies and won a parliamentary seat for Dunedin City in 1871. In his later years he encouraged many Scots to settle in New Zealand. But it was gold which showed the true colour of the man. As Otago struggled with central government to assert its rights in relation to the South Island goldfields, John went public declaring that he favoured separation, even volunteering to lead the Scottish company and seize the customhouse!

Chapter Eleven
Hail, the Flexible Scot!

L EARNING NEW WAYS, bending with a breeze which might occasionally threaten to flatten you, were skills which the Scots had soon to master in their adopted home. Flexibility and adaptability combined with the previously mentioned steely determination to succeed made the Scots formidable pioneers in many spheres, from songwriting to rugby-scrummaging.

Similarities between the American West and pioneering days in the Australian outback were marked. Alex Scott, whose family immigrated from Midlothian to Queensland, would have been a tough cookie in any setting, a natural-born frontiersman. He would not have been out of place in Dodge City. Alex left his home at Bouldercombe in 1912, aged only thirteen years, and became a stable hand for Cobb & Company, the famous stagecoach company, at their Emerald depot, learning about horses and their awkward ways. After five years he moved on to a station called Mount Cornish where he began his career as one of Queensland's most celebrated breakers of wild horses. His son, Bill Scott, who now lives in Barcaldine (QD), recalls that his dad got off to the most unpromising of starts when he killed the very first horse he tried to break. Despite this early setback he was soon recognised as a master of the art of horse-breaking.

The equivalent of the Wild West rodeo was the Buck-Jumping Riding Show and in 1926 at Muttaburra they could not produce a horse capable of throwing Alex. He was remembered as the only person ever to perform this feat. It was also at Muttaburra that Alex, in truly theatrical style, rode his horse into the bar and ordered a drink. Of course, the upright citizens were having none of this uncouth behaviour and Alex was arrested and called before the local magistrate.

Though born in Australia Alex had grown up in a home environment

Alex Scott, one of Queensland's most celebrated horse-breakers and a man whose Scottish accent landed him in trouble. (*Bill Scott, Queensland*)

where only broad Scots was spoken by the older members of the family and he had always had a beautiful, lilting Scots accent. Unfortunately the magistrate was also Scots and when he heard Alex answering in broad Scots he was convinced that he was being mocked and fined our horseman £50 for contempt of court.

During the late 1930s Alex turned his hand to horse racing and trained many of central Queensland's leading horses in the 1940s and 1950s.

TARTAN MONOPOLY ON ANTHEMS

'Waltzing Matilda' and 'Advance Australia Fair', one the people's song and the other the official national anthem, were both penned by Australian Scots who found no difficulty reconciling their roots in the auld country with a strong sense of patriotism for their new nation.

War correspondent and author of *The Man from Snowy River*, Andrew 'Banjo' Paterson, the bush balladeer, was the son of a grazier from the Scots community in New South Wales. As well as writing extensively he also collected popular songs. The verse 'Waltzing Matilda', which has made him immortal was contained in an otherwise unpromising volume – *Saltbush Bill JP*. The melody was based on an old piano tune which Paterson had heard played by a squatter's daughter.

Peter Dods McCormick was born at Port Glasgow and went to Australia to take up a teaching post. Composed in 1879, 'Advance Australia Fair', McCormick later admitted, had been drafted on a bus on the way home from a concert where a massed choir had sung the anthems of the world's nations. The Scot had felt aggravated that there was 'not a note for Australia'. Peter set things to rights.

As a girl Helen Mitchell charmed the audiences at the Caledonian Society of Melbourne's regular get-togethers with a selection of the old favourite Scots songs. The daughter of an immigrant from Forfar, Helen is better known to the world as Dame Nellie Melba (1861–1931) and is still regarded as one of the 20th century's greatest operatic sopranos.

A CREATIVE PERCH

Maybe there's something in the air of South Australia which brings out the poet in young men from a Scottish background. That can be the only explanation for the cluster of Caledonian poets in the far southeast of the state, an area heavily settled by the Scots.

Adam Lindsay Gordon (1833–1870) committed suicide in Melbourne after learning that he had failed in a bid to inherit the family estates at Esslemont in Aberdeenshire. From a privileged background, Gordon was a friend of prizefighters and horse trainers in his younger days and was despatched to Australia by his father for 'some colonial experience'. After various adventures in the mounted police, he started jotting down rough poems. Subsequently he bought a farm, became interested in politics and maintained his love of horses through steeplechasing. However, poor investments plagued his business life.

Will Ogilvie was inspired by Gordon's ballads and left for Sydney in 1889. As his biographer Margaret Muller tells us, he arrived in a period of nationalistic fervour in the run-up to the Federation of the States in 1901. Ogilvie went to Penola and found the Scots inhabitants of the district so hospitable that it was impossible to get through a day on less than a bottle of whisky! The Scots names – McAdam, McKean and McConnichie – made Ogilvie 'hear the sound of the bagpipes and the gurgle of whisky from a special reserve bottle'.

He contributed poems under the pseudonym of Glenrowan to a number of local papers including the *Border Watch* in which he examined the beauty – and the harshness – of the South Australian landscape. Ogilvie also meditated on the majesty of the horse. Returning to Scotland, he married and lived in Selkirk for the rest of his long life. There is a memorial cairn to his memory on the hill road between Ashkirk and Roberton.

The image of the Scot remains a powerful one within New Zealand society. Witness these cheeky wee adverts for a Wellington off-sales.
(*Thanks to the Robbie Burns Shoppe, Wellington*)

Born in Penola, John Shaw Neilson's father, however, hailed from Stranraer and was himself a published poet. Following the family tradition, Neilson was a keen observer of the bush surroundings. A tough upbringing with poverty a constant companion shaped his view of life and hence his poetry.

If indeed the hard school of life is a prerequisite for writing meaningful poetry then the story of Glasgow's Mary Foott proves the point. Her father had been a Glasgow merchant before the family migrated to Melbourne. Mary married in 1877 and took up land with her husband in southwestern Queensland. Seven hard years saw the early death of her husband through overwork during a fearsome drought and coloured much of her outlook on life but she still retained an optimism about the Australian experience and her part in it:

> But the Past is past – with all its pride –
> And its ways are not our ways.
> We watch the flow of a fresher tide,
> And the dawn of newer days.

Forced off the land by the many difficulties, she settled eventually at Rocklea near Brisbane and launched into a new career in journalism.

From the hallowed halls of the *Airdrie and Coatbridge Advertiser* and *Rutherglen Reformer* journalist John Liddell went to New Zealand in 1881 where, as well as reporting, he found time to write poetry and gathered it together in a volume called *Heather and Fern* in 1901.

Shipbuilding on the Clyde seems an unlikely springboard to a career as a poet but John Barr from Paisley migrated to Otago in 1852 and became a kenspeckle figure around the settlement, eventually living at Water of Leith in Dunedin. He is considered to be Otago's first poet and his particular skill seemed to be writing humorous verses for almost every conceivable social occasion.

Being born to the shipping business does indeed seem to have been something of a passport to literary success for immigrant Scots. James Brown of Irvine went to New Zealand on the foundation of Canterbury College in 1875 to teach classics. He wrote novels and published extensively on the Polynesian people. His wife Helen was the first female M.A. in New Zealand.

Bridge of Weir man William Gay (b. 1865) was starving in London when some friends joined together to help him to a fresh start. Working as a purser on a cruise vessel in New Zealand's fjord country, he was commissioned to write text for a travelling academic. In a life marked by hardship, poverty and illness this proved a turning point. He was appointed to Scotch College in Melbourne and published poetry on a universal theme, also tutoring at a number of homes in Melbourne. Sadly he died aged only thirty-two.

George MacRae from Leith (b. 1833) wrote short stories based on Aboriginal legends after making his home in Melbourne. Skye-born Catherine Martin wrote widely but is remembered in particular for *The Incredible Journey*, the story of an Aboriginal woman's trek across desert country to recover her lost son. It was considered a sympathetic appreciation of the native standpoint.

These artistic Scots could enjoy their fun moments amidst the serious business of settling. *The Mayor's Fancy Ball*, a series of satirical essays poking fun at civic dignitaries who attended the very first fancy dress ball in Australia at Sydney in August 1844, was the work of Aberdeen-born artist and author John Rae, who had arrived in New South Wales five years previously.

SLEEPERS AND SIDES OF BEEF

Traditional skills developed by Scots engineers meant that they were destined to play an important role in the young countries, the immigrant nations, whether it was in the village foundry or in some grandiose plan for a railroad spanning the continent.

John Anderson from Inveresk, Musselburgh, served his apprenticeship as a blacksmith before joining the North British Railway Company at Leith. Although a Presbyterian he came with the Canterbury Association to Christchurch, an Anglican settlement, in 1850 and spent his first night, like so many other newly arrived Scots, with the Deans family at Riccarton. John set up in business as a blacksmith. By 1857 he had opened an engineering plant and foundry and as his family grew so did his business. Soon the company was manufacturing steam boilers and in later years it gained a national reputation for rail and bridge construction.

As you would expect, among the immigrating Scots engineers were many committed to the goal of railway development as the way ahead for land transport. Among them was Perthshire's James Stewart who in the 1870s helped develop the rail network around Auckland and as a private consultant built the Thames and Rotorua railroads. His interest extended to tramways and he was also an inspector of steamers.

Islay, in the Western Isles, is not known as one of the world's great railway centres, nor yet for its many bridges. However, William Blair, a native of the Argyllshire island was an engineer/surveyor responsible as Under Secretary of Works in New Zealand for important sections of lines, viaducts and bridges. David Lennox of Ayr (b. 1788) is recognised as the first notable bridge-builder in Australia, having worked with Thomas Telford before leaving Scotland.

Thomas Brydon from Peebles-shire could rightly claim a unique double in the industrial sphere. Before migrating he was a partner in 'Paraffin' Young's oil company in West Lothian in 1866, while in New Zealand he is considering a founder of the frozen meat and dairy industry, being responsible for the first shipment of frozen meat from New Zealand to London.

In Australia the pioneer of meat preserving was another Scot, James Harrison (1816–1893) from Renton in Dunbartonshire, a journalist and inventor who saw the potential for refrigeration as early as 1850. It was 1873 before he exhibited his fridge at Melbourne confirming that mutton, beef and poultry could be preserved for long periods. In that same year he sent a large shipment of frozen meat to England but technical defects in the freezing chamber led to the meat going bad and Harrison, who had put most of his own cash into the venture, was ruined.

Harrison also launched and edited a number of newspapers and for a time held the editorial chair at the *Age* in Melbourne. After a number of years back in the United Kingdom he returned to Geelong where he died in poverty. Poignantly, over his gravestone was inscribed: 'One soweth, another reapeth'.

Even though the Scots were often at the cutting edge of the developing technology it was not always a comfortable experience. When cars started

The pipeline across the wilderness bringing water to the gold towns of Kalgoorlie and Coolgardie (c. 1902). (*Battye Library, Perth, Western Australia: 3184P*)

to become more widely available in New Zealand the Scots migrants were, naturally, among the first to get behind the wheels. The Adams family of Oamaru in north Otago has a lovely story about Alexander Adams from Portsoy in Banffshire, who came to New Zealand in 1872.

Alex ran a family bakery at Albury and the first vehicle to replace their horse-drawn wagon around 1911 was a large rugged, model from Dodge Bros of Detroit. The dealer drove down from Timaru in Canterbury and an official handover took place with all appropriate ceremony. Auld Alex with his sons and grandsons then embarked on a trial run round the neighbourhood with the senior Adams at the wheel. Everything proceeded smoothly and on returning to the yard the new truck was lined up for the shed entrance but as they cruised inside Alex pulled back on the wheel and shouted 'Whooooah!' Of course, unlike the nags who had pulled the bakery wagon, the Dodge ignored the appeal and continued steadfastly through the rear wooden wall and on to the adjoining property.

During my inquiries in Australia I was delighted to discover that a certain John McCosh Hewitson (no direct relation that I know of) who left Glasgow in the 1860s had, after working on a variety of jobs on the Richmond River, launched a pioneering auto sales business – selling the Model T Ford to northern New South Wales.

ENTER STAGE LEFT, UNEXPECTEDLY

William Begg, born in Edinburgh, became a Shakespearean actor of international standing more or less by chance when in Dunedin (OO) he took over his brother's role in an 1872 amateur production. His brother's fiancée had threatened to break off their engagement if he went ahead with the role of Mr Potter in *Still Waters Run Deep*, so in stepped William and it was immediately clear that he had found his element.

His father – a big man with a leonine head and a voice like rushing wind, apparently – had been a leading figure in the Free Church movement in Scotland and partly because of his father's strong objections to the theatre, and because William thought his name might be open to ridicule, (he feared that some louts might shout 'poor beggar') he changed his name to Walter Bentley. He made his professional debut in Christchurch the following year before removing to London where he became junior lead to the legendary Henry Irving. He toured the world and returned to Australia and New Zealand to find that, despite the Depression, audiences were plentiful. Retiring from the stage he opened a College of Voice Culture in Sydney.

Bentley struggled throughout his life to improve the working conditions of actors and even stood unsuccessfully for parliament representing the Women's National Party – his mother, perhaps surprisingly bearing in mind their strict family background, had been a great advocate of women's rights. On one occasion while playing Rob Roy in Melbourne he was mugged after leaving the theatre but true to the valiant deeds of the hero he was playing on stage he beat off his attackers and, triumphantly carrying one of their hats, reported the assault at the nearest police office.

CEMENT MIXERS AND SEWAGE CARTS

When John Campbell left Greenock for Melbourne in 1874 it was to supervise the construction of a sugar refinery. However, he founded a dynasty which has included engineers, surveyors, a lord mayor of Melbourne and a clerk to the Victoria legislative assembly. We find many such stories.

Aberdeen-born George Fraser established one of the most successful machine-making companies in New Zealand. In this highly skilled business George, who reached Auckland in 1856, was responsible for agricultural equipment, marine engines and gold mining machinery. His obituary describes him as a pioneer industrialist of Auckland and there was scarcely an industry in and around the town which George did not have a hand in developing. During the Maori Wars he earned the capital to expand his business by supplying bakers field ovens for the troops.

It's a little-known fact that early problems of sewage disposal in Wellington fell on the lap of Charles McKirdy, a Rothesay-born engineer and contractor. After marrying at Invercargill (SD) in 1864 he moved north where as well as numerous roading contracts with Wellington city council he also held the infamous and euphemistically titled 'Night Soil Contract'.

There were many problems with sewage disposal in Wellington in the 1870s with almost everyone having their own suggestion as to where the waste should be dropped – usually as far from their own front door as possible. For a period Lyall Bay, where Wellington International Airport stands today, was in vogue. The tidal flats were dangerous and on one occasion the horse and cart became stuck fast; with the tide advancing menacingly, the sewage operative had to swim for shore. The horse (dead, of course) and the cart were washed up in Port Nicholson Bay a week later.

McKirdy went on to build railway lines and bridges and had a finger in many of Wellington's commercial pies in the late 19th and early 20th centuries. He is remembered by railway enthusiasts at the Silverstream Railway Museum on the outskirts of Wellington who have named their station 'McKirdy' in his honour.

CEMENTING THE RELATIONSHIP

Being flexible and adaptable was all very well but equally important was the ability to seize the moment. Again the Scots displayed this ability in good measure.

As Nathaniel Wilson tramped miles across the hills of the Muhurangi Peninsula north of Auckland to take orders for his shoemaking business it's unlikely that he ever thought he would make his fortune from cement. He had arrived in New Zealand from Glasgow in 1842 with his parents and brother, settling near the village of Warkworth. His health forced him to quit the cobbler's trade and he took up farming while at the same time building a kiln to make use of the limestone deposits on the farm. By that time hydraulic lime was in great demand for all sorts of construction work in the growing towns and cities – for harbours, tunnels and city buildings.

In *The Rock and the Sky* Mabbett tells us that by 1878 Nathaniel was sending shiploads of lime to Auckland. New kilns were installed and after much experimentation he began producing Portland cement, relying on the importance of fine grinding to give a quality product. Many problems had to be overcome – when the quality dropped away, adding shell to the product

From itinerant cobbler to cement magnate: Nat Wilson's cement works at Warkworth (AD). (*Rodney District Council*)

restored the high standard; when there was a slump in orders the plant only kept going when the workers agreed to have their wages postponed! By 1893 the plant was producing 100 tons of Portland cement and 100 tons of hydraulic lime weekly. Nathaniel the shoemaker had struck dust that was as good as gold.

MISSING THE CATHEDRAL

When Dunedin's cablecar system finally closed in 1965 an interesting link with Scotland and with the world-famous Market Street in San Francisco disappeared. It is a little known fact that a man called Hallidie, an engineer whose parents came from Dumfries-shire, designed San Francisco's cablecar system after observing the plight of horses which had to drag heavy loads 'halfway to the stars' up Market Street. With its grid system of streets the scheme presented little difficulty to the engineer once the basic principle had been calculated.

At about the same time, around 1880, another engineer from a Scots background, George Smith Duncan of Dunedin, heard about Hallidie's unique system and set about getting together all the reading material he could muster with a view to inaugurating something similar in the principal city of Otago.

The proposal made it off the drawing board but one rather important obstacle lay in the line of his cableway – St Joseph's Roman Catholic

Cathedral, the focus of the Catholic community in Otago. George had to find a way to curve the track around this religious edifice. Finally he came up with the 'pull curve' pulley technique, an intricate combination of drum pulleys easing the cable around beneath the street while still allowing the grippers of the car to maintain their hold. This imaginative solution came to Hallidie's attention in California and during correspondence between the two Scots engineers Hallidie asked for and was given details of the invention.

The Dunedin cablecar system may be no more but outside the cable barn at the top of Market Street, looking out over San Francisco Bay, where the route curves sharply before dropping again to Fisherman's Wharf, George Duncan's masterpiece operates beneath the street to this day.

CREW OF THE BLACK EAGLE

It is a generally accepted fact among those in the know that the greatest cricketer produced by New Zealand up until the 1920s came from a family which left behind industrial Lanarkshire for a new life in Canterbury.

Daniel Reese's father, by the same name, came south in the *Zealandia* in 1862 and after trying his luck on the West Coast goldfields made his home at Christchurch, following his trade as a building contractor. He was responsible for the construction of the Central Post Office.

Young Daniel played cricket in Australia and in England, where he was a friend and team-mate of the immortal W.G. Grace; he also played county cricket and sought work as an engineer. Back in New Zealand Daniel was every Christchurch schoolboy's idol and seemed always to save his best for international matches.

His father also had a sporting claim to fame as a rower of repute and a member of the crew of the legendary Black Eagle which achieved a result at the 1863 New Year's Day regatta at Lyttleton, a result which lives on in rowing folklore.

Daniel Reese Snr had joined a family called Dawson, all expert oarsmen, in the crew of the Black Eagle. In a moment of daring, some said madness, they decided to row their boat round to Lyttleton Harbour from Christchurch. Only a few days in the year was such a risky operation possible because two miles of the journey had to be negotiated in the open sea. This was all safely accomplished, however, and they were on the last leg to Lyttleton when the wind changed direction and swamped the boat, throwing the crew into the water. Daniel, a big strong Scot, took the little coxswain on his back and they all clung to the boat, treading water, until a rescue craft reached them.

Earlier in the day the immigrant sailing ship *Brother's Pride* had arrived from Scotland and anchored in the harbour. Daniel's future bride, from the same part of Lanarkshire, witnessed this drama from the deck of the boat but did not meet Daniel until some time later at a social event in Christchurch.

To complete this exciting day the Black Eagle won the four-oared championship at the regatta and the brave lads carried their boat back over the hill, now undercut by a tunnel, and rowed over to Christchurch victorious.

A BRUSH WITH DESTINY

Scotland's early contribution to art in Australia were few – but significant. The real trailblazer must surely have been Sydney Parkinson, who was the botanical artist on Cook's *Endeavour* expedition.

First professional artist to live and work in Australia was Dumfries-born Thomas Watling. Unfortunately he wasn't there by creative choice – he had been transported in 1792 for forging guinea notes of the Bank of Scotland. His interest was in painting natural history but he also produced landscapes and his collected works depicting the fledgling colony at the end of the 1700s, wildlife, Aborigines and their lifestyle and the views of Sydney, are now housed at the British Museum. Watling was eventually pardoned and returned to Scotland only to be charged with forgery for a second time.

Scots artists were to play their part in the cultural growth of both countries. John and William Gibb, father and son, were both painters, the father being noted for his Clydeside landscapes. Even before reaching New Zealand at the age of fifteen, young William had been studying with his father and went to work in the National Gallery at Melbourne, exhibiting there while still only eighteen years old. Again his forte was landscapes.

David Hutton from Dundee came to Otago in the *Christian McCausland* as a drawing master under the provincial government and established the School of Art in Dunedin where he was principal until his death in 1910. Lerwick-born artist John Irvine specialised in portraits and after settling at Dunedin in 1863 he painted the portraits of many of the province's founding fathers including Dr Burns and William Cargill.

John Mather from Hamilton made his living in Melbourne in the 1880s as a house decorator, painting landscapes in his spare time until he was well-enough known to devote all his time to art. Today his paintings can be found in galleries all across Australia. Harry Kirkwood, a law graduate of Edinburgh University, left Scotland in 1876 to work in an office in Dunedin but within a decade he had made art his life, moving around the country and painting the spectacular New Zealand landscapes. Glasgow painter James Nairn was the first artist in New Zealand to conduct classes for the study of the nude figure in the late 19th century.

Oil painting depicting the Hastie boys, William and Thomas, of Dunedin in
their kilts. The boy's father, Alexander, was an Edinburgh carter who came to
Otago with his wife and nine children on the *Jura* in 1858.
(*Otago Settlers Museum, Dunedin*)

STENHOUSEMUIR'S ARTIST OF THE OUTBACK

In the middle of the Indian Ocean, on his way to a fresh start in Australia,
twelve-year-old Harry McVey from Stenhousemuir was a witness to one of
the most spectacular events of the 20th century. For four nights everyone

'Scotty' – the image of a timeworn Scots immigrant as portrayed by Harry
McVey from Stenhousemuir who settled in Queensland in the early 20th century. (*Betty Markwell*)

on board the immigrant ship *Orantes* bound for Queensland was treated to
a wonderful display of Halley's Comet. It was a memory which stayed with
him all his long life.

The family of nine had only £5 when they made landfall and jobs were
the immediate priority. Harry soon found himself working on a dairy farm
and this was to be the first job in a lifetime on the land. However, the Great
War intervened and Harry served and was wounded in the trenches of France,
where he swore at the mud just as much as the exploding shells. His conclusion was that the war had been a dreadful waste of time and lives.

By the age of twenty-six Harry had saved enough for a farm of his own, concentrating initially on dairy farming then moving on to beef cattle. Between times he had married Ivy and raised four daughters.

Established in the community of Beaudesert, Harry launched into his poetry and painting, the latter being inspired by the opportunity to paint backdrops for the local drama group. Harry would explain that he was only persuaded to do the work after being plied with drink in the bar of Beaudesert's Grand Hotel. Harry's trademark was that he painted on any type of article he could get his hands on. Over the years he adorned frying pans, cowbells, bottles and trays as well as the more orthodox canvases. Many of his pictures reflect the history and development of the Beaudesert district with horse teams, hotels, gum trees, camp fires, bush cottages, friends and family.

THE WIZARD AND THE BIG CHOOKY BURDIE

Novelist Sir Walter Scott was a 19th-century superstar in Australia and New Zealand as he was throughout the English-speaking world. But there is also a tantalising possibility that, with a bit more imagination, he might have pioneered emu farming in the Borders two centuries before big chooky burdies like ostriches began to appear on the Scottish scene.

Such was the hero-worship of the exiled Scots for the Laird of Abbotsford, The Wizard of the North, that his fan mail was of global proportions. One Australian immigrant by the name of Harper threw the great man into a tizzy when he announced his intention to send Scott a brace of black swans, emus or kangaroos. Take your pick, he offered, clearly convinced that the exotic creatures would grace the lawns of Abbotsford. Scott filed the letter and hoped the whole affair would die a death. However, in 1827 the persistent Mr Harper landed in the United Kingdom with a brace of emus in tow. By this time Sir Walter had discovered that these great lumps of birdlife could grow six feet in height and were notorious wanderers. The novelist sensed trouble.

In July of that year Robert Cadell of St Andrews Square in Edinburgh, Scott's publisher, received a letter from the man himself outlining the problem and asking Cadell's advice about this 'great & uncommon scrape' in which he found himself. Scott admitted:

Now I knew no more what an Emu was like than what a phoenix was like but supposed them sort of large parrots . . .

Sir Walter had imagined they might perch in the hall amongst the armour. Now that he knew the scale of the beast he feared their arrival would soon be followed by the whole mob of Melrose. The suggestion was that Mr Harper should be gently advised to offer the emus to the King for housing in the Royal menagerie at the Tower of London or sold at the Exeter Exchange. Either way they never made it as far as Abbotsford.

ENCOUNTERS IN A NATURAL WORLD

Many Scots officials in New South Wales were keen amateur naturalists, if not before they arrived then certainly after they had seen the amazing variety of wildlife and landscape.

To the eldest son of a provost of Wick goes the title of 'Father of Australian Zoology'. Alexander Macleay (b. 1767) went to Australia in middle age as colonial secretary of New South Wales. He had always been intrigued by insects and extended his studies to Australian birdlife, sending specimens back to the Linnean Society in London.

His house at Elizabeth Bay became famed for its rare plants, and visitors were stunned by the ability of this son of Caithness to make the garden flourish in what were considered to be sterile conditions. Macleay might also claim the title of founder of ornamental gardening in the Antipodes. He died in a carriage accident in 1848. His son Sir George Macleay joined an expedition into the interior with his friend Charles Stuart.

The weather often played a significant part in the destiny of many immigrants. Alexander Hunter, a Scots builder, arrived in Auckland in the early 1850s but lost his business in a cyclone. The Ormond family from Aberdeen who bought a small sheep station in Victoria quickly learned of the hazards of a very different climate. In 1851 a bush fire swept across their corner of the state. It passed through Ormond's run and although they were able to save some stock the place was burned out. It looked like their great adventure was at an end. However, the fire proved a blessing in disguise. A large part of the station had been covered with thick scrub. When the rains came the grass sprang up everywhere and Ormond was able to sell the station for a profit and buy better land.

WITH THEIR HEADS IN THE CLOUDS

In a unusual career Sir Thomas Makdougall Brisbane managed to combine the role of Governor of New South Wales in its formative years with a lifelong interest in astronomy. When the Largs-born career soldier was appointed to Sydney he had soon constructed – much to the amazement of the down-to-earth settler community – the first properly equipped Australian observatory, inland at Parramatta. How he found time for stargazing while he was working on land reform and the development of democracy in the colony is anyone's guess but he is known to have kept in regular touch with his two assistants at the observatory and visited as often as was practical.

Brisbane also takes the credit for encouraging groundbreaking expeditions to the north and south which were eventually to lead to the colonisation of both Queensland and Victoria. He was also a forceful advocate of free immigration which he believed would improve the status of the colony.

However, life as governor was not an easy one. Various factions were fighting for control within New South Wales, and Brisbane, a sitting target for complaint, was on one occasion accused of conniving in sending female prisoners to the Emu Plains for immoral purposes – a charge which failed to stand examination by a committee of inquiry. Almost inevitably there were accusations that his passion for astronomy had led to neglect of official duties. Again, these appear to have been without foundation. The consensus seems to have been that New South Wales was fortunate to have such a man at the helm as it moved from penal colony to establishing a broader-based society.

INSECTS IN THE OBSERVATORY

Another stargazer, James Dunlop, a weaver's son from Dalry in Ayrshire, had constructed his own telescope at night while working in a thread factory at Beith during daylight hours. When he was twenty-seven Dunlop made the acquaintance of Sir Thomas and when he went to Sydney in 1821 Dunlop went with him as scientific assistant, working at the Parramatta Observatory. Without any formal training Dunlop had a natural flair for the work and in less than three years had catalogued 7,385 stars. After Brisbane left Australia in 1825 Dunlop also returned to Britain but was appointed superintendent back at Parramatta in April 1831. To his dismay he found the observatory in a derelict state, parts of the ceiling had fallen in and records had been destroyed. After Dunlop had put in much improvement work the building was attacked by white ants and fell into decay. Dunlop died a disappointed man.

WIND OF CHANGE

A New Zealand rugby internationalist, one of the famous All Blacks who was truly larger than life, was Sandy Paterson. He could claim the title of the most eccentric New Zealander ever to pull on the famous black jersey.

Born in 1855 this gentle giant once lifted a cart-horse off the ground outside the Robbie Burns pub in Dunedin – for a bet. Story is that when his adversary refused to cough up the cash Sandy hooked him by the coat to a street light. The great loves of his life were said to be rugby, rabbit hunting and beer. He carried around his stud ferret inside his jacket, as one careless pickpocket found to his cost.

According to Bill Milburn of the *Otago Daily Times*, Sandy's rugby career was almost cut short 'because of his love of tripe and onions and a slack sphincter' and he is possibly the only rugby player formally penalised for flatulence. After a Saturday lunch of his favourite dish washed down by a couple of jugs of beer the scrum became a seriously dangerous place. His team-mates complained and eventually Sandy was forced to choose rugby over his diet.

His debut in representative rugby was like a fairy tale. Drinking on the terracing at Carisbrook with his mates at the 1907 match between Otago and Southland, Sandy was called out of the crowd to lock for the second half when both Otago locks had been injured. He was thereafter a household name and represented New Zealand on several occasions, notably in a tour of Australia in 1910.

OUT OF POLLOKSHAWS

Out of Glasgow's Pollokshaws in 1912 came the Hanlin family who were to make a significant impact on the sporting life of New Zealand. Mother Rachel Hanlin was destined to become one of Otago's special Scots. The Hanlins, with nine children, set up home in the mill town of Mosgiel just outside Dunedin in a house which they called The Shaws. The children variously starred on the Highland dancing circuit, played hockey for Otago, represented their province at soccer and Rachel herself became the first life member of Mosgiel soccer club, founded in 1913 by her son David.

Her grandson Peter Johnstone was captain of the All Blacks in 1949, appointed for the fourth test against the British Lions (which they won) and led the team on their unbeaten tour of Australia in 1951. Two other grandsons played provincial rugby. A granddaughter Nancy was New Zealand shot putt champion. The Hanlin descendants also figured in national basketball and cricket sides. During World War II Nancy and her sister Peggy helped raise funds for the Red Cross by becoming the country's first women rugby players. Into the present day the Hanlin great-grandchildren continue the sporting tradition and have added Australian Rules football, skiing, snow-boarding, baseball, golf, tennis and athletics to their achievements.

The story is told that Rachel while watching a soccer match with her friend Mrs McCloy became so incensed with the referee's handling of the game that, brandishing their umbrellas, they chased the unfortunate official

Glasgow-born Rachel Hanlin waves New Zealand troops, including her nephew
Bill Johnstone, off to war from Dunedin rail station (1942).
(*Nancy Whittlestone, Dunedin*)

Scots descendant Peter Johnstone leads out the All Blacks against the British
Lions in 1950. He captained the side to a 10–8 victory.
(*Nancy Whittlestone, Dunedin*)

from the park. He was last seen sprinting towards the railway station to catch the first train back to Dunedin.

THE CUT OF THEIR JIB

Although rough craft may have been put together by stranded sealers and whalers in the earliest days, historians generally accept that Gilbert Mair, the Peterhead trader who settled at the Bay of Islands in the far north of New Zealand, built the first ship in the country. This was the 60-ton mission schooner the *Herald* which operated between the Bay, Sydney and the Bay of Plenty with the pioneering missionary the Rev. Henry Williams. It was eventually wrecked on the bar at Hokianga harbour.

Shipbuilding skills were exported to both Australia and New Zealand by the early Scots settlers. Around Auckland for instance, we find, by the early 1840s, Henry Niccol, son of a Clyde shipbuilder, at work on his first ship the *Thistle*. Niccol had arrived on the *Jane Gifford* in 1842 in one of the first parties of Scots immigrants. He went on to build a series of splendid vessels for both coastal and international trade. By 1864 he was at North Shore across the water from the city of Auckland, where his first steamer, the 300-ton *Southern Cross*, was on the stocks. Many more steamships and successful racing yachts followed. By 1887 he had built the impressive total of 181 vessels.

Robert Logan from Dumbarton, who had served his time with Steele & Company, Clydeside shipbuilders, was in Auckland by 1874 with his wife and five sons. His move was prompted by a request from his cousin James – already installed in New Zealand – to design and build a steamer called *Eclipse*. Like other colonial ships, *Eclipse* was prefabricated in the United Kingdom and shipped Down Under. By 1878, with three of his sons – Archibald, Robert Jnr and William (the other two having gone into house building) – Robert started his own boatbuilding yard at Devonport on the north side of Auckland harbour. Using the magnificent local kauri timber the Logans built fast racing yachts based on the style of William Fife under whom Logan had studied.

According to Paul Titchener, former mayor of North Shore City and marine historian, the timbers were laid up diagonally, creating a strong, leak-free, ribless hull:

> Eleven keelers Logan built over a century ago are still afloat and sailing –
> a great tribute to the Logan skill.

The Logan boys then branched out on their own in a new yard where they built yachts for the international market. Archibald was the best known and his son Jack built yachts until his death in 1978. The Logan designs have strongly influenced modern yacht construction in New Zealand, says Paul Titchener. Among vessels from the same slipway is *Black Magic*, which won the America's Cup.

Chapter Twelve
Spirit of Adventure

A GROUP of rather shadowy individuals from a Scottish background have been mentioned among the first European 'settlers' in New Zealand. As early as 1809 – just over twenty years after the establishment of the New South Wales penal colony – surveyor George Bruce was adopted by a Maori tribe in Whangoroa (ND), just one of a number of adventurers who, for one reason or another, 'went native'. Also in this category was John Rutherford, who was rescued from the Maoris in 1826, ten years after being captured while landing to take on fresh water. Others who have been listed as early settlers with a Scottish heritage include James Cadell, a sealer who used Stewart Island as his base, whaler John Love in Taranaki, Barnet Burns, a flax trader at Mahia and, of course, Gilbert Mair, probably the first genuine Scots settler.

Of the many 'firsts' which the Scots can claim in Australia, perhaps the most unusual must be the funeral of Forby Sutherland, a crewman on Cook's *Endeavour* who is said to have been the first British subject buried in Australia. Sutherland Point commemorates the burial of Forby, who hailed from the island of Flotta in Orkney's Scapa Flow. In the earliest days of the pioneer communities there was seldom either a cemetery or an undertaker so the family would simply place the body in a rough box and pack it with thatching grass to stop the deceased from rolling around on the way to the burial.

William Scott from Aberdeenshire arrived in New Zealand via Ontario in Canada in 1865. He was determined that his last resting place in the Paterangi Cemetery (WO) should have a fitting memorial and several years before his death he arranged for a huge granite stone to be imported from the quarries of Aberdeen.

WAIPU — SAFE HAVEN AT LAST

Arguably the most romantic story of the Scots pioneers in New Zealand – a tale which is of legendary proportions in the Antipodes and Canada but strangely not as well known in Scotland as it should be – concerns the Highland settlement at Waipu in Northland. This is an adventure with all the ingredients for an epic film, a big screen spectacular in which actual events outstrip the imagination of the scriptwriter.

In the first years of the 19th century Norman McLeod from Assynt in Sutherland joined 400 fellow Highlanders who sailed away from Clearances for a fresh start in Nova Scotia. The year was 1817. By the time the *Frances Ann* had reached Pictou, McLeod, a failed theology student, had been accepted as their minister.

The group settled at St Anns after an abortive attempt to join a Highland colony in Ohio and for thirty years honed their skills in fishing, farming and boatbuilding. Norman McLeod, having finally qualified as a minister in

This historic photograph taken in 1901 shows eight of the original group of settlers who arrived at Waipu (ND) from Nova Scotia in September 1854. Alexander Mackay (*second left, back row*) was first to step ashore when only a teenager. (*Waipu Museum – House of Memories*)

The clipper *Breadalbane* which brought a group of colonists to the Waipu settlement of Nova Scotian Scots in Northland in 1858.
(*Waipu Museum – House of Memories*)

New York, was unchallenged as their leader both in the spiritual and temporal
fields. All breaches of civil and moral law were tried by him.

By 1847, after a series of hard winters, poor harvests and finally a potato
blight, the community was unsettled. A letter from McLeod's son Donald,
a seafaring adventurer, spoke of favourable prospects in South Australia. So
it was that McLeod and his people decided to try again, on the other side
of the world. In 1851 the first group, which included Norman McLeod and
his family, set sail for Adelaide in the vessel *Margaret*, built and equipped
by the Highland folk themselves. But after the arduous sea journey, Adelaide
proved a disaster. The Scots' austere way of life was not suited to the brash
and busy atmosphere of the developing city and three of Norman's sons
died of typhoid fever.

Following in Donald's tracks they moved on to Melbourne where, being
maritime people, they turned down the offer of land in the interior. New
Zealand beckoned. Sir George Grey volunteered to find them a suitable
settlement location and in September 1854, the advance party landed at
Waipu, close to Whangarei. Eventually 47,600 acres were set aside for the
clansfolk, the first settlers having to pay for the land, later arrivals receiving
a land grant.

The Waipu Caledonian Society says that by 1860 there were about 1,000
Gaelic-speaking Nova Scotian Scots living in the Waipu area. Their input to

The Fraser graves in the distinctly Highland settlement of Waipu (ND) where a
large group of Nova Scotian Scots settled in the mid-19th century.
(*Paula Preston, Auckland*)

the development of New Zealand in very specific areas was enormous, despite the close bonds of family and clan. Before 1900, for instance, there were fifty-three Waipu Scots commanding vessels not only around the New Zealand coast but in foreign waters also.

In 1950 a proposal to protect the heritage of the Waipu pioneers by building a museum attracted support from descendants throughout New Zealand and others gave voluntary labour to help in the construction. As well as genealogical records the House of Memories, as it is called, contains many artefacts and records from the earliest days of settlement. The little community still has its Scots kirk and stages an annual Highland gathering.

There is another McLeod story of do-it-yourself immigration which ranks alongside the Waipu saga for sheer enterprise. That ended with the family of Scots descendants establishing a sawmill operation at Helensville, north of Auckland.

These McLeods from the Canadian province of New Brunswick were timber people through and through. When economic conditions worsened in Canada they decided to sell up and sailed around the world to a new home amid the kauri forests of New Zealand's North Island. In 1861 two McLeod families purchased a 257-ton schooner *Sea Gull*, advertised for more passengers and cargo and sailed for Auckland. The journey, including a dreadful storm off Tasmania in which the masts were ripped away, took 173 days. Altogether thirty Canadian-Scots, about to become New Zealand-Canadian-Scots shared in this expedition. Their heritage is easily identified from the passenger lists which included Andersons, McPhersons and a clutch of McLeods. From a diary kept on the voyage it's clear that the skills of the McLeod boys in working with wood came in handy, particularly during the Tasmanian storm when they had to cut away the damaged masts.

THE 'NEW ZEALAND DEATH'

The Waipu colony shows the value of strength in numbers and of co-operative action but the rigours of life in the new lands could occasionally overwhelm the more solitary settlers. Newspapers and local histories are scattered with sad reports of suicides. There are dozens of lonely graves on the Eyre Peninsula (SA), for example. One of these belongs to James Miller, aged forty-six, who died on 7 November 1861. Research has shown that he took strychnine while depressed over a broken love affair with a lass who was still in Scotland. He staggered as far as the Ulney Station but died before the farm-hands could hitch up the bullock cart and summon assistance.

Robert McKenna chose to hang himself in a hut conveniently situated next to the Narrogin Cemetery (WA). A report in the *Narrogin Observer*

Sun-bonneted and dressed in the Sunday best as if for a stroll, early tourists are pictured on the Franz Josef Glacier. Scots helped to open up New Zealand's fjord country to tourism. The blur in the centre of the photograph is a shaggy dog. (*Alec Graham: courtesy of Westland National Park*)

of August 1923 identified McKenna as a forty-two-year-old Scot who had arrived in Australia about three years previously and who had been doing odd jobs around town. Laterally he had been unemployed and local Scots turned out in force at his funeral.

John McRae from Dingwall in Ross-shire (b. 1838) took up land on the Burdekin River in Queensland but the times were hard and he failed to cope. At first when he was found in the paddock it was thought that he had died from a kick from a horse but a revolver was found beneath his body. The grave fell into dereliction but has recently been restored thanks to the local historical society.

The death in 1908 of Robert Bennie of Dunfermline who worked on the railroads but was based in the gold town of Coolgardie (WA) still remains a puzzle. While self-inflicted cyanide poisoning was given as the official cause of death, the family wonder to this day. Bob had returned from work out of town to find his wife had been admitted to the small hospital – they thought Mary Jane had typhoid. The family speculate that to prevent a panic the authorities kept Robert in the dark. It is known that he returned home that night distressed.

Death by drowning was so common in the earliest period of settlement it was called the 'New Zealand Death'. According to the Edinburgh-born mountaineer and surveyor Charlie Douglas, the better you could swim the more likely you were to take chances. Certainly the casualty list from drowning is a long and harrowing one.

James Balfour (1831–1869), a cousin of Robert Louis Stevenson, was born and educated in Edinburgh and went to New Zealand with a reputation as a marine engineer. Perhaps his most famous works were the designs of the Cape Campbell and Farewell Spit lighthouses, landmarks on the fringes of Cook Strait which separates the two main islands and which were familiar to many thousands of immigrants. He was drowned while landing at Oamaru to attend the funeral of another Scot, railway engineer Thomas Paterson who, tragically, had also drowned in the Kakanui River.

Haddington's Peter Hogg, a sub-collector of customs at Port Nicholson (Wellington), moved from region to region within New Zealand as he was promoted, reaching the position of chief collector of revenues in Auckland. With the terrain so difficult to negotiate, sea journeys between settlements were the norm for most of the 19th century. Having clocked up thousands of sea miles in his duties, Hogg was lost in a shipwreck around 1850.

Quinton McKinnon, having served in the French Army against the Prussians, married a Shetlander and came to New Zealand where, in the late 1800s, he could be correctly described as a pioneer of the tourist industry in the wild southwest. Having qualified as a surveyor he was passionate about his mountains and spent years in Otago living in a hut on the shores of Lake Te Anau. He had the contract to carry mail across to the West Coast at Milford but disappeared in the lake. His body was never found although his upturned boat was discovered. It was assumed he had fallen overboard.

Botanist Andrew Sinclair was born in Paisley in 1796. Originally drawn to medicine he was soon in the botanical front line taking part in expeditions to the Americas and by 1841 visited New Zealand. He was still travelling back and forwards between London and Sydney but a chance meeting with Captain Robert Fitzroy changed his life forever.

Fitzroy was on his way to New Zealand to take over the governorship and Sinclair tagged along, having offered to conduct exploration work free of pay. The officer whom Fitzroy had planned on making colonial secretary had suffered wounds during his voyaging in Australia and by the time the party reached the Bay of Islands, Sinclair found himself appointed to the secretaryship. In the following twelve years Sinclair effectively created New Zealand's first civil service before retiring in 1856. Sixty years of age and still active he devoted the remainder of his life to exploration. In the Southern

Alps he had put up at a homestead called Mesopotamia and, setting off one morning to trace a mountain stream to its source, was swept away in the swollen waters and drowned. His grave lies beside the old farmstead and, in the Alps, 7,000-foot Mount Sinclair is a permanent memorial to the man.

Another member of the Sinclair clan, Francis, originally from Prestonpans, and his wife Elizabeth decided to migrate from Stirling to New Zealand in 1840 sailing on the *Blenheim*. The land they bought, as often was the case, was not yet available so they sailed in a whale boat along the coast to Wanganui, stopping to sleep on the shore each night. The family did not settle in Wellington and after constructing a 45-ton schooner, Sinclair set off to explore South Island. In 1843 using his schooner (which he later sold for thirty head of cattle) Sinclair brought the Scots who pioneered the Christchurch area. After establishing a successful dairy business in Canterbury, they then built several schooners and traded between the Banks Peninsula and Wellington. Tragically Sinclair and his son George vanished when their new schooner the *Jessie Millar* was lost at sea with all hands. Elizabeth Sinclair, clearly a formidable adventurer in her own right, then set off across the Pacific, visiting Vancouver Island before settling eventually to a farming life in Hawaii.

Mac's Hotel, opened by native-born Scot John MacDonald in 1864 in Mount Gambier (SA), became one of the district's most famous watering holes. However, John's arrival was touched by a tragedy which is still recalled on the Victoria-South Australian border to this day. Four of his party drowned in the Glenelg River at Nelson when their punt capsized crossing over to South Australia.

BABY AND THE BATHWATER

Unknown to one another, in the year 1912 Isobel Brand from Torphins and Charlie Robertson from Aberdeen both migrated to New Zealand. Soon they met up and were married in 1921. Making their home south of Auckland, near the town of Pukekohe, there were soon three youngsters to be cared for and while they waited for the new house to be built they slept on the site.

One of the children, Belle Avery from Auckland, recalls how one night she and her little brothers Athol and Keith were wakened by their mother. The bedroom was filled with smoke and flames licked at the door. With no water supply and no fire brigade to alert, Isobel and Charlie fought the blaze with the remainder of the tank water then, dressed only in their night clothes, fought their way down a dense bramble-covered bank to collect water from a nearby burn. The children, with nine-year-old Belle in charge, had been left in the T Ford farm truck and could only watch the drama unfold. Belle remembers:

> Fire fighting continued until Charlie and Isobel were exhausted and still it not been completely beaten, Isobel then remembered that she had not emptied the baby's bathwater that evening . . . and it was all that was required to extinguish the last of the flames.

Forgetting to empty the bath was such an omission for the methodical Scots mum that they later agreed it must have been God-given foresight. Next morning the restoration programme began.

STRAIGHT OUT OF THE COMIC BOOKS

Pioneer aviator Sir Ross Smith was brought up very much in the Scottish traditions, his parents having moved from Scotland to South Australia where his father was manager of the Mutooroo Station. He left the hardware company where he had been working to enlist at the start of the Great War and by 1915, after serving at Gallipoli, he was in the Air Force during the Palestinian campaign. There he did bombing and observation work and was given the job of flying Lawrence of Arabia to Sharif Nazier's camp to arrange Arab co-operation.

Almost as soon as the war was over he was involved in some spectacular long-distance flights and in 1919 with his brother Keith he went after the £10,000 prize offered by the Australian government for the first machine manned by native-born Australians to fly from London to Australia. Along the way they met with a series of Boys Own adventurers, even having to ask a group of Indian lancers to help prevent their plane – a Vickers aircraft – from being blown away at Baghdad. In the Dutch East Indies the plane got bogged down on an improvised runway and only with the assistance of an army of locals who laid a 350-yard surface of bamboo mats did they get

Scots descendant Sir Ross Smith was a pioneer of Australian aviation and a World War I pilot, notably in the Middle East. (*National Philatelic Collection: Australia Post*)

Grahamstown, named after a Lanarkshire pioneer of New Zealand's North
Island, seen in its heyday during the Thames gold rush (1875).
(*Alexander Turnbull Library, Wellington*)

under way again. The amazing journey was completed in twenty-eight days.
A round-the-world flight was planned but Ross Smith was killed testing an
amphibious plane in 1922.

Another Scottish contribution to pioneer aviation down under came with
Malcolm McGregor (1896–1930), also a pilot in the Great War, and recognised as the prime mover in organising New Zealand's air mail and passenger
services.

As we've seen, having some feature of the landscape named after you was
a kind of daft settler's dream. It mattered not if it was a rock outcrop, a
bend in the river or mud track or whether it had been invested with a more
colourful Maori or Aborigine name since the dawn of time.

Lanarkshire's Robert Graham went one better. He had a town named
after him. Graham (b. 1820) was the son of a farmer and mine owner and
became a leading light in the development of the Thames goldfield in New
Zealand's North Island. Arriving on the *Jane Gifford* he went into trade
with his brother in Auckland initially but Robert became a potato speculator
and sent cargoes to California where he spent three years. Back in Auckland

he was involved in a variety of development projects, and one of his own pet schemes was opening spa facilities which anticipated the boom in health tourism. His other achievements included laying out the Ellerslie horse racetrack, now situated in the heart of modern Auckland. For five years he was superintendent of Auckland and was a staunch opponent of the ultimately successful moves to relocate the capital to Wellington.

THE GOLDEN THREAD

Although there can be no question that the first spark of Scots colonisation in Australia came with the convict age, it reached a peak in the mid-1800s with the gold rush days. Up until this frenzied period immigration had been progressing in a fairly calm and organised manner but gold mania saw a flood of people from within Australia to Victoria and New South Wales, as well as a legion of immigrants from all over the world anxious to try their fortune at the diggings.

The Scots seemed to gravitate into each other's company in the rowdy camaraderie of the gold rush camps. The fact that many men simply walked off their jobs to follow the golden thread also opened up opportunities for Scots immigrants in less romantic occupations.

Stuart Baillie spent time at the Broken Hill goldfields in New South Wales and gave a vivid description of a lively place, awash with money. He wrote of Sunday morning wrestling matches in the horse yards of the Pig and Whistle Inn and of the busy shooting galleries. He left during a strike in the 1890s when the town was by contrast in a pitiful condition with many half-starving.

Many Scots coal miners headed for Australia, and the first major coal development was pioneered at Newcastle by the Brown brothers, who employed many Scots. A Scot called McLaren, looking for water in central Queensland, came across coal and today the location is one of the largest open cast mines in the world – a place called Blair Athol. The Scots were also found in shale-oil mining and to a lesser extent in copper mining.

In the gold rushes the Scots seem to have fared no better than other ethnic groups and while a few, like J. B. Watson at Bendigo and J. A. Wallace at Rutherglen, made a fortune the majority had enough hard luck stories to fill a library. After the gold rush fever on the Otago fields of New Zealand beginning in 1861 had subsided, Scottish diggers who had arrived via California and Victoria were absorbed into commerce, farming and industry.

The town of Wonthaggi (VA) was planned in 1910 with the opening of a coal mine. Streets were named after politicians of the day, many of whom were Scots. Thus we come across Murray, Cameron, Campbell, McKenzie,

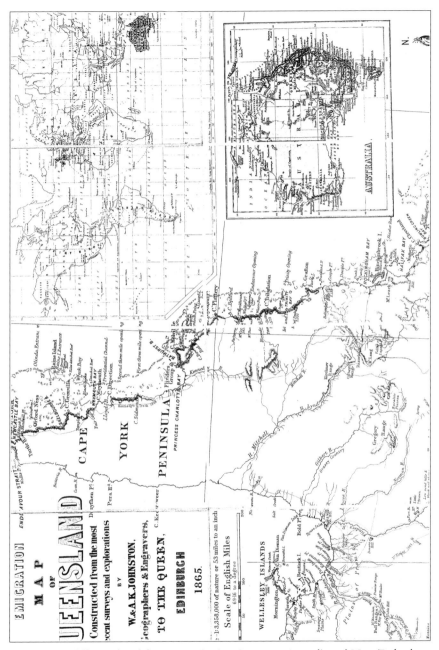

Maps specially produced for prospective immigrants to Australia and New Zealand by the Edinburgh firm of W. & A. K. Johnston – Queensland (1865) above and Auckland (1876), see page 265. Although based on contemporary topographic maps, they also contain a range of additional information of potential value to settlers. (*By permission of the Trustees of the National Library of Scotland*)

An armed escort prepares to leave the Thames goldfield for town – the possibility of the gold shipment being ambushed was ever present.
(*Turnbull Library, Wellington*)

McLeod and Graham Streets. A further Scots connection is found in the
Agnes Chambers Maternity Wing of the Wonthaggi Hospital, named for a
lady from Broxburn in West Lothian who founded and was president of the
first Miners' Women's Association in 1934. The Miners' Union, with Scots
on its executive, set up a committee to feed families of striking miners during
a dispute in 1934 and built a theatre, Co-op store and dispensary.

PROFILE OF A GOLDSEEKER

George Fairweather Moonlight, so it was rumoured in the pioneer community along the Buller River on New Zealand's South Island, was a
foundling discovered in an Aberdeen backstreet on a bright night of pleasant
weather and clear skies. At least so the story went.

Such a romantic pedigree suited the man although the truth is that he was
born in 1832 at Glenbervie near Stonehaven, his name a corruption of the
Angus name Munlichty. Moonlight deserted ship to join the California gold
rush (his cousin was a governor of Wyoming) and he followed the golden
thread to Australia and then to the goldfields of Otago. Here we become
aware of a twist in the tale. Moonlight, it seems, merely enjoyed finding the
gold, something for which he seemed to have an uncanny knack. He never
made a fortune; the thrill was in the exploration. Moonlight Creek near
Queenstown in the far south, and Moonlight Gully on the West Coast bear
testimony to his discoveries. Another Scots goldseeker with a Scots pedigree
described Moonlight as possibly the most intrepid and self-reliant man who

ever trod the soil of New Zealand. Something in the Glenbervie porridge, surely?

Another consequence of Moonlight's search for gold was in the opening up of the country. He is credited with the discovery of many routes through the mountains and is the man largely responsible for the development of the Upper Buller River. In a little twist in the naming game he left creeks which

Glenbervie adventurer and goldseeker Thomas Moonlight who was famed along the Buller River on New Zealand's South Island, pictured with his dog in 1868.
(W.E. Brown Collection, Nelson Provincial Museum)

Moonlight's Commercial Hotel in the gold mining district of Buller.
(Tyree Studio Collection, Nelson Provincial Museum: F255D)

bear the American Indian names of Rappahannock, Shenendoah and Min-nehaha as reminders of the family connection with the States.

Marrying and opening a supply store, Moonlight sent pack teams along the valley to remote outposts. Based in Murchison, at the junction of the Buller and Matakataki Rivers, he bought the Commercial Hotel in 1877 and also operated as the town postmaster. At a stroke Moonlight became first citizen of the little township – postmaster, storekeeper, hotel owner – and unofficial lawman. Despite a disastrous flood which forced rebuilding of the hotel, Moonlight prospered.

Deep in the mountains of the Upper Buller you will find an area called Ataura where some of the biggest gold nuggets found in New Zealand were unearthed, including the 79 oz Pessini nugget. *Ataura* is Maori for Moonlight – a tribute from the native races to an extraordinary man.

When his wife died and the hotel failed Moonlight took to prospecting again to provide for his children and on one of his sorties he disappeared. A search was organised and Moonlight was found dead beside a stream, looking for gold to the last.

At every goldfield location the Scots seem to have realised that the service industries could prove highly profitable with a lot less hard graft and risk.

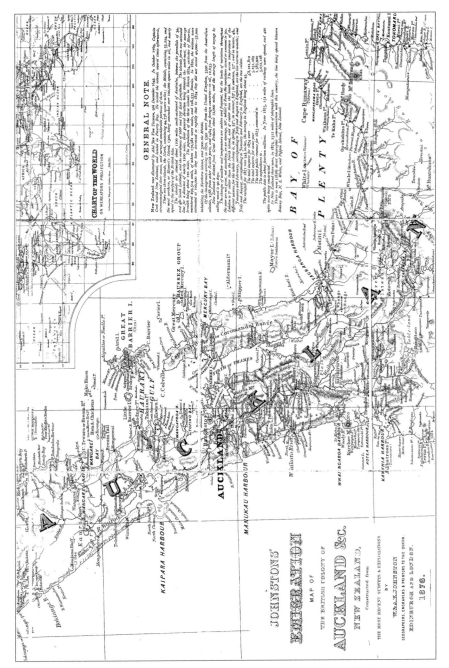

Detail from Johnston of Edinburgh's settler's map of Auckland.

Many supplied food, clothing and mining equipment to the goldfields. Gabriel's Gully in Otago experienced one of the most intense gold fevers and William Murray from Berwickshire was among those making healthy profits selling meat to the hungry miners.

Donald Reid was born at Newton Farm, Strathtay, Perthshire, and was on his way to New Zealand before he was sixteen, determined to be a successful farmer. Harvesting in the summer and cutting hay in the winter he had, within three years, saved enough capital to buy twenty acres south of Dunedin where everything went smoothly until the gold rush. In 1861, right across Otago, in fact right across New Zealand, farm labourers downed tools and headed for the diggings. In view of the difficulty in keeping labour Reid made a pact with his men that if they stayed with him until the summer work was over they would all go in search of gold in the winter months, with Reid promising to provide the transport, equipment and rations. Unlike many other farmers, he kept his workers and, just as importantly, he kept them happy. Reid went on to become a cabinet minister.

The story of Arthur Scoular's arrival in New Zealand has all the characteristics of the goldseeker. He hailed from Stewarton in Ayrshire where from the age of seven he was involved in making Kilmarnock bonnets. He became an apprentice cabinetmaker and in 1854 sailed for Australia as carpenter's mate on the *Contest*. He tried his luck at the Victoria diggings and was attracted to Otago by the Dunstan gold rush. There he made enough money to start his own cabinetmaking business in Dunedin.

In among the diggers were men whose engineering skills and vision saw the rapid development of the goldfields. Scots descendant James Wilkie introduced steam power on the West Coast where he was a mine-owner.

Often the entire family followed the gold discoveries. Such was the experience of the Rose clan from Elgin who moved around Queensland with each new strike in the late 1800s and early 1900s. From Gympie to Bouldercombe to Mount Perry they went. Margaret Rose's husband Tom was badly injured in an accident at the Mount Perry mine and when his broken leg set the nerve was trapped in the break. The constant pain caused him to behave violently and, unaware of the problem, the medical authorities wanted him committed. Margaret steadfastly refused to sign the committal papers and eventually found a hypnotist who identified the problem; the leg was rebroken and Tom recovered. At their final stop off on the gold rush circuit – at Many Peaks – Tom, unable to work any more, opened a billiard hall.

Occasionally the hard graft on the goldfields could help achieve some unusual ambitions. James Chisholm (b. 1843) hailed from the shores of Loch Leven. Arriving in New Zealand with the *Three Bells* he worked with his father for a few years and then went to the Gabriel's Gully diggings and won sufficient gold to allow him to return to Scotland to begin university study from which he emerged as a minister.

First settled minister on the Otago goldfield in the 1860s was James Copland of Edinburgh who came to New Zealand as a ship's surgeon. In the rough and ready environment of the mining communities he was called on to give medical as well as spiritual aid and in later years gave some of the earliest socialist lectures heard in New Zealand.

Like Thomas Moonlight, for some Scots the exploration was everything – and the bustle of the goldfields, a nightmare. Such a man was William Docherty from Glasgow who after coming to New Zealand spent thirty years as a lone prospector in the western districts and fjords of Otago. Copper, coal and asbestos were among his discoveries but never in the quantities which would have made his fortune. Just the way Willie would have wanted it.

The contrast between the lifestyle chosen by Docherty and the bustle of the gold mining towns could scarcely be more marked. For example, Coolgardie (WA) in the late 1800s suddenly went from a tented village to a town of 25,000 people with twenty-six hotels, three breweries, a mosque, a horse racing circuit and seven newspapers – all in the space of half a dozen years.

THE WRATH OF TARAWERA

Inverness emigrant Joseph McRae was a leading light in the village of Te Awairoa, in the shadow of Mount Tarawera on New Zealand's North Island – he ran the community's two hotels, the bakery, store and other shops. However, in one night in 1886 the mountain blew itself apart, destroying McRae's village and two others and killing 153 people.

Joe, who sailed to New Zealand on the *Blue Jacket*, tried his hand at sheep farming in South Island before making his home on the volcanic plateau. On the night of the eruption he was wakened by a terrifying earth tremor which set the hotel swaying. A second shudder of the earth threw him out of bed and as a third shook the village he saw from his window the top of Tarawera burst into an inferno. Red hot stones began to fall. One which hurtled through the window had to be cooled with buckets of water to prevent the hotel catching fire. Gathering his guests together in the substantial drawing room, Joseph could only watch as the rest of the town burned under the downpour of rocks and debris. When the ceiling began to sag they took refuge in a nearby *whare* or Maori dwelling, one of only four houses in the village to survive.

Joseph then decided to try to negotiate the deadly cloud of falling ash and stones to check out a Maori meeting house quarter of a mile away. However,

he was struck by a stone and lay unconscious, waking to find himself surrounded on all sides by streams of hot mud. At the meeting house he was
able to reassure himself about the safety of the guests who had been staying
there. But at the nearby residence of the schoolmaster he found that the lady
of the house was trapped beneath a pile of rubble and so he led the rescue
effort. Mrs Hazard was found pinned to the ground by the fallen roof, alive
but cradling two children who, sadly, had been crushed by the falling debris.

The man who rightly deserves the title of Hero of Tarawera remained in
the hotel business until retiring to a sheep farm in North Auckland. He died
aged ninety in 1938.

Explosions, man-made this time, lead us to two fascinating individuals on
New Zealand's South Island. Mosgiel today is a town of around 10,000
people on the western outskirts of Dunedin. Big Alex and Little Alex were
two itinerant Scots farm workers. Although they did most jobs around the
farm, Big Alex was a dab hand with the explosives, or so he thought.

The duo carried all their tools on a four-wheeled wagon including the
blasting powder, gelignite and fuse wire to blast the tree stumps which
peppered the countryside. This was a highly risky but vital occupation with
land clearance being a necessary preliminary to agricultural development.

Inevitably accidents happened, though rarely serious. On one occasion the
two Scots were on stump clearance detail. The procedure was to dig a hole
below the stump, pack in some powder and try to blast it out of the ground
or at least weaken the roots sufficiently to allow the horses to drag it out
of the soil. Unfortunately, a burning sliver of wood after one blast did a
skyrocket act and landed on a coil of unused fuse wire which immediately
started to fizz. Lyn Young, who witnessed this all of seventy years ago
remembers the incident as if it was yesterday. The box of powder went off
with a hiss; uncompacted, it did not explode, but Big Alex got in among the
burning fuse wire frantically chopping with his axe because it was burning
in several places. When the panic was over, so the story goes, they were left
with a 50-foot coil of fuse wire chopped into neat six-inch lengths.

South Australia's community of Penola recognises Alexander Cameron,
who hailed from Inverness-shire and was brought up in the shadow of Ben
Nevis, as its principal founding father. As the Clearances took their toll,
Alexander, a shepherd, found his way to Australia with another 101 Camerons on the *Boyne* which sailed from Cromarty in 1838. He already had
family Down Under – two uncles who quickly organised their clansfolk to
act as drovers moving their flocks to the new pastures of the Port Phillip
district (Melbourne). This epic journey took two years to complete, a trek
of some 1,500 kilometres with a convoy of bullock wagons which averaged
only sixteen kilometres daily. Some of the Camerons settled on the outskirts

of what is now Melbourne while others pushed west through Victoria and into what is now South Australia.

Possibly the first to cross the border with a flock of any size, Cameron established himself in the new land which had been declared a colony only ten years previously. His biographer Peter Rymill observes that Cameron must have sensed the irony that the profitability of the very sheep which had driven him out of the Highlands was providing the foundation of his new venture and ambitions. As more business passed his way Cameron opened the Royal Oak Hotel and the Penola Station became a focus for settlers – particularly Scots.

EYEBALL LICKING FOR BEGINNERS

Combining the occupations of payroll escort and stand-in nurse Christina Prouse, daughter of a Perthshire couple, was a modest celebrity in the growing community of Levin in the Manawatu district of New Zealand. Her husband operated one of the town's sawmills but the bank was sixty miles away in Wellington and it was Tina who made the monthly train journey to collect the payroll. She timed her visit to Wellington so that she had only twenty minutes to reach the bank and set off on the return leg. The opening of a bank branch seven miles from the mill ended her escort duties.

In the pioneering community she was often called on to tend to broken limbs and gashes before the train was flagged down to take the most serious cases to hospital in Wellington. She became accustomed to the bizarre as well as the mundane, such as the man who anticipated the medicine of the late 20th century by producing his toe from his pocket after he'd sliced the appendage off with an axe, fully expecting that Christina would replace it.

Riding through the muddy bush she would, in her role as unofficial midwife, attend the births in the remotest homesteads and earn herself the nickname of 'Granny Prouse'. In her book *Petticoat Pioneers* Miriam Macgregor tells how Christina cured a boy poisoned by eating berries by feeding him kerosene. Even more remarkably, on a train journey to Wellington she restored the sight of a man blinded by smoke while fighting a bush fire by licking his eyeballs until the smoke film had been removed from his pupils. The reaction of the other passengers is not recorded!

If Dunfermline's most famous weaving family were the Carnegies, producing young Andrew who as a steel king in America became one of the world's richest men, it's worth remembering the less trumpeted successes of others from the Fife town. Alexander Hay left Dunfermline in 1838 as a teenager and gave up his job as an apprentice weaver to set sail for South

Australia. (Down the street Andrew Carnegie was still a toddler.) In Adelaide his grocery and hardware business flourished and in 1845 he married a Glasgow girl, Agnes Kelly, remarrying after her death in 1870. For his second wife, Agnes Gosse, he built Mount Breckan, a vast mansion house on a hill overlooking the town of Victor Harbor, their summer retreat.

By this time a member of the first House of Assembly in South Australia, Alex was a rich man and the two-storey building with its twenty-two rooms and 80-foot tower reflected his achievements. The house cost £25,000 and is said to have been paid for by the return of one year's wool clip from his sheep stations.

Alexander died suddenly in 1898 and his death was followed in the next few years by further family tragedy. The house was burned out after a fire in 1909 and while insurance claims were being settled Mrs Hay and her youngest daughter Dolly were lost when the Clyde-built *Waratah* vanished between Durban and Cape Town. A disappearance unexplained to this day.

Mount Breckan is now in private hands and the intention is to restore it to its former glory.

Too often the great adventure could end in tragedy but not always in such bizarre circumstances as that of Orcadian Alexander Miller. He immigrated in the 1860s and worked as a labourer in the town of Waikouaiti north of Dunedin which, as we've seen, attracted many Orkney folk.

With Charles Miller (no relation) and two other Scots, Alexander made for the Otago gold diggings in August 1864. The men set off walking and after buying provision and a tent, set up camp for the night. The plan was that they would push northwest in the morning to seek their fortune. For Alex and Charles that day never dawned. They cooked their meal over an open fire which they then stoked for the night to keep warm. Sadly they failed to make sure the flames were extinguished before hitting the sack and as they slept soundly after the long hike the flames spread into the roots and the tree fell on them during the night, fatally injuring the two Millers.

A survivor of what the local paper called this 'melancholy incident', John McGregor from Stirlingshire, married Alexander Miller's sister and was involved in gold mining and sheep rearing before becoming proprietor of the Waihemo Hotel in central Otago. They both died before World War I, leaving a large number of descendants in the Otago area.

THAR' SHE BLOWS!

In his book *The Story of New Zealand* A.H. Reed tells the marvellous tale of how a convict ship approaching Port Jackson (Sydney) in the late 1790s found the sea around teeming with whales; they were watched from mid-day to sunset, spouting as far as the eye could see. Whaling was to become Australia and New Zealand's first real export industry and ports were constructed specifically to service this lucrative trade. Among the tough whalers and sealers were a significant number of Scots. Whaling centres like Bluff in New Zealand's Southland were bustling and bawdy places and yet we can find Scots who enjoyed the atmosphere. One settler at Bluff felt that the presence of the whalers added a 'zest and piquancy to an existence that otherwise might have grown monotonous and somnolent'.

One of the earliest professional whalers to arrive in the area (1809) was Captain William Stewart, a self-declared Jacobite after whom New Zealand's third island – Stewart Island – takes its name. Robert Campbell, the Greenock-born merchant and pioneer Sydney businessman, was the single biggest employer in the sealing and whaling business.

As early as 1792 a party from Sydney under the command of John Leith landed at Dusky Sound at the southwestern tip of New Zealand, collecting 4,500 seal skins in a year.

The majority of whalers who reached the Australian coast were of British origin and many were known only by their nicknames such as 'Long Bob' or 'Black Peter'. 'Scotch Jock' was John Nicol who worked as a whaler and traded on the Kapiti coast of New Zealand's North Island voyaging with his Maori wife in the 1830s up and down the coast in a fragile lug. John and his wife later kept a boarding house.

These were tough, independent and resourceful men, staunch friends and dangerous enemies but according to one commentator they were not slow to pull up a seat made from whale vertebrae beside the fire and offer you a drop of grog.

Despite his Teutonic surname Charles Schultze hailed from Edinburgh, the son of a merchant in the West Indies. By 1831 he had established a whaling station at Otago Harbour, seventeen years before the Scottish emigrant ships arrived to establish Dunedin.

Many Orcadians and Shetlanders, noted seafarers and some of them already with valuable experience with the Hudson's Bay Company, joined the early whaling expeditions around New Zealand's South Island. When the industry collapsed many opted to settle around the old whaling camps. For example, Traill and Leask descendants are still to be found on Raikura (or Stewart Island). The romantic Maori name for New Zealand's southernmost isle means Land of the Glowing Skies, in recognition of the Aurora Australis or Southern Lights.

Kaikoura on the northeast coast of New Zealand's South Island is considered to be one of the best locations in the world to go whale watching. The deep waters of the Pacific run almost to the shore and whales gather in impressive numbers. How many of the whale watchers will know, however, that the first European settler at the Kaikoura Peninsula was Robert Fyfe, baptised in 1811 in the parish of St Martins about five miles from Perth.

Robert entered the tough whaling business in Australia after running away to sea at the age of nineteen. With backing from a Wellington merchant Robert had his first whaling season at Kaikoura in 1843 and with forty men working for him that winter, Kaikoura proved to be the most lucrative fishing ground in New Zealand during the 1840s; but by the end of the decade Robert Fyfe was having to supplement his income by farming. In 1854 he was joined by his cousin George, who had been a law student at Edinburgh University, and when Robert drowned taking whale oil to Wellington, the younger man took over. The Fyfes' residence in Kaikoura, a heritage site, is the only building standing from the whaling station days. George's wife Catherine came from Scotland to marry but the hard life continued to take its toll and George was killed when he fell from a jetty into the sea.

South Australia's Encounter Bay was another major whaling centre which attracted many Scots to a typically rough-and-ready community. George Fife Angas was a pious Scots financier who had done much to bring South Australia into being and in the prospectus of Angas's South Australia Company strong emphasis was made on the pursuit of the whale and seal. The importance of other fisheries and the curing of fish for export were all central to the development of the colony.

Whale oil provided much of the lighting in the developed world of the 1830s and almost every feature of the whale found a market whether it was making corsets or fine porcelain. Targets for the whale hunters at Encounter Bay was the Right Whale. Angas's company had three ships operating out of the bay at the deep sea work but whaling in the bay itself was to prove more lucrative. By 1854 declining numbers led to the closure of the operation which was the most successful and enduring of the shore-based whaling stations in South Australia.

Among the Scots associated with the Encounter Bay/Victor Harbor area was Alex Ewen, a ship's carpenter from Glasgow who arrived in 1848. Alex told his family of the days of bay whaling – adventures when they harpooned a calf and the furious mother split the boat in half, breaking a couple of Alex's ribs; and of the occasion when one of the Aborigine whale watchers collapsed and died having spotted a school of whales. To prevent the Aboriginal rowers who arrived on the scene breaking off into the traditional death ceremonial, Alex told them that their companion was simply having a sleep at the bottom of the boat. Out they went, captured their whale and the bad news was broken to the crew on their return to shore.

Chapter Thirteen
A Sense of Continuity

A LTHOUGH only a small proportion of the great Scots legion in Australia and New Zealand are actively or regularly involved in Scots-interest groups and activities, you'll be told that the customs and values brought from Scotland generations ago are still at work in family settings – and these seem to persist at a much deeper level than the superficialities of bagpipes and heather.

I don't know what they do to the enemy, but they scare the living daylights out of me. The Mount Morgan Scots (QD) on parade around the turn of the century. (*John Oxley Library, Brisbane, Queensland*)

The Caledonian groups do flourish. It is estimated that there are well over 100 Scottish clubs, clan societies and organisations in Sydney alone. There is clearly a need to express Scottishness also in a more flamboyant manner. This may possibly trivialise Scottish culture Down Under but, as Malcolm Prentis points out, it would be worse to lose it altogether.

LEANS OUT OF THE CLOSET

In at least one notable case the move to New Zealand allowed one Scots family to reassert their heritage and their nationality, to resurface from a self-imposed exile. To all intents and purposes the Lean family of Blislands, Trehudreth, Cornwall, were a reasonably well-to-do West Country family seeking a fresh start. However, when Robert and Every Lean migrated to Pakuranga, now in the suburbs of Auckland, in 1850 they stepped off the *Constantinople* as the Macleans. The family had fled Scotland after the Jacobite Uprising of 1745 and found sanctuary in Cornwall.

The newly-outed Macleans, after a century in England had, however, lost much of their Scottishness. They settled at their new home which they dubbed Bleak House (Dickens novels being popular at the time) and are remembered in part for their role in setting up the Pakuranga Hunt, the first in New Zealand, formed in 1872 to chase hares.

Families with Jacobite traditions could be found in all the principal areas settled by the Scots. A memorable character in the Rangitikei district of New Zealand's North Island was John 'Henech' Cameron from Argyllshire whose great-grandfather had been killed at the Battle of Prestonpans during the '45 Uprising. John had reached his century when he died in 1881. Fittingly a piper led a cortège of buggies and horsemen to big John's funeral. The first chief justice of New South Wales, Francis Forbes, came from a Jacobite family who had settled in Bermuda after the Uprising.

While it is generally accepted that the Scots managed to blend in well with their new environment Down Under, there were occasions when the patience of even the most fair-minded Scot was stretched beyond endurance. In Victoria the misuse of the term 'English' to mean British was a common enough occurrence. When it became known that the Queen's Jubilee celebrations in 1885 were to be marked by illuminations in which the 'Queen of England' display would feature, 'study Jacobite' Theodore Napier went to war and after an energetic campaign succeeded in having the plan overturned. There were always Theodores around to remind backsliders of their roots but the majority of the Scots simply dispersed into the community, finding no difficulty being Scottish, British and Antipodean at one and the same time.

WHEN NEIGHBOURS BECOME GOOD FRIENDS

But even 12,000 miles from home there was nothing the Scots liked better than to poke fun at the Auld Enemy. One joke which has stood the test of time and still does the rounds of the clubs and societies runs like this. God made the earth and stood back to admire his handiwork. However, he was questioned about the fact that he'd given Scotland natural beauty and such a proud, sensitive and patriotic people. Wasn't it unfair that Scotland had so many advantages? Yes, saith the Lord, but wait till you see who I've given them for neighbours.

Social historians argue that the centuries-long struggle to remain free of English domination bred a special resilience in the Scots, a toughness and mindset which made them formidable immigrants; those who had been unsuccessful or oppressed at home sought a promised land, those who had been successful, fresh challenges. Almost without exception, the New Zealanders and Australians with this Scottish background, despite fears about the changing character of the relationship with the old country, are optimistic about the future.

From time to time, however, these folk are reminded that Scottish spice is only one ingredient in the ethnic and cultural broth. Gordon Smart, Auckland haggis-maker, is a man steeped in the Scottish traditions. Only natural then that he should want to fly the Saltire in his back garden. He was somewhat deflated, however, when a neighbour phoned to ask why the Greek flag was flying above the Smart residence.

With the passing of the years an interesting, subtle change has taken place within the Scots-interest groups in both countries. Fewer now have Scots-born leadership, perhaps only one or two Scotsborn members – some none at all – but there remains a boundless enthusiasm for all things Scottish.

OH, FLOWER OF SCOTLAND

When the *Bengal Merchant* pioneers reached Port Nicholson from the Clyde in 1840 they were already making plans for their first St Andrews Day celebrations. As New Zealand historian W. L. Pearce tells us, this 1840 picnic at Petone, round the bay from where the great city of Wellington stands today, was notable for one historic event – the planting of seeds of the thistle especially imported from the old country. Quantities of grass imported in subsequent years must also surely have carried the thistle seeds but the Petone ceremony indicates just how important the settlers regarded the symbolic sewing of the national seed.

A similar scenario is discovered in Australia and although we cannot trace any Petone-like event, in western Victoria where Highlanders were found in large numbers the thistle was already declared a pest by the 1850s. It is generally accepted that it was introduced to this area by Scots settlers suffering what Malcolm Prentis has called 'misguided homesickness'. Although officially outlawed in the 1850s, by the middle of the following decade it had achieved a firm hold. Letters from Scots settlers in Hampden Shire, for instance, said the local authority had begun to fine landholders who showed a reluctance to keep the bonnie thistle in check. No improvement was in sight and, in fact, one grazier from a Scots background managed to persuade the Shire Council in Warrnambool to abandon their anti-thistle legislation altogether.

In Queensland settler George McKay from Thurso sent the council men packing when they arrived to cut down his 'Scotch thistle' which had been spreading like wildfire on his farm east of Boonah. Seeing his national emblem put to the scythe was more than old Geordie could stand.

More innocently, heather was widely planted in both Australia and New Zealand by the Scots incomers and generally flourished. Right at the southern extremity of New Zealand there is a legend that an exiled (and unnamed) Jacobite princess planted the heather carpets which decorate the island to remind her of home.

There seems no doubt that Scots traditions, often much diluted, do persist.

It doesn't get much more Scottish than this. In the Queensland bush we find the heather clad slopes of Lochnagar. (*Bill Scott, Queensland*)

One old-timer in Southland ventured the opinion that 'porridge, heather and the Psalms of David last to the third generation' in the foreign lands.

Edinburgh-born Edward Cargill was a son of the first superintendent of Otago, William Cargill, and was a pioneering merchant and ship-owner in his own right, having his fleet of steamships built on the Clyde. He is best remembered as a reactionary, one who called for the original settlers to stand together and preserve 'The Old Identity', a nickname he carried for the rest of his life.

SHAMAER, HUGHONSHIRE

The great dream of Australian and New Zealand Scots is now to be able to retire early with sufficient capital to make the journey back to Scotland at least once. More than a few realise this goal, as I can testify from the accents in Kirkwall's Broad Street in the summer months. Although many know exactly where they are headed and may even have family to board with, the links are sometimes very tenuous and some folk seeking to explore family histories can find it difficult to get a foothold on the genealogical ladder. Mrs Chris Milroy in Collie (WA) knows only that her forebears, the Milroys, came from Scotland to the Victoria goldfields in 1856. However, the family records show the birthplace in Scotland as Shamaer, Hughonshire. Inquiries are continuing.

The growth of genealogy and the search for family roots has been so spectacular in recent years that many libraries across the English-speaking world are struggling to cope with demands for information. Gradually even district libraries and historical societies in Australia and New Zealand are building up a database of local pioneers which is assisting descendants in tracing the wanderings and watersheds in the lives of their Scottish ancestors.

READY FOR THE ROLL CALL

One particularly imaginative and demanding project currently under way is being co-ordinated by the Scottish Interest Group of the New Zealand Society of Genealogists who are compiling, and intending to publish, a register of all Scots-born immigrants to New Zealand arriving before 1921. A mammoth task. This register is likely to become one of the most important research tools available in making Scotland-New Zealand connections.

Older people tried to instil a gentle love of Scotland and things Scottish in their Antipodean grandchildren. Several folk wrote telling me how they still sat occasionally with the family singing songs like 'Granny's Heilan' Hame'. That particular melody, one lady in her eighties confided, always seemed to bring a lump the size of an egg to her throat – and the nearest she'd got to Scotland was watching Andy Stewart on television. The truth, however, is that young Australians and New Zealanders belong to the 21st century and their interests are international; they are unashamedly citizens of the world. This realisation can often hit grandparents like a sledgehammer.

The story is told among the Scots groups of Grandpa sitting on the verandah dreaming of the Scotland he had left behind. He stares out over the Queensland bush as the sun dips low in the west.

'Can you make a noise like a frog, Granpa Keith?' chirps wee Jimmy, his grandson, but every inch an Australian.

'What's all this nonsense?' says the veteran, annoyed at the interruption to his reverie. 'Go down to the creek if you want to hear a frog.'

But the wee chap is insistent: 'Go on, Granpa, make a noise like a frog.'

Exasperated, and with his dreams of Caledonia over for the evening, the old man asks: 'What's this all about, James?'

'Mum says that when you croak we can go to Disneyland.'

An interesting phenomenon in relation to homesickness was the widely reported fact that a trip to the old country often provided a once-and-for-all cure . . . involving as it does the sudden realisation of all the advantages that living in the Antipodes offers and allows any romantic fancies about Scotland to be finally dispelled. Kittie, daughter of New Zealand land reformer John McKenzie, once famously remarked after a visit to her father's homeland that while Scotland was pretty it was 'not equal' to New Zealand.

REWRITING THE RULE BOOK

Interest in the Scottish heritage seems to have waxed and waned over the years with all sorts of factors such as war, economic depression and significant anniversaries playing their part. The Burns Supper in Stratford (TI) in 1912 was used as the occasion for the announcement of the formation of the Taranaki Provincial Scottish Society. The first chief, William McLaughlin Kennedy, spoke with feeling about the need of patriotic Scots to remember their roots as reflected in the number of Caledonian Societies. But he had a warning:

> The idea of a Scottish society did not imply that a few old topers should meet together on special occasions to get 'fu' but that they desired a so- ciety where Scotsmen and descendants of Scotsmen should be banded together.

Meeting together from time to time they would keep alive in their breasts love 'for the land of our sires', for her tradition, history and cultivate a fuller

The Hanlin girls from Dunedin, Jean, Margaret and Helen. The family came from Glasgow in 1910 and held fast to the Scots traditions. Jean (*left*) was in a foul mood, the family recall, and after the photo session went outside and spread the mash all over the chicken run. (*Nancy Whittlestone, Dunedin*)

knowledge of her literature. Younger generations were apt to forget in these far-away lands, said the distinguished Mr Kennedy, the rock from which they were hewn. Oh yes, and there would be a wee drink afterwards.

Time and again in examining the constitutions of these Scots groups it's clear that the members were keen to remind the world of the three truths which were fundamental to the Scottish people – they loved their God, they loved their country and they loved to be educated.

The Turakina Caledonian Society on New Zealand's North Island was formed as early as 1865 and still stages an annual Gathering of the Clans to this day. The local newspaper the *Rangitikei Advocate*'s news report in 1924 noted a change in the character of the event:

It was a gay orderly throng who met to perpetuate the memory of Bonnie Scotland, the home of their parents which, alas, is fast losing its hold on the young generation . . . Time passes and with it the order changes.

It was in the 1920s that Rule 8A in the constitution adopted by a number of Scottish societies had to be overturned as it threatened the very existence of the Scots-interest groups. It held that only Scots-born were eligible for

Even in death the Scots hold fast to the traditions of the auld country.
(By kind permission of Chippers, Funeral Directors, Perth (WA).)

membership. No matter how enthusiastic or interested a New Zealand-born wife and children might be, they were excluded. The Scottish Society of Manawatu, realising that this rule was threatening the numerical and social growth of the society, threw it out in 1927. A special meeting substituted the phrase 'of Scottish descent' for 'Scottish born'. It was a far-seeing move which now allows fifth or sixth-generation New Zealand Scots to participate in the celebration of their heritage.

In more recent years these groups have attempted to broaden their 'cultural outlook' by starting Gaelic classes, ladies' step dance classes, singing groups, even re-enactment clubs. Other slightly more off-beat events have crept into the social calendar. At the Scottish stronghold of Bothwell in central Tasmania there is an annual 'Highland Spin-In' where spinners, weavers and wool-growers from all over the world gather. Among these new-style events the 'old-timers' are still going strong. At Maryborough (VA), Highland Games have been held on New Year's Day (Antipodean midsummer) since 1859 and have been described as the oldest continuing event of its kind in the Commonwealth.

As well as organising Highland Games from Waipu in the north to Invercargill in the south and encouraging pipe bands and Highland dancing, the Scots in New Zealand regularly run Scots nights or 'Ingleside'. In the past these were alcohol-free and for all ages but they may be passing out of favour because of the demand today for drink to be available at social functions. Dancing was a highlight of these evenings, the Eightsome Reel, the Dashing White Sergeant and the Gay Gordons among the more popular dances.

For many years before the establishment of these secular Scots-interest groups and societies, the Presbyterian Church was the main vehicle in both countries for the continuing expression of Scottish identity.

Anniversaries now take on special significance in the celebration of things Scottish. Among the more significant and imminent, 1998 sees the 150th anniversary of the Scots foundation of Otago. Although this is unquestionably a Scottish enclave historically, there have been rumblings of late. A group of Indians settled on the coast near Dunedin before the arrival of the emigrant ships and there were Welsh whalers and sealers around at the same time. One Welsh descendant wrote mischievously to the Press suggesting that because of this Welsh connection the town's name should be changed to Dineddyn, or if this caused problems of pronunciation they should revert to the Maori name for the district – Otepoti.

A SENSE OF PLACE

What precisely did the expatriate Scots feel for their homeland? Australian-Scots poet Allan McNeilage tried to explore this strange longing in his poem 'Day Dreaming':

Oh, I ken this land is unco fair, an' friends around me monie,
Fu' kind o' hairt an' cheerie, I hae tried an' proved them true;
But the links o' love, unbroken, bind me to yon land sae bonnie . . .

Sir Robert Menzies, Prime Minister of Australia and a man quite openly proud of his Scottish heritage, identified what he saw as the principal factors which had enabled the Scot to succeed when transplanted to a foreign field – a sense of continuity and a spirit of independence. He saw nothing wrong with nostalgia and the celebration of the Caledonian roots. Australian Scots, by and large, he felt, were in the happy position of 'having memories, but no regrets'.

THE AULD SCOTS FAILING

Oddly, for an ethnic group often accused of being clannish and introspective we do have this familiar habit of scrapping amongst ourselves. It seems that this was a talent exported to New Zealand and Australia along with the porridge oats and tartan shawls. If we're looking for examples we need go no further than that scrapper John Dunmore Lang. He fought with Scots

Governor Sir Thomas Brisbane over what he saw as lack of official government support for the Scots Presbyterian church in the face of what he perceived to be the Catholic/Irish menace and he went apoplectic over an enthusiasm expressed by one of his professors, Henry Carmichael, for the secularisation of schools. Anathema to the street-fighter Lang.

While the Scots would deny clannishness or nepotism they often found it mutually rewarding to share business ventures with their countryfolk – the Queensland Steam Shipping Company being a good example. This was created by an amalgamation of three pairs of Scots entrepreneurs – Burns and Philip, McIlwraith and McEachran and Gilchrist and Watt.

George McKay from Thurso was the wild member of his family, as neighbours in southern Queensland were to find out in the 1860s when it came to selecting and establishing a claim to land. After putting his stock on a block at Fassifern, George went out with his son Alex on horseback to check the animals. They came across a neighbour, Campbell McDonald (short odds on him being a Scot!), busy chasing stock off their selection. McKay let out a yell and took off after McDonald. They raced around the gum trees and swamps, clearing fallen logs, McKay cutting him off on occasions but never getting close enough to bring him to a stop. When McKay's horse began to tire, McDonald made a break for it. Young Alex had enjoyed a grandstand view of this exciting passage of play.

Years later Campbell McDonald was watching the election results being posted at Boonah when he heard people behind him saying goodnight to a Mr McKay. 'Are you the son of the old Scotsman who had a property at Twelve Mile?' He got the nod. Said McDonald: 'Ferocious old devil. If I hadn't been on a good horse that day he would have killed me.' He wandered off still muttering under his breath. 'Ferocious old devil.' The years had not dimmed the memory of that skirmish.

On the social front it is certainly true that the Scots who felt a keen sense of nationality were always busy organising their Scottishness. Among the Scots a favourite quip told of the two Englishmen shipwrecked on a desert isle who still hadn't spoken to each other five years later when rescued because they hadn't been introduced. Meanwhile two Scots in a similar situation had within hours formed a golf club, Caledonian club and laid the foundation stone for a Presbyterian kirk. And it is true, as we've seen in previous pages, that the Scots did work together for mutual benefit. The Scots Mafia, Caledonian Phalanx and the Highland Brotherhood are just three ways which have described the virtual stranglehold the Scots held in certain areas of Australian and New Zealand life.

In Tasmania the Cook family from Dundee settled in the southeast. One of the nine children, James Cook was a 'dour Scot' if there ever was one.

He was in the habit of using the legendary Edinburgh greeting when his German neighbour Manfred Rollins came visiting – 'You'll have had your tea.' Whenever they met going about their chores on the land James and Manfred would immediately launch into a debate on some obscure topic which they would chew over until they were left with the bones. Practical as ever, and not wanting to lose a good neighbour, James prevented the disagreements becoming too deeply entrenched by persuading Manfred that come hell or high water the topic for debate would change every fortnight. And it did, regular as clockwork.

THE SKIRL O' THE PIPES

You might expect it, but there is a claim, among the Scottish lobby who want credit for a Caledonian involvement in every historic event since the construction of the ark (MacNoah, perhaps not!), that the bagpipes were the first musical instrument heard in New Zealand, which, unlike Australia, is a didgeridoo-free zone. Not as unlikely as it might sound, first of all because of the portability of the instrument and secondly because there certainly were Scots sealers and whalers among the first white faces to appear in New Zealand waters in the early 1800s.

Haggis, we're told, was served on Cook's *Endeavour* as it rounded New

Australian Scots at play and not a kilt in sight. The 1977 informal gathering of Victorian Scots at Bob Monro's farm at Corinella (VA). (*Joan Fraser, Victoria*)

Zealand in 1769 to mark the birthday of one of his officers. What is often omitted from this story, for decency's sake I suppose, is the fact that the haggis contained dog meat cooked in the hound's stomach. As to whether this appetising feast had a bagpipe accompaniment, the histories are imprecise.

What is not in dispute is that wherever the Scots settled there was sure to be a piper in the company, whether it was in the rough gold mining camps of Victoria or the kauri forests of Auckland, or more recently at Anzac Day parades which would seem bereft without the pipes. Organised pipe bands are a relatively recent phenomenon and the first pipe band in New Zealand – the Caledonian of Southland (1896) – claims the distinction of being the oldest pipe band south of the Equator. In true Scottish style it was born in the midst of a rammy over personnel. Their stated goal was a simple one, 'to play and encourage the cultivation of bagpipe music' and for this purpose the Southland bandsmen would walk many miles to practice.

Even when the pipes were missing the Scots would improvise. David Drummond from Fife was an accomplished bagpipe player – without a set of bagpipes. When he ended up in 1842 in the forests of New Zealand's Nelson region he had brought with him his precious Jew's-harp with which he would twang away lustily of an evening.

Romantic they may have been but the new Australian Scots were certainly not dyed-in-the-wool traditionalists. They were willing to experiment. At the Maryborough Highland Games in the early 1920s goat-racing was the boom sport, with the animals harnessed up to little carts and the lads who drove them decked out in racing silks and caps – the whole business being taken very seriously.

Often the tale is re-told of the famous day when Edward, Prince of Wales, visited Bendigo (VA) and the Maryborough pipe band was invited to take part in the celebrations. A couple of planks with side safety rails extended as a walkway across the street from one high building to another and a Maryborough bandsman was nominated to pipe his way across the overhead companion-way as the prince passed below. With a fine bag o' wind and a skirl that plucked at the Highland heartstrings he began his crossing. However, at this moment, as part of the welcome to His Royal Highness, someone released a flock of pigeons. There was the piper, above the cheering throng, engulfed by a flock of squawking birdlife. The piper struggled to keep his foothold in this explosion of music, feathers and wild hurrahs from the onlookers. The prince was said to have been most amused and the only injury was to the piper's pride.

Although Australian pipe bands tend to be very cosmopolitan outfits these days, the bonus of a Scots piper is much sought after. In the mid-1990s, for example, Brian Lamond from Inverkeithing in Fife took a year-long working holiday and when he wasn't busking on Melbourne's Princes Bridge he was in the ranks of Victoria Police Pipe Band, even travelling back to Scotland for the World Pipe Band Championships in Glasgow where the Victoria finished the world's top police band and fourth overall.

Highland Balls across New Zealand, often held to raise funds to support local pipe bands over the years, could be spectacular affairs with the entire company marching to the hall. At locations where it was illegal to have liquor on the premises many a visit would be made to the 'broom cupboard' for resuscitation.

Should you think for a moment that the pipe band scene is really just a superficial pastime, a bit of fun, then think again. In the summer of 1996 the University of Otago's Jennie Coleman presented her doctoral thesis devoted to the history of the bagpipes in New Zealand. Appropriately she was piped into the ceremony by veteran Dunedin piper Airdrie Stewart.

Political economist Duncan Macgregor from Aberfeldy in Perthshire, as a lecturer at the self-same university, influenced many of the leading thinkers in New Zealand in the late 1800s but he too enjoyed the skirl of the pipes and was a regular attender at Otago's Highland gatherings.

The first pipe band contest in New Zealand took place in Christchurch (CY) during the International Exhibition of 1906–7 with only three bands taking part. There are now numerous pipe bands, with some cities sustaining three or more.

The formation of the Wanganui Highland Pipe Band in 1939 followed a familiar pattern. Drum rolls were practised on chair seats – they had no drums. There was a great debate before McLeod of Lewis was chosen as their tartan then abandoned. Then the local Scottish Society said they favoured Macgregor. Once again the band came up with a list of alternative tartans. McIntosh looked like a runner when a local businessman of that name offered sponsorship but the band stood on their dignity. Eventually Mackenzie was selected and the Wanganui pipe band blows strong to this day.

Up the road the Manawatu Pipe Band had to make do with some unusual practice venues in the early days including a garage, a bakehouse and a funeral parlour. And boy, has the Manawatu band had its moments. Old-timers recall with glee the rather puffed-up drum major and his first parade which also proved to be his swan song. He led the band on a circuit of the square with his kilt on back to front. Then there was the legendary occasion when the Manawatu and Wanganui pipe bands combined. Pipe Major Bob Thompson had to march solo as the seventh man on the right flank and was pushed so far to the side of the road that he disappeared into a storm drain. Up to his waist in water he continued to play. That same day the Drum Major went for a particularly impressive toss, sending his mace seemingly into orbit because it never returned to earth, having become entangled in decorative draping and streamers above the street.

Many bands both in Australia and New Zealand were sadly depleted during World War II but in 1945, with people keen to get back to normality, Scots-interest groups were among those who experienced a boost in membership, yet another indicator of how interest in things Scottish has ebbed and flowed over the years.

The first time traditional Scottish music was played at the Annual Race Week in South Australia it caused a sensation. Alex Cameron, the so-called 'King of Penola', arranged for a piper on a cart to race through the town playing full blast. Most of the Scots present hadn't heard the pipes since leaving their native heath and got a bit overheated, coming running in the direction of the sound shouting: 'It's the pipes, by God.'

The Mackenzie pipe band, based in the town of Fairlie in Canterbury, was formed when an expatriate Scot who worked in the district as a wool classer heard three young Scots playing the pipes in the main street and on the spot offered £5 to anyone who would help organise a band.

One Scots lady in the town of Stratford (TI), who, with fifteen children, you'd have thought might have had little time to feel homesick, devised a novel method to cure the blues. The arrival of the telephone changed her life. When she began to feel low, particularly at weekends, she would pick up the

Parade Day on Broadway, Stratford (TI) 1889 captured for posterity by immigrant Scots photographer James McAllister.
(*McAllister Collection, Alexander Turnbull Library*)

telephone and call a Scots friend living locally who played the pipes to her over the phone, much to the disgust of the other twenty folk on the party line.

FORGET NOT THE PEOPLE

Trevor Ross of Palmerston (OO), whose grandfather immigrated from Achnahannet in Moray, has converted his house into a temple in honour of Scotland and has a memory second to none of that part of New Zealand between the Wars.

When the Gaelic-speaking folk from Waipu on North Island visited in the mid-1930s, Trevor, then a schoolboy, sang the 'Brown Haired Maiden' and the 'Skye Boat Song'. He remembers travelling about with his father to monthly Scots gatherings where young Trevor was always called on to sing. Some bizarre echoes of the Scotland they had left behind were still found. Says Trevor:

> At these gatherings I remember well how the tickets were sold at the office and the doorman, who knew everyone, directed Campbells to the left and McDonalds to the right.

World War II was a watershed in so many ways because, by 1950, when Trevor was providing the entertainment for Clan Campbell gatherings

Trevor Ross of Palmerston (OO) among his collection of Burns memorabilia, part of a temple – it began as a garage – to Scotland and its culture flourishing on the other side of the world. (*Trevor Ross*)

nobody raised an eyebrow when he sang 'Glencoe'. At Glencoe in Southland the Clan Donald members in the region unveiled a cairn early in 1997 to commemorate the massacre. While people who had visited the genuine article in Argyll found it an eerie place, the hope is that the New Zealand location will be a friendly, welcoming spot.

Towards the end of 1996 a petition was handed into the University of Otago organised by the student association's Highland Society demanding a Gaelic-Celtic Studies course. The cover of the petition carried the old Gaelic proverb 'Forget not the people from where you came'. A Gaelic history course was to be set up in 1993 but funding became tight and it was dropped in favour of an Asian course. The petitioners argue that forty per cent of New Zealand's population is of Gaelic origin.

When Highland Games became popular the tough Highlanders at Waipu produced some formidable competitors. Especially remembered were the tug-o-war teams of giants who on one occasion arrived in Auckland for a competition to find the opposition had evaporated at the thought of facing the iron men from the north.

Middle-distance champion D. N. McMillan seems to have been a bit of a show-off. Having won his race he amused the crowd at the finish line by jumping back and forth over a fence while waiting for the other competitors to stagger home. N. R. McKenzie tells us that in early Waipu the undisputed champion of the caber was Donald Rory Og. At one meeting, after he successfully tossed the tree trunk stewards had to lop three feet off the caber before anyone else was able to toss it.

It is clear then that homesick Scots pioneers Down Under happily embraced the symbols and images of a dying Highland way of life and reworked them as their staff and comfort in the new lands.

Although it does seem that the Caledonians have a high profile in Australia and New Zealand, certain matters Scottish, as far as the world at large is concerned, remain shrouded in almost Masonic secrecy. Gordon Smart is one of the world's top haggis-makers, operating from his base at Auckland. Recently he told me that he was required to airfreight a large haggis to Australia for a Scots wedding. This, of course, meant lots of form-filling for the agricultural authorities in Australia; they needed to know the ingredients and weight of the haggis. Faxes and phone calls zipped back and forward between the two countries. Finally, a message came from the Australian authorities saying they were quite happy to let the haggis into the country but wanted to put it in a field to graze for three weeks after its arrival.

Long may the mystique of the Scots, at home and abroad, flourish.

Sources

A Dictionary of New Zealand Biography edited by G.H. Schofield, Wellington (1940)

The Dictionary of Australian Biography by Percival Searle, Sydney and London (1949)

The Scots of New Zealand by G.L. Pearce, William Collins (New Zealand) Ltd (1976)

The Scots in Australia: A Study of New South Wales, Victoria and Queensland 1788–1900 by Malcolm D. Prentis, Sydney University Press (1987)

That Land of Exiles: Scots in Australia by various authors, Her Majesty's Stationary Office (1988)

Encyclopedia of Australia compiled by A.T.A. and A.M. Learmonth, Frederick Warne, London (1968)

The Scots Overseas by Gordon Donaldson, London (1966)

The Scottish in Australia by Malcolm D. Prentis, AE Press, Melbourne (1989)

Piping in a Rough Equality – the Scots Contribution to the Making of New Zealand by Tom Brooking (1996)

Petticoat Pioneers by Miriam Macgregor, A.H. & A.W. Reed (1975)

Brisbane's Forgotten Founder, Sir Evan Mackenzie of Kilcoy by John H.G. Mackenzie-Smith, Brisbane History Group Studies (1992)

Caledonia Australis – Scottish Highlanders on the Frontier of Australia by Don Watson, Collins of Sydney (1984)

A Legacy of Scots edited by Charles Walker, Mainstream (1988)

History of the Dargo Traills by Bill Traill (1993)

Burghers o' Westray by Jeff Burgher *et al.*, Personal Publications (1992)

In addition hundreds of individuals, family groups, libraries and local authorities assisted my inquiries by providing papers, pamphlets, cuttings, family genealogies and local histories, too numerous to list.

Index